The Wonders of
Waldorf Chemistry

Table of Contents

Preface.	8
Developing Scientific Thinking.	9
Creating a Sense of Wonder in Chemistry.	16
Teacher's Guidelines.	21
The Process of Learning.	23
Teacher's Scheme.	24
Tasks for the Teacher.	25
Enthusiasm.	27
How to Read Science.	29
Laboratory Equipment.	31
Safety.	33
Disposal of Chemicals.	39
Prologue to the Chemistry Main Lesson.	44

The Seventh Grade

Outline of Course.	46
Themes in the Seventh Grade.	47
A Brief History of Chemistry.	48
The Nature of Chemistry.	49
Combustion.	51
The Candle.	56
The Plant.	59
Chemicals in the Home.	70
Oxygen.	72
Calcium.	75
Class Reading – Nathaniel Hawthorne.	76
Limestone.	78
Sulfur.	83

Phosphorus	84
Sulfur, Phosphorus and Carbon	85
Acids and Bases	86
Salts	94
pH	95
Rock Sugar Crystal	96
Smoking	97
Chemistry Skit	99
Spelling and Vocabulary	101
Building a Portable Lime Kiln	102

The Eighth Grade

Outline of Course	110
Themes in the Eighth Grade	111
Three Branches of Chemistry	112
Water	114
Crystals	118
Chemicals in a 100-Pound Student	122
The Metals	123
The Blast Furnace and Industrial Chemistry	136
Photosynthesis	140
Class Reading – Rutherford Platt	142
Sugar	143
Starch	147
Cellulose	150
Experiments with Sugar, Starch and Cellulose	151
Alcohol	152
Carbon Dioxide Generator	153
Hydrogen	154
Proteins	155
Oils and Fats	157
Spelling and Vocabulary	158

The Ninth Grade

Outline of Course	160
Themes in the Ninth Grade	161
The Lab Sheet	167
Carbon	168
Carbon Dioxide	171
The Bunsen Burner	173
Bending Glass	175
Oxidation/Reduction Experiment	176
Phlogiston	178
Photosynthesis	179
Class Reading – Jan Ingenhousz	183
Sugar	192
Polysaccharides, Starch and Cellulose	196
Microscopic Lab on Carbohydrates	201
The Transformation of Cotton into Nitro-Plastic	202
Commercial Use of Plants	203
Rarefaction/Solidification	206
Chromatography	207
Hydrogen	210
Fermentation	211
Distillation	213
Esters	214
Proteins	218
Fats, Oils and Waxes	220
Saponification	221
Textiles	223
Synthetics	227
Plastics	228
Rubber	230
Hydrocarbons	233
Making Aspirin	235
Drugs	236

Biographies of Selected Scientists	239
Chemicals and Supplies	267
Bibliography	273

Preface

You are about to delve into a wide-ranging collection of topics harvested from the notebooks of a teacher with a breadth of experience, both in elementary class teaching as well as in high school science. David has taught chemistry in these three classes over a dozen times at the request of class teachers. This book will be a valuable resource for preparing the chemistry blocks in the seventh and eighth grades, and also for the introductory high school chemistry block in the ninth grade, along with other resources on the Waldorf approach to science and especially the books on chemistry mentioned in the introduction.

David has woven the fruits of his classroom work into sections, sharing tips on classroom pedagogy, the wonder of chemistry, the role of enthusiasm, as well as a good deal of practical material on experiments and safety information. There are also lovely selections of poetry and aphorisms which can be wonderful artistic additions to enrich the blocks. I hope you enjoy all this material as much as I do.

– John Petering, editor
May 2001

The author expresses gratitude to Graham Kennish and Robert Mays for their careful reading of this book and for advising me of the corrections to be made.

– David Mitchell
February 2004

Developing Scientific Thinking

Education is not to fill a bucket but to kindle a fire.
– Herodotus 485–425 BC
The Father of History

Waldorf education works with the developmental stages of growth in children. The harmonious unfolding of the personality depends on the healthy maturation of each developmental stage, and each progression builds upon the one before it.[1] Strengthening a child's later cognition in science begins with the building of a strong foundation in the early years, initially by parents and family and later by teachers.

Pre-school children are informed about the world through their bodily or sense impressions. The wonder in the world passes directly into their physical, sensory organization through every experience they encounter. Impressions are stored as cellular memory as the organs of the body are being sculpted. Young children have a feeling of "oneness" with the world, and the world is their teacher. These sensory engravings later become the basis upon which scientific cognition is founded.

What can parents do to help their children? Parents have the opportunity to enrich this time of development by surrounding their children with beauty, rhythm and activities which appropriately stimulate the senses. The nourishment the parent provides for the child builds security in the world and allows for the gradual awakening of the individuality or self. In the early years everything coming toward the child from the environment requires adult attention and discretion; sounds, tastes, light sources and all outer impressions which could possibly over-stimulate the child's sense life and throw it into imbalance need to be monitored.

To constructively aid development, adults could arrange activities so the children are consciously exposed to different smells (acrid, sweet, pungent), tastes (salty, sweet, sour), surfaces (smooth, rough, soft), and so on. They could be encouraged to practice balancing on logs and stones; they could jump rope and be introduced to other games requiring rhythmic movement and spatial awareness. Warm, cool, hot and tepid should become living experiences, and lightness, heaviness, bigness and smallness should be understood through wakeful activity. All of the primary senses need to be set to work.[2]

A good place to do this is the kitchen where science underlays every activity. The children can experience the smell of yeast as the bread rises (fermentation) as well as the transformation of the bread as it is being baked; they could on special occasions experience the old traditional kitchen tasks of boiling fruit and jelling jams with pectin, the caramelizing of sugar, the separation of whey from milk, and the aroma of eggs being fried or custard being baked with nutmeg. In the kitchen, the mother and father become resident chemists, and if they ensoul their activity with love, they will fill the child's soul with warmth, and the child will help develop a loving relationship for learning and experimenting as he observes and imitates the parents. These participatory activities become the foundation stones for a later acquired scientific thinking.

Between ages three and five is the time when the children are learning to comprehend weight (mass)—but understanding it directly through their limbs and senses. Once, at a birthday party for one of our four children, I made the mistake of cutting the birthday cake disproportionately. My four-year-old daughter complained to me that her older sister had received a larger piece. Quietly, I reached over and cut hers in half and said, "There, now you have two," and she was satisfied. This would not work with a child past the age of seven.

Try never to answer a child's scientific questions with dead, intellectual concepts. A young child does not have the ability to fully comprehend scientific abstraction. For example, a friend and father of a child in my fifth grade class disputed this with me. He was a highly educated scientist—a missile engineer at Raytheon Corporation in Massachusetts. One day after a long day at work, he came home and decided to soak his stress away in the bathtub. His young son, Jason, a kindergartner, was happy to see him home and accompanied him to the bath to talk. Jason saw the bath water rise when his father entered the tub and asked him why this happened. His dad thought for awhile and then explained to him in detail Archimedes' principle. Throughout the conversation Jason nodded comprehension. The next morning at breakfast he decided to see what Jason remembered so he could have fun with me at our next meeting. He asked Jason, "Do you remember what we talked about last night while I was in the bathtub?" Jason nodded. The father continued, "Can you remember the name of the man I told you about?" Jason could not remember. The father continued, "Do you remember you observed that the water in the bathtub rose when I got in and I told you why?" Jason said yes, he remembered. The father continued, "What was the point of the story I told you about Archimedes?" Jason replied, "The bathtub will overflow if two people get in at the same time!" His father and I had a wonderful laugh as he related this story to me and acknowledged that he now understood the futility of too early intellectualization with young children. They are, by nature, very practical and use pictorial thinking, as Jason demonstrated.

Children need living pictures that fill their souls with wonder and surprise, not lifeless, abstract reasoning. Their inner imaging becomes vitalized when an observation awakens a feeling of reverence. Reverence and a sense of wonder are the groundwork that Waldorf education uses to build its science curriculum.

It is interesting to consider the derivation of the word "science." It evolved from the Latin word *scientia* which means "knowledge." In science knowledge is acquired through observation. The task for teachers and parents of young children is to encourage them to carefully observe, love and feel the wonder of the phenomena in the world around them. The stimulation of observation in the early years strengthens the thinking needed for science when they reach puberty.

How does one observe? The word "observation" has the roots of two words within it—"serve" and "object." This is the key to the activity of looking at something; we ask the children "to serve the object." In other words, we ask them to put aside their feelings, their sympathies and antipathies, their preconceived notions and to ultimately allow the phenomena themselves to speak directly to them, to fill their soul.

Some of the activities which help lay a healthy foundation for scientific thinking in the elementary school child involve activities in nature—walks on which the adult helps stimulate the child's observation to notice the seeds in the swaying grasses, the pattern of the bark on different trees, the glitter within a rock, the geometry of a particular leaf or flower, the reflection in a puddle, and so on. The important thing at this stage is not to allow judgments or concepts to become fixed. Rather, let the observations stand, expand upon them, and provide opportunities for experimentation and comparison.

In the Waldorf first grade the children meet the metamorphosis of the butterfly and the wisdom imbedded in the various fairy tales. Minerals are available in the classroom as are a terrarium and plants which require human care and consciousness. Academically, the teacher refrains from dry facts or platitudes and strives to build up inner pictures of living organisms. The children's minds are allowed flexibility and expansiveness. The "wholeness" and security in the world is emphasized.

In the second grade the class meets the fables. In a fable, such as "The Wolf and the Lamb" by Aesop, the teacher can ask questions which the class can answer out of their own collective observations. How do the wolf and the lamb walk? Both walk on four feet. What are their skins like? The lamb has soft, white, fluffy wool, and the wolf has rough, matted, shaggy fur. What are their teeth like? The lamb has small, chisel-shaped front teeth (incisors) which it uses for cutting grass. The wolf has predominantly sharp, pointed teeth (canines) which it uses for ripping meat. Both have flat strong back teeth (molars) for grinding and chewing. How do they live? The lambs live in groups or herds and are dependent on each other for safety. The wolf is a loner and hunts independently for his daily meal but can also travel in a pack to overwhelm prey. In such a way the second grade teacher can build up objective and accurate pictures from within the animal kingdom which will return in future zoology classes.

The third grade is involved in farming, gardening, house building, measuring, weighing, analyzing soils, identifying grains and other practical activities which develop and solidify their scientific knowledge. This particular year finds the children going through physical changes. Their heartbeat slows down to a 4 : 1 ratio with their breathing. This is the ratio of the adult.

Also at this age the psychology changes; the children are able to discern a separation between the self and the world. The special tree no longer has a name—it is now objectively a tree! The children begin to lose the complete trust in the world that they had in the early years of childhood. They undergo a transformation from the imaginative, moral treatment of the kingdoms of nature to one in which they stand opposite natural objects in a more objective way—and they now need to understand them. This is developmentally the right time for a more objective science to be taught.

The fourth grade meets this need through the main lesson on zoology which continues into the fifth grade when botany is added. The question for the teacher is, "What is expressing itself in the plant?" The plant should be examined as an integral part of its environment, but again pictures should be the vehicle for this knowledge, not dry, dead facts.

While teaching botany to my fifth grade, I asked the class one day what a seed was. One of my more imaginative students replied, "A seed is a little box with its lunch inside." The image contained in this response is greater than the fact it conveys. It is an example of metaphorical thinking and is another building block for the scientific reasoning which will blossom in the teenage years.

In the sixth grade mineralogy is introduced by way of the qualitative character of particular landscapes. Limestone landscapes such as the Mammoth Cave area in Kentucky are compared with granite landscapes such as the White Mountains of New England. What are the distinctive plants of each? How does each landscape react to acid rain? What are the different qualities of granite and limestone? Physics—including acoustics, optics, heat, magnetism and static electricity—is introduced in the sixth grade as well. Optics is evolved from their experiences with watercolor painting and acoustics from their experiences in music. The children are now asked to accurately describe the phenomena from the demonstrations. These observations then lead to the discovery of the laws which underlie the phenomena.

Precise, accurate, observations (free of attempts to figure out "what is causing it" behind the senses) are the activities which are reinforced for the next two years in the seventh and eighth grades as chemistry is introduced, physics is deepened, astronomy is explored, and human physiology is studied.

The Waldorf approach to these subjects is different than what you yourself might have encountered in your public or traditional private school education. Historically, the scientific method is taught by the teacher or the textbook, wherein a hypothesis is presented and the students are told to prove it. This method is linear, has predicted results, and does not stimulate everyone. Physicist Victor Weisskopf objected to this sterile approach when he said, "Science is not flat knowledge, formulae, names. It is curiosity, discovering things, and asking why…

We must always begin by asking questions, not by giving answers." And he added, "You can teach only by creating interest, by creating an urge to know." The German poet/scientist Goethe said even more strongly, "Hypotheses are lullabies for teachers to sing their students to sleep!"

Therein is the reason that Waldorf schools use a totally different approach. Waldorf teachers begin with a phenomenon which the students observe. They then take their observations inward and later accurately write about what they saw. The class discusses the observations, thinks about them, wrestles with them, perhaps repeats the experiment, and then strives to arrive at a conclusion. Why did such and such happen? In this process the students' thinking is active. They arrive at the concepts through their own inner thought activity and worked-at judgment. They re-discover what Cavendish or Priestley is credited with discovering, but they own the experience of finding it themselves, they own the concept they have derived. Later the acquired activity of thinking will be of use to them in life when encountering problems requiring discrimination, whether they continue to study science or not.

In the ninth and tenth grades of a Waldorf high school, rigor is applied to the thinking. Now the students must do more than just observe. They must bring discipline to their thinking. There must be logic in their statements. They must understand the working of the internal combustion engine. They must know the glands of the endocrine system and how they function. They must comprehend the properties of metals and understand chemical reactions. Their thinking must become vital, and they must appreciate that it is thinking which has created the modern world. They must learn to value their own thoughts.

When a foundation of observation and disciplined thinking is established, the high school science teacher now introduces a new type of thinking, while still strengthening and building upon the first two. This "new" thinking is called phenomenological thinking. Quite simply it can be explained as follows: First, a phenomenon is carefully observed; second, the rigors and the laws of thinking and science are applied and the phenomenon is contemplated; third, everything up to now is laid to rest, the mind is cleared, and the phenomenon itself is allowed to speak. The student quietly observes what comes forward while keeping the mind from straying. Finally, the student will write what the phenomenon revealed in his life of thought. This activity opens one up to new possibilities.

This type of thinking is freed from the senses and allows the universe to speak through to the individual. It is a type of thinking which is truly moral and can be the fertile ground for the "new" science of the 21st century.

The aim of conventional education is to lead the child into particular fields of knowledge. Waldorf education has the opposite aim—it strives to transform fields of knowledge into "education" in a way that encourages the child's healthy development.

The intention of this book is not to tell you what to do but rather to give you many examples to draw from so that you can be successful as the author of your own lessons.

ENDNOTES:
1. See *Natural Childhood* by John Thomson, New York: Simon and Schuster, 1994, pp. 26–61.
2. See *Will-Developed Intelligence* by David Mitchell and Patti Livingston, Fair Oaks, CA: AWSNA Publications, 1999, pp. 74–75.

Creating a Sense of Wonder in Chemistry

The most beautiful thing we can experience is the mysterious. It is the source of all true art and science. He to whom this emotion is a stranger, who can no longer pause to WONDER and stand rapt in awe, is as good as dead: His eyes are closed. ... to know that what is impenetrable to us really exists, manifesting itself as the highest wisdom and the most radiant beauty which our dull faculties can comprehend only in their most primitive forms—this knowledge, this feeling, is at the center of true religiousness.
– Albert Einstein

Wonder is an experience which blossoms in the soul when one is suddenly surprised and amazed by the attentive consideration of something rare, astonishing and extraordinary. When we feel wonder we feel enlivened through our own vitality and feel a direct connection with an archetypal spark in the Universe. Wonder is the seed of knowledge.

The ancient Greek civilization knew its educational aims. The foundation for all learning was wonder—otherwise there would be no impulse to explore. In the early years of a child's education, poetry, music and movement were developed so that, in more mature years, there would be an understanding for mathematics and philosophy. To guide the social life the religious leaders gave moral instruction through the great dramas written by Euripides, Aeschylus and Sophocles.

The 17th century mathematician and philosopher René Descartes considered wonder a universal human experience. To him the importance of wonder was intellectual rather than religious.[1] Wonder compelled people to study objects until they became familiar and understandable. For this reason, wonder was an important feeling to be attained by scientists who were observing natural phenomena.

Robert Boyle, the British chemist and physicist, for example, decided to observe natural and artificial phosphors. He included in his study not only exotic stones and precious diamonds, but also less elegant substances such as putrefying meat and fish, and even a distillate from human urine. Late one night his servant discovered a rotting veal shank in the larder that was glowing green; he summoned Boyle who worked through the night recording the color and intensity of the light emitting from each part of the meat. Boyle was energized with wonder at the phenomena he was recording. Many scientific discoveries during this time were made based on wonder and careful observation.

During the 18th century, social and religious changes turned wonder into the hallmark of the unsophisticated and credulous. Wonder was discarded as the frivolous activity promoted by magicians. The appreciation of wonder as the foundation of scientific inquiry ended. Intellectuals became infuriated when undiscerning priests, medical quacks and political revolutionaries invoked natural wonders like comets and meteor showers as signs of divine intervention. Wonder began to be associated with ignorance and bad taste, and the intelligentsia became more and more materialistic in their thinking.

We are now at a turning point. There was a historical necessity for thinking to pass through the stage of materialism. The nadir has been reached, and some of the symptoms are apathy and incidences of violence in our schools. The quality of empathy is in the process of being snuffed out like a candle flame, and this leads to apathy, or indifference, which is the arch-enemy of education. The antidote for apathy is the cultivation of empathy and gratitude while allowing students to experience the wonder within the natural world. Gratitude focuses one outwardly. Ingratitude causes estrangement; it cuts one off from the world. The new millennium is desperate for novel ideas about the teaching of science; the souls of youth ask to be kindled with creative passion.

Gratitude is an internal disposition to see the wonder of the world about us, to recognize good things as bounty bestowed and to delight in the beauty and goodness of things given. Empathy allows an individual to merge with others also experiencing their experiences and founding new community. Gratitude is both a spur to learning and byproduct of it. The intellectual journey begins exactly where the virtue of gratitude begins—in wonder: wonder at the unknown, awe-filled appreciation of the mysteries that surround us. The pre-schooler asks, "Why do flowers have colors? Why is the sky blue?" The older student wonders, "How is it that music lifts my heart and spirit? Why does a painting touch me to the inner core of my being?" Teachers need to fan this spark of "wonder" by providing the students with knowledge. The students need to engage in a participatory science. Discovering concepts does not extinguish wonder but rather fuels it, intensifies it and elevates it to a new level.

Teachers need to inspire students with biographies of men and women who saw life as a gift and who struggled through adversity to achieve their goals. We need to share stories about individuals who have come from little, but have accomplished much. We need to relate about those who came from plenitude and, yet, felt the need to give to others. We should stress the works and lives of those who have chosen to give back to humanity—to be faithful stewards of the earth and of their fellow human beings.

We must move away from materialistic, fixed models and create living, inner pictures that can sustain the students through life. For example, in astronomy we might ask the students how many stars they think they can see from a hill on a dark night. After collecting their answers we might then ask them how many grains of sand they have in their hand when they scoop a handful from the beach. They may be surprised when they learn that it is ten thousand grains. That is also approximately the number of stars they can see with their naked eye on a dark night; yet there are as many stars in the heavens as there are grains of sand on the earth.

Or we might borrow an example from a book entitled *Earthsearch* by John Cassidy.[2] He instructs us to find a large open space and place a soccer ball in the center to represent the sun. He then directs us to walk 10 paces in a straight line, stick a common pin in the ground. The head of the pin stands for the planet Mercury. Then take another 9 paces beyond Mercury and put down a peppercorn to represent Venus. Step 7 more paces on and drop another peppercorn for Earth. One inch away from Earth, another pinhead represents the Moon. Take 14 more paces and place a peppercorn for Mars, then 95 paces to Jupiter and place a ping-pong ball. Take 112 paces further and place a marble to represent Saturn.

He then inquires, "How far would you have to walk to reach the nearest star, Proxima Centauri?" He instructs you to pick up another soccer ball to represent it and set off for a walk of 4200 miles. As for the nearest other galaxy, Andromeda, he suggests, don't even consider it!

These two exercises become part of one forever. They create a lasting image in the soul and open you to the enormity of life. They invoke wonder.

Science teaching needs to utilize new techniques based on the old wisdom. This requires a combination of kindling the sparks of imagination, quieting the soul so the inspiration can be heard, and presenting intellectual material so that intuitive truths can be experienced. When we do this we attend to both content and character. We help students move from apathy to wonder, from wonder to knowing, and from knowing to gratitude.

ENDNOTES:
1. See *Wonder, the Rainbow and the Aesthetics of Rare Experiences*, by Philip Fisher, Cambridge, MA: Harvard University Press, 1999.
2. See *Earthsearch* by John Cassidy, Palo Alto, CA: Klutz Inc., 1994.

Sense of Wonder

by

Rachel Carson

If I had influence with the good fairy who is supposed to preside over the christening of all children, I should ask that her gift to each child in the world be a sense of wonder so indestructible that it would last throughout life as an unfailing antidote against the boredom and disenchantments of later years, the sterile preoccupation with things that are artificial, the alienation from the sources of our strength.

If a child is to keep alive his inborn sense of wonder without any such gift from the fairies, he needs the companionship of at least one adult who can share it, rediscovering with him the joy, excitement and mystery of the world we live in. Parents often have a sense of inadequacy when confronted on the one hand with the eager, sensitive mind of a child and on the other with a world of complex physical nature, inhabited by a life so various and unfamiliar that it seems hopeless to reduce it to order and knowledge. In a mood of self-defeat, they exclaim, "How can I possibly teach my child about nature—why, I don't even know one bird from another!"

I sincerely believe that for the child, and for the parent seeking to guide him, it is not half so important to know as to feel. If facts are the seeds that later produce knowledge and wisdom, then the emotions and the impressions of the senses are the fertile soil in which the seeds must grow. The years of early childhood are the time to prepare the soil. Once the emotions have been aroused—a sense of the beautiful, the excitement of the new and the unknown, a feeling of sympathy, pity, admiration or love—then we wish for knowledge about the object of our emotional response. Once found, it has lasting meaning. It is more important to pave the way for the child to want to know than to put him on a diet of facts he is not ready to assimilate.

Teacher's Guidelines

What are the important steps for a successful chemistry class? Waldorf educator and chemistry teacher Frits Julius says that the teacher of Waldorf chemistry must pay attention to four important points:

1. Anything you present in chemistry has to be in correspondence with what is happening within the developmental stage of the child.
2. The teacher must develop an all-embracing world outlook.
3. The students must understand and remember the material—which means we must involve the whole person in their feeling-life, doing-life and thinking-life.
4. The teacher must remember that it is not the amount of material that is covered, but rather how the teacher allows a "breathing space." A phenomenon is shared, a lapse of time is permitted, and then the phenomenon is brought back in memory. (Goethe called this "exact sensorial imagination.")

I would further add:

- It is vital that the students understand that thinking is important and can change the world. Chemistry is a subject where this lives as a reality.
- Have the students recapitulate each demonstration or experiment after it is completed. Refrain from giving explanations. Allow the inner pictures to form purely.
- At the beginning of the next class ask the students, once again, to recapitulate. This process will build mental confidence in the students. They gain surety of thought as they see it with their imagination and strengthen their associative thinking as they translate this inner picture into words.

Demonstrations:
You must develop good "stage" presence for your experiments.

- The display area should be immaculately clean and empty save for the equipment you will be using.
- Consider how the students will be seeing the demonstration. Is the background appropriate? You may need a large, black or white sheet of cardboard so that the phenomenon can be seen clearly.
- Is the lighting adequate for good observation? Should the room be darkened? Should a lighting box be placed under the experiment?
- Is the air in the room fresh? Did you open windows and air-out before class?
- Have all extraneous noises been eliminated? Should the heat be temporarily turned off so that the heating sounds won't overwhelm the acoustics of the experiment?
- Are you wearing a white lab coat so that the colors of your clothing won't be distracting from the phenomenon?

The purpose of this book is to guide teachers, especially those who need assistance in mastering the practical aspects of Waldorf chemistry in grades 7–9. It is assumed, and encouraged strongly, that the reader is already familiar with the contents of at least one of the books below and has an understanding of why Waldorf chemistry classes are taught in the way they are and why this method is developmentally important for our students. The key books are:

Julius, Frits. *The World of Matter and the Education of Man.* Forest Row, UK: Steiner Schools Fellowship, 1987.
———. *Fundamentals for a Phenomenological Study of Chemistry.* Fair Oaks, CA: AWSNA Publications, 2000.
Kolisko, Eugen. *Elementary Chemistry.* Fair Oaks, CA: St. George Books, Rudolf Steiner College Press, 1978.
Ott, Gerhard. *Fundamentals of Chemistry.* Only available in manuscript from private libraries, 1972.

The Process of Learning

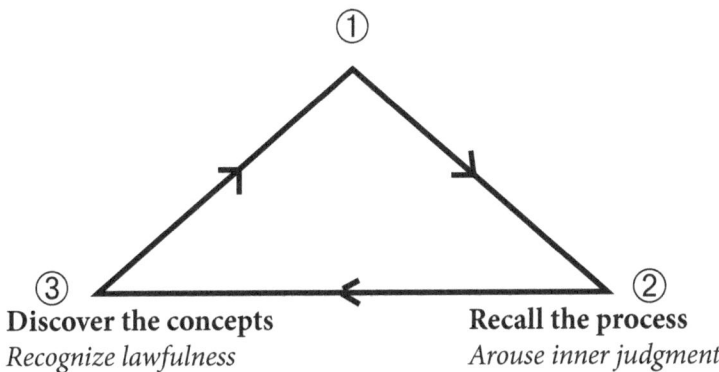

1. Activate the feelings of the students for the subjects being taught. Give them the material they need to stimulate their judgment. Do not give them premature concepts or hypotheses.

2. Arouse their will: Give them an assignment or ask them questions. Pause for several seconds after you have asked the question; do not always call on the first person to raise her hand. Instead, allow the students to struggle inwardly so that they learn to discriminate and arrive at their own individual understanding.

3. Recapitulate and then draw out of them various judgments, always showing the merit of each one until one student hits upon the concept or law toward which you have been shepherding the class. This concept must be alive and useful and should move the students to the next dimension of experience in the subject matter you are teaching.

Teacher's Scheme

Prepare the lesson and lab in great detail.

Practice the lab.

Put notes aside.

| Do not memorize it | "Read" your students. | Do not just wing it |

or

read it

or

deliver it

regardless of students' response.

Respond to their feelings and needs.

or

disregard preparation

or

be too random

or

omit to prepare.

Let the ideas flow through you because:

1. You are confident of the material.
2. You care about the students.
3. You are "reading" the situation.

Orchestrate the lesson and the class.

Tasks for the Teacher

- Have an active review from the previous day with quick questions peppered around the class to wake them up.

- Begin with feeling, then thinking, and then willing or doing.

- Paint the big picture first—"whole to the part."

- Invoke mental pictures in the students.

- Explain things from different points of view.

- Use analogy, story, color.
    Invoke both laughter and quietness.
    Dramatize with facial, eye and body movements.
    Vary tonal inflection.
    Be unpredictable.
    Role-play the subject.

- Encourage imagination, intuition and original thought.

- Put questions … then pause … at least 5 whole seconds before expecting an answer.

- Don't answer your own question—draw it out of the students.

- Use activities to allow students to discover the concept.

- Stress understanding instead of memorization.

- Show why a process works, not just how it is done.

Points to Consider after Each Day

1. Did I arouse the interest of the children?

2. Was there "soul breathing" in the class? Did they laugh and also feel deep introspection? (A lesson without a laugh is a lost opportunity.)

3. What real images were brought as opposed to judgments or pre-formed concepts?

4. Were different senses of the children properly stimulated?

5. Was the phenomenon experienced by the students?

6. Was the review of the experiment with the apparatus in place successful?

7. Was the recapitulation of the previous day's experiment without equipment successful?

8. Was a concept or "law" arrived at by the class?

9. Did I prepare the children properly for the night?

10. Were the questions that arose from the morning lesson stimulating?

11. Did they give back through the will today what went through the senses yesterday?

12. What new skill or knowledge did the children receive today?

13. Was every child acknowledged, and did they each produce effort?

14. What was done to get the children moving in some way?

15. How can I better apply all of the above tomorrow?

Enthusiasm

Nothing great was ever achieved without enthusiasm.
— Ralph Waldo Emerson
Circles

In a class students are typically doing one of three things. They are either paying attention, daydreaming, or sleeping. We can catch ourselves doing the same thing whenever we listen to a lecture. Obviously the teacher's goal is to engage the students for the entire lesson. Teacher enthusiasm plays a vital role here.

Enthusiasm is infectious! If the teacher is genuinely filled with enthusiasm for the material, then the students will share the mood for the subject. Through questions, projects and other Waldorf methods, the teacher helps the students to translate this mood of enthusiasm into real learning.

Living is learning. When we are most alive, using most fully our energies, senses and capacities, we are learning the most.
— John Holt

1. Awaken feelings for a subject
2. Think about it
3. Do something with it

When binoculars are properly focused, we are aware of the objects within our gaze, not the binoculars. We momentarily forget the medium as we enthusiastically inhale the new vision.

In the same way, occasionally the student is highly interested in the lesson, and the teacher's method of teaching is consistent with the student's natural style of learning. When this occurs, the student may enthusiastically experience the material undistracted by the medium through which he is learning.

We all express our enthusiasm in different ways. We don't have to be overdramatic to fire the students. Sincerity, expressed through a tone of voice, a facial expression, a turn of phrase, a pregnant pause, may be enough.

The main point is to allow the students to arrive at the concept through their own activities and judgments. If we as teachers give the students the space to uncover the concept themselves, they will benefit in a two-fold way. First, students will "own" the concept they have derived. Second, the students will benefit because their thinking has been active in a process of discovery. They will be able to use this process in life when encountering other problems requiring discrimination.

The Goethean approach to chemistry is to observe:

- changes in substances
- the quality of the process
- the order in the different qualities of the process.

How to Read Science

It is important to teach our students "how" to read a difficult science text. Reading science is unlike reading a novel in which clear images come forward to entertain you. Reading an article, paragraph, magazine or book on a scientific topic requires a strategy.

First, imagine that you are being confronted with a picture puzzle. What is it you look for first? Usually you try to find the four corners to give a boundary to the puzzle. You can attack your science reading in the same manner.

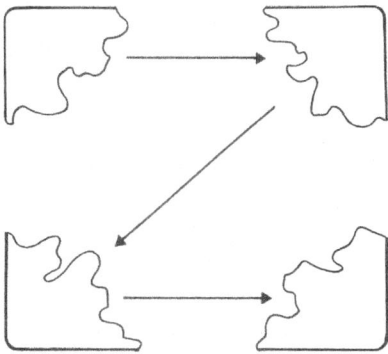

Before you start to read you have to familiarize yourself with the article and recognize that the author is trying to point out his or her observations to you. The following four steps, preliminary to actually reading the text, will help you.

1. Read the title and ask yourself what you already know about the subject.
2. Then thumb through the reading and acquaint yourself with the chapter or paragraph headings, the graphs, the pictures and illustrations. Familiarize yourself with the graphics and ask what the author is trying to get across.
3. Go to the end of the article or book and read the final paragraph or summary. This will give you a clear idea of where the article is heading. Then glance at the topic sentences from a few of the paragraphs.

4. Finally ask yourself questions that you hope to find the answers to as you are reading and then start to read with a highlighter in hand (or a pencil to underline or a notebook to make notes in as you read).

This strategy will save you a great deal of time as you read and will improve your comprehension.

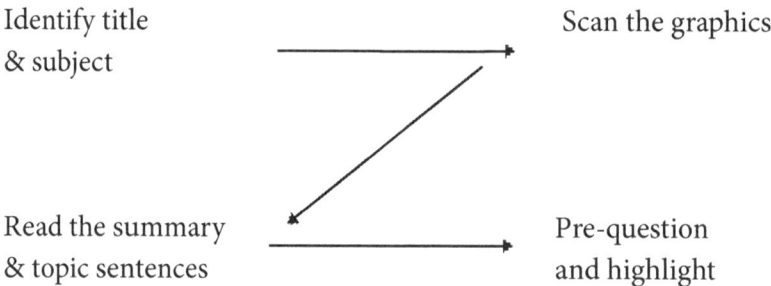

These are the four corners of the puzzle which will give you a strategy to master difficult scientific readings.

Equipment in the Chemistry Lab

It is important that the students know the names of the equipment they will be using, as well as the correct spelling of each. Some of the equipment is illustrated below:

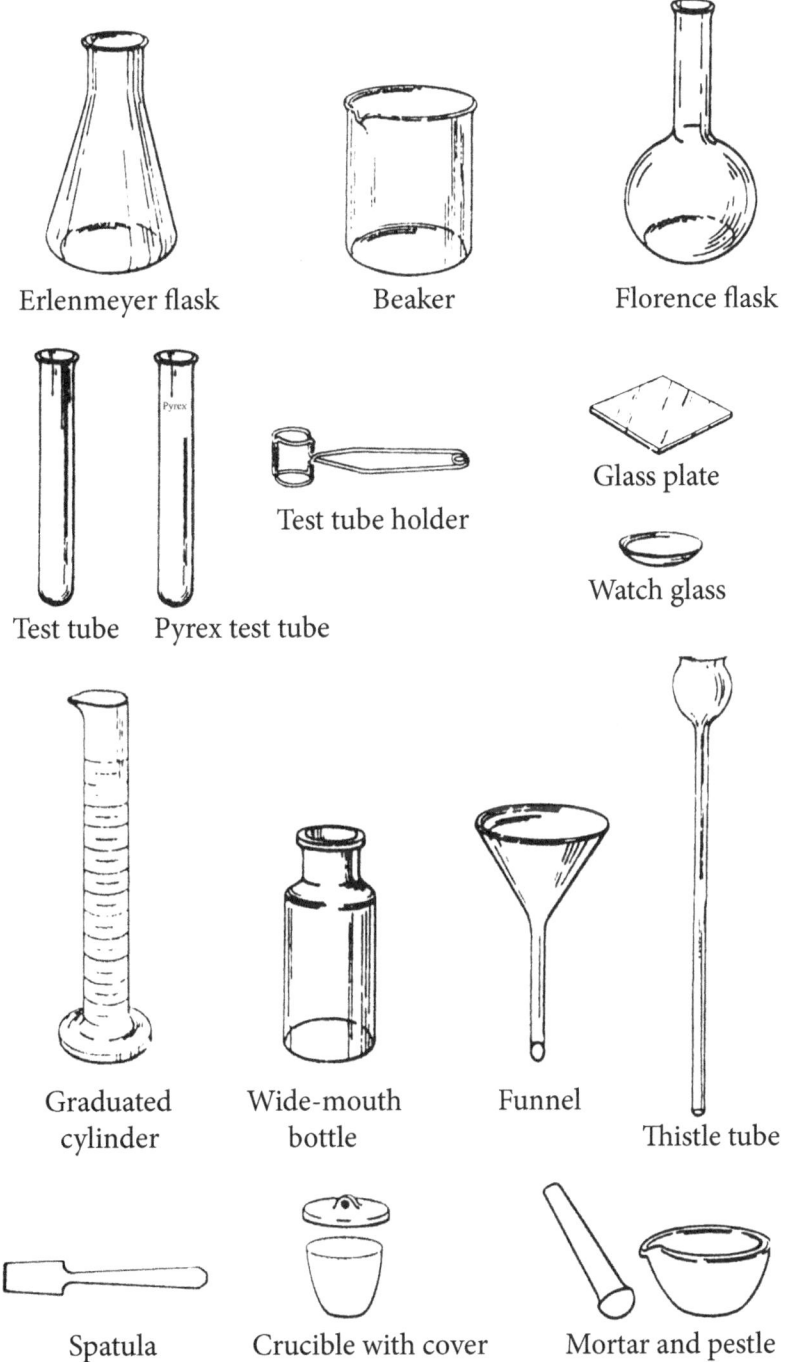

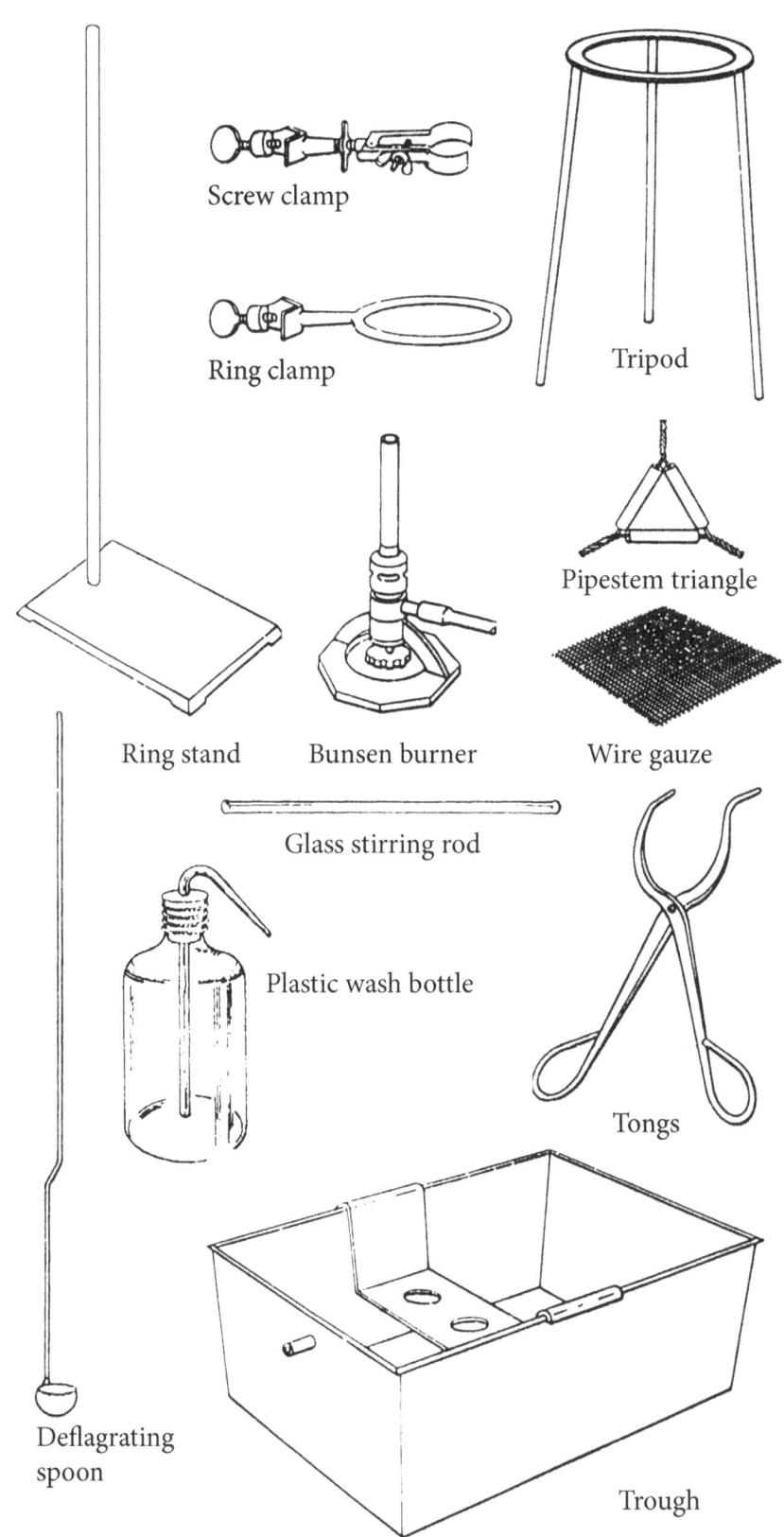

Safety

A teacher's first concern is that of the safety of the students. Chemistry is a safe subject when one uses common sense and follows a few guidelines.

1. The teacher sets the example and therefore must be awake to all safety concerns.
2. Always use correct procedure. (If you don't know, ask someone who does!)
3. Always wear eye protection while demonstrating and have any student who is helping you have on a pair of safety glasses. If students sit close to your demonstration table, they also should have on protective glasses.
4. Have two, properly coded fire extinguishers available—one at the front of the classroom and one at the rear.
5. Wear a lab coat, apron, or other protective clothing.
6. Use only Pyrex glass when heating.
7. Always have an eye wash station or eye wash bottles available.

Follow the illustrated safety procedures below:

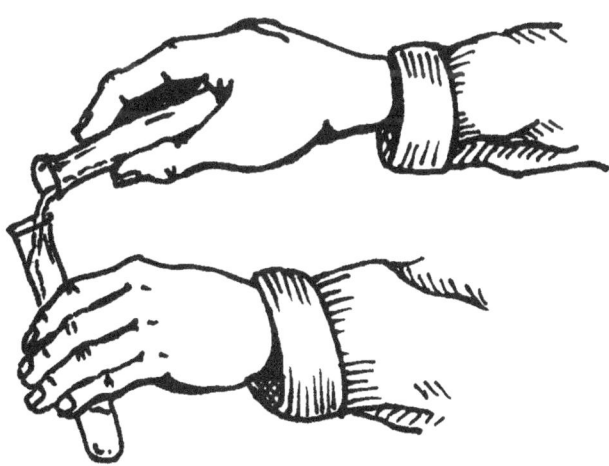

When pouring a liquid from one test tube to another, always extend your arms fully away from the body and pour the liquid down the side of the test tube.

When pouring an acid to a beaker, use a glass rod and stream the acid down the rod into the beaker. Always mix acid into water!

When heating a liquid in a test tube, always tilt the test tube away from your face and gently swirl the test tube through the top of the flame of the Bunsen burner. Use boiling chips to prevent splattering due to violent, sudden boiling.

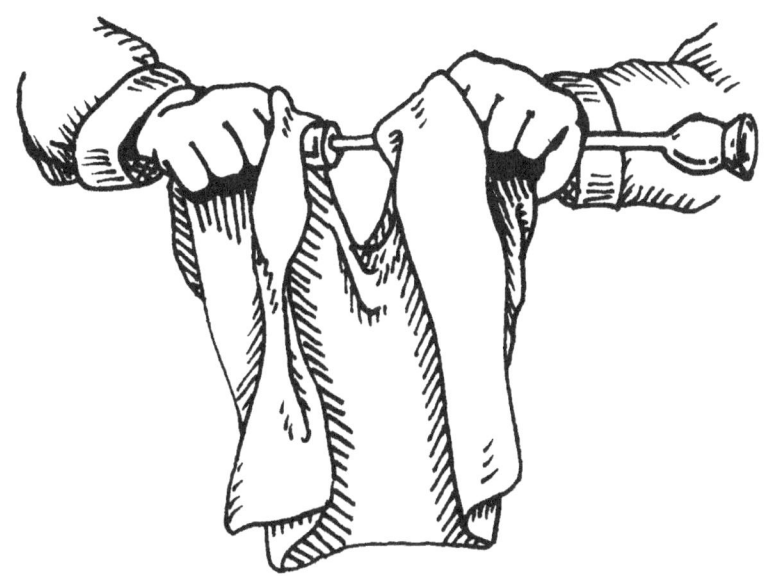

When placing a cork or rubber stopper on a thistle tube or glass tube, always use a cotton towel to protect your hands in case the glass should break. Lubricate with a few drops of glycerin.

When smelling the vapors of any substance, always gently waft the vapors toward your nose with your hand. Never smell the vapors by placing the test tube directly next to your nose.

Use common sense!

Always practice an experiment by yourself before you demonstrate to the class. Use good judgment and *never* take chances.

Ventilation:

This book talks a lot about proper ventilation. I do not mean an open window! I mean a movement of air by a fan or venting system.

If possible the school should have a table with a vacuum venting system which draws in fumes before they rise to face level. A demonstration "hood" vented into an exhaust system or set by an open window with an egress fan is a good investment.

Chemicals:

You should have a three-ring binder with the MSDS sheets (material safety data sheets) listing all the precautions for handling the chemicals in your inventory. (In many states it is a law that these be kept in the vicinity of the chemicals.)

The following are some chemicals with which you might come into contact. Know the potential of all chemicals you use by reading the safety literature which accompanies them. Save all literature in a three-ring binder for future reference.

Compound	Effect	Precaution
Acetone	Headache, drowsiness, skin irritation	Proper ventilation
Ammonia	Irritant to eyes, caustic to lungs, serious when in strong solution	Use diluted with soap and water; corrosive vapors!
Benzene	Intoxication, coma, respiratory failure; alleged carcinogen	Use alternative solvent.
Chlorinated Hydrocarbons	Dissolve fatty layer of skin; cause liver and kidney damage	Avoid if possible; ventilate, wear neoprene rubber gloves; toxic.
Copper Compounds	Oxide, can irritate lungs, intestines, eyes and skin	Ventilate when heating; wear gloves when handling.
Phosphorus	Extremely flammable	Keep locked up in tight-sealed glass container under water.
Lead	Damages brain, central nervous system, red blood cells, marrow, liver, kidneys; fumes are especially dangerous	Avoid if possible; ventilate well; minimize handling, wash hands after touching.
Mercury	Damages brain, nervous system and kidneys	Avoid fumes and skin contact; toxic.
Sulfur	Noxious fumes	Provide ventilation.

Silver Compounds
Absorbed into the skin as vapor or dust
Silver dust in the eyes can cause blindness.

Wear goggles, gloves and a respirator.

Zinc Compounds
Dust and fumes attack the central nervous system, skin and lungs.

Ventilate and wear respirator.

Acids
All acids will burn the skin and cause blindness if they touch the eye. All acids will cause respiratory irritation if inhaled. Some acids, when spilled on clothing, will dissolve the material.

Wear goggles, rubber apron and insure proper ventilation.

Neutralize with a base such as baking soda and flush with a lot of water.

Sodium
Will burn right through the hand

Must be locked up and kept under oil in a sealed bottle. Hazardous!

Aqua Regia
1 part nitric acid
3 parts hydrochloric acid

Caustic acid

Mix carefully, with good ventilation.
Keep in glass, not tightly stoppered. Do not store in a small space.

Gases
Hydrogen
Oxygen
Propane

Explosive and flammable

Use with **CAUTION**, in small amounts.

Esters
Can be noxious

Use **CAUTION** not to spill on clothing.

Turpentine
Skin irritant; brain and lung damage possible

Ventilate; wear gloves.

Benedict's Solution
When hot, it is damaging to the eyes; contains ammonia

Always have an eye wash bottle present.

NOTE: Always use the minimal amount of any material and never place unused material back in the original bottle—it will undoubtedly have been contaminated.

Disposal of Chemicals

All chemicals must always be stored in a locked room or cabinet to take away the temptation they provide for curious teenagers who will, most assuredly, cause mischief with them.

The safe disposal of all chemicals is essential and is the responsibility of the teacher. All local Health and Safety codes should be understood and available in a three-ring binder stored with all chemicals. This binder should also include:

- An emergency poison telephone number
- An emergency chemical assistance number
- The complete set of DOT paperwork which came with the chemical when it arrived
- Date of arrival should be noted on the paperwork
- The manufacturer's factual information on the chemical
- Disposal/recycling directions

Further, insure that every chemical is labeled.

Nothing should be washed down a drain because of the corrosive property of many chemicals which will eat away the plumbing and cause major damage. It is possible to install a stainless steel, laboratory-quality sink with glass pipes and chemical traps if you have the resources. Otherwise it is important to have large brown bottles (to prevent reaction initiated by sunlight) for all liquid wastes.

- Trash should be emptied daily into covered metal containers. At all costs avoid storing oily rags or paper towels which can spontaneously combust. These should be immersed in buckets of water before disposal and removal from the premises.
- A separate container should be made available for all broken glass.
- All ash and solids should be placed in plastic bags and stored in metal containers in the shade. Contact your local disposal service for instructions on how to dispose of legally.
- Recycle as much as possible. Consult a high school chemistry teacher for directions.

- Spent chemicals which contain highly-reactive compounds, water-reactive compounds, concentrated strong oxidizing or reducing agents should never be mixed with other chemical waste. This type of waste should be kept separately in sealed bottles which are made of materials compatible to the waste.
- Always wear splash-proof goggles, gloves and a laboratory coat when handling chemical waste.
- Small amounts of metals or metal salts can be disposed of in the "Spent Metal Solution" container. If a waste meets one or more of the following four "characteristics," it is considered a *hazardous waste*.

◆ **Flammables**

Any liquid having a flashpoint of less than 140° F is an "ignitable" material. This includes almost all organic solvents. Some common examples are:
- aromatics, alcohols and alkanes

and the following miscellaneous examples:
- benzene, methanol, hexane, acetonitrile, toluene,
- ethanol, heptane, acetone, xylene, propanol,
- petroleum ether, ethyl ether, pseudocumene,
- butanol, lacquer thinner, ethyl acetate
- and all compressed gases (propane, methane, etc.).

◆ **Oxidizers** (e.g., potassium nitrate, sodium nitrite)

It is not a liquid and is capable, under standard temperature and pressure, of causing fire through friction, absorption of moisture, or sponataneous chemical changes and, when ignited, burns so vigorously and persistently that it creates a hazard.

◆ **Corrosives**

1. Any aqueous material having a pH less than or equal to 2.0 or greater than or equal to 12.5 is a corrosive material.
2. Any liquid which corrodes steel (SAE 1020) at a rate greater than 8 inches per year at 130° F is a corrosive.
3. All common organic and mineral acids are considered corrosives. Aqueous bases, such as sodium hydroxide or potassium hydroxide, have the characteristic of corrosivity.

The following are examples of corrosives:

Mineral Acids	Organic Acids	Bases
nitric acid	formic acid	ammonium hydroxide
perchloric acid	acetic acid	potassium hydroxide
sulfuric acid	trichloroacetic acid	sodium hydroxide
hydrochloric acid	propionic acid	phosphoric acid

◆ **Reactives**

A waste material is considered "reactive" if it meets any one of the following definitions:

a) It is normally unstable and readily undergoes violent change without detonating.
b) It reacts violently with water or forms potentially explosive mixtures with water or, when mixed with water, forms toxic vapor or fumes.
c) It can form hydrogen cyanide or hydrogen sulfide gas when exposed to pH conditions between 2 and 12.5.
d) It is readily capable of detonation or explosive decomposition if it is subjected to a strong initiating source or is heated under confinement.
e) It meets the definition of a Department of Transportation (DOT) explosive.

Some common examples of reactives are:

Metals	Cyanides	Sulfides	Water reactive
lithium	potassium cyanide	sodium sulfide	calcium hydride
sodium	sodium cyanide	potassium sulfide	sodium methoxide
potassium	silver cyanide	ammonium sulfide	sodium ethoxide
rubidium	ferric cyanide	aluminum chloride	
cesium			

♦ **Toxicity Characteristic Leaching Procedure (TCLP) Wastes**

Any waste product is considered "TCLP toxic" by RCRA regulations if it contains any one of forty named metals, solvents or pesticides in specific quantities. Regulated quantities are in fractions of, or parts per million.

The following chemicals are found under the Toxicity Characteristic and are regulated in parts per million concentration:

Metals	*Organics*
arsenic - 5.0 ppm	benzene - 0.5 ppm
barium - 100 ppm	carbon tetrachloride - 0.5 ppm
cadmium - 1.0 ppm	chlorobenzene - 100 ppm
chromium - 5.0 ppm	chloroform - 6 ppm
lead - 5.0 ppm	cresol - 200 ppm
mercury - 0.2 ppm	methyl ethyl ketone - 200 ppm
selenium - 1.0 ppm	nitrobenzene - 2.0 ppm
silver - 5.0 ppm	pyridine - 5.0 ppm

Most metals are toxic to humans and aquatic life in these parts per million concentrations. Metals are a persistent problem because they cannot be broken down into less toxic materials.

NOTE: I strongly recommend that everyone obtain a free copy of the Flinn catalog from:
> Flinn Inc.
> PO Box 219
> Batavia, IL 60510
> 800 / 452-1261 phone
> 630 / 879-6962 fax

This catalog has an extensive section on chemical and laboratory safety.

A recent study shows that the highest percentage of accidents takes place in ninth grade chemistry labs, the chief reason being that instructions were not read or understood.

Suggestions:

1. Identify and label all chemicals and have defined methods of disposal of all wastes.

2. Store your hazardous wastes in a secure storage area located away from areas frequented by the students.

3. Review and inspect obsolete equipment prior to disposal to ensure that it does not contain hazardous components that need to be recycled or disposed of as hazardous waste. Potential items of concern include: batteries, ballasts, capacitors, mercury switches, cathode tubes, computer components and lamps.

4. Inform your colleagues about your hazardous waste management procedures. Their support and participation are necessary for your efforts to be successful.

5. Promote methods to eliminate, conserve or recycle the hazardous materials in your inventory as a means to decrease the volume of hazardous waste generated by your school. This approach can improve the health and safety of your school while also decreasing your disposal costs.

Prologue to the Chemistry Main Lesson

During puberty and adolescence, it is especially important to recognize the individuality of each student. The handshake and the look into the eyes at the beginning of each main lesson allow for warm personal contact as do the few brief words of exchange between the teacher and student.

Once gathered, the class stands and centers itself. When quiet the morning verse is recited followed by a song, poem, or recorder piece. Next comes the awakening of the mind. Tongue twisters are spoken and humor is experienced. The pace is lively, and everyone in the class is included both collectively and individually. The class stands up.

The teacher then speaks a short number series (say, 7562) which the class repeats. Then a student is challenged to say it forward and then backward. If successful they sit down. The number series is lengthened as they show their sharpness (98564, 314878, 7489032, 3035419244). The largest numbers are telephone numbers of students in the class. When they realize this it adds to the excitement.

After they have all earned the right to sit down again, we look at vocabulary. First, there are several scrambled words on the blackboard (shohuropps = phosphorus, or cenices = science, and so on). The class unscrambles them. Second, they are asked the meaning of the week's vocabulary.

Now that they are warmed up in their thinking, they recapitulate the previous day's lesson. The teacher guides the process with short, clearly formulated questions which are peppered around the classroom. Then the pace slows and the students are asked if anything from the day before was unclear. If necessary, the other students provide further clarity with the teacher acting as a guide. They are now prepared to explore and articulate the "law" behind the phenomenon.

The appartus for the next experiment is set up, and the the next experiment proceeds. Allow a few moments for the phenomenon to be digested and then, with the apparatus still assembled, ask the students to describe what they observed. Go slowly so that every detail from the class can be considered.

Seventh Grade Chemistry

*O, Nature, from thee are all things,
In thee are all things,
To thee are all things returned.*
— Marcus Aurelius

*Those sciences are vain and full of errors
which are not born from experiment, the
mother of all certainty.*
— Leonardo da Vinci

Seventh Grade Chemistry

Introduction
    Themes for the teacher to consider
    Brief historical background of chemistry

Combustion
    The anatomy of a small bonfire
    The study of the candle
    The plant
    The phenomena of different burnings
        plants - roots, stems, leaves, flowers
        animal - hair, fat, hide, feather
    Opposition of light and weight
    Spontaneous combustion
    Explosions

Gases
    Study of oxygen and biography of Joseph Priestley

Salt formation/ limestone cycle
    Nature of crystallization in formation of chalk
    Limestone in nature/ the limestone cycle

Sulfur and phosphorus
    Physical observation and description
    Properties of combustion
    Relationship to human beings

The burning of carbon
    Physical observation and description
    Properties of combustion

Acids and bases
    Properties and uses of acids and bases
    Litmus—cabbage water
    pH scale
    Acids and bases in the human body
    How acids and bases react to form salts

Crystallization

The chemistry of smoking

Themes in the Seventh Grade

The block begins with combustion, and Rudolf Steiner advises us to startle the students with a bonfire. This opens the door for observing and experiencing a wide variety of realms of chemical phenomena. The chemistry teacher should not characterize chemistry by restricting its field of study, but rather through a path of questioning which leads to a spiritual penetration of the transformations of matter and the forces which shape it.

Fire or combustion is the first image we encounter as we contemplate the flame stretching upward, radiating illumination, with gray mineral ash remaining consumed by the process.

The next image is that of the lime cycle. Remnants of life in the form of exoskeletons, shells and calcified bone fall to the bottom of the sea over immense periods of time. They become compacted and then are lifted up on the shoulders of geological upheaval to become limestone mountains. We heat the rock, break it down to desiccated powder, then add water and sand to revitalize it into a bonding mortar for bricks and stone. We also use the lime to explore salt formation and crystallization. This leads nicely into the study of acids and bases and finally, if there is time, into the metals.

The teacher navigates the students to observe ever more carefully as each demonstration unfolds. The class collectively reviews each phenomenon so that new insights can present themselves.

There are many diversions and side paths the teacher can take along the way. What cannot be done in one year can be picked up in the next. The following represents the path taken by one teacher and is presented so that you might be inspired to find your own way.

In lecture #2 of Curriculum, Steiner advises the following:

> *Make your start with a process such as burning, and from such an ordinary process you try to achieve a transition to simple chemical concepts.*

A Brief History of Chemistry

Chemistry is one of the youngest of the sciences. It began when mankind learned to keep a fire going. The earliest evidence of this is from an area around Bejing, China, where ashes and charred bones were found and have been carbon-dated to two hundred thousand years ago.

Fire was first used for metallurgy when an observant relative noticed a rock melting by a hot fire. This rock was most likely pure copper. Evidence has been found to suggest that metal smelting was taking place in 7800 BC in Asia and 7000 BC in Peru. Bone, antler and stone implements were now replaced by metal ones. Soon metals were mixed (alloyed) to produce stronger tools.

Clay also was found to become hardened by fire. This chemical transformation was the birth of pottery. Pots dating back to 6000 BC have been found in Egypt and to 2500 BC in China.

Sand under a hot fire was transformed into a hard, smooth substance in the city of Ur in Mesopotamia around 3000 BC. The people of Ur controlled this process and made glass beads. The first glass for windows was made in Rome around 100 BC. This glass looked like the bottom of a glass soda bottle and was translucent not transparent.

The alchemists of the Middle Ages followed Aristotle's views and believed that all matter consisted of mixtures of the four elements—water, earth, air and fire. Some sought to transform one substance into another, such as lead into gold. Others attempted to meet the practical needs of the people on the one hand, and while experimenting to find an elixir for immortality on the other. This age brought forth great healers like Phillipus Paraceles (1493–1541) from Switzerland, who studied nature through observation and imaginative meditation, and the Belgian Jan van Helmont (1577–1644), who studied air and gases.

The last two centuries have seen more discoveries in chemistry than in all of the other sciences combined; it has changed the way most modern human beings live.

Chemistry is the study of the inner nature of substances and how they interact. Today all science is built upon the marriage of perception and understanding.

The Nature of Chemistry

Chemistry is the science dealing with the inner nature of substances as revealed through their transformations, their characteristics and their composition. When water changes from liquid into solid (ice) or into gas (steam), we call these changes *physical* changes. When iron rusts, its inner nature is altered. Rust is no longer the same substance as iron and will not become iron again if it is merely heated or cooled. Thus iron has undergone a *chemical* change.

If cream is separated from skim milk, *physical change* has occurred, but if whole milk is allowed to curdle, the inner nature of its substance has changed, and we say that a *chemical change* has taken place, or as soon as a bite of food enters the mouth and our saliva starts to work upon it, a *chemical change* has begun.

Chemistry, then, is the science in which people observe and study the inner nature of the substances and follow the changes which take place when these substances are combined or are separated.

Of all the forces in the world which can produce chemical changes, the most active is fire. In every burning process a chemical change takes place. Fire (combustion) is a chief tool of chemistry and has played a central role in the history of chemistry.

Anatomy of a Bonfire

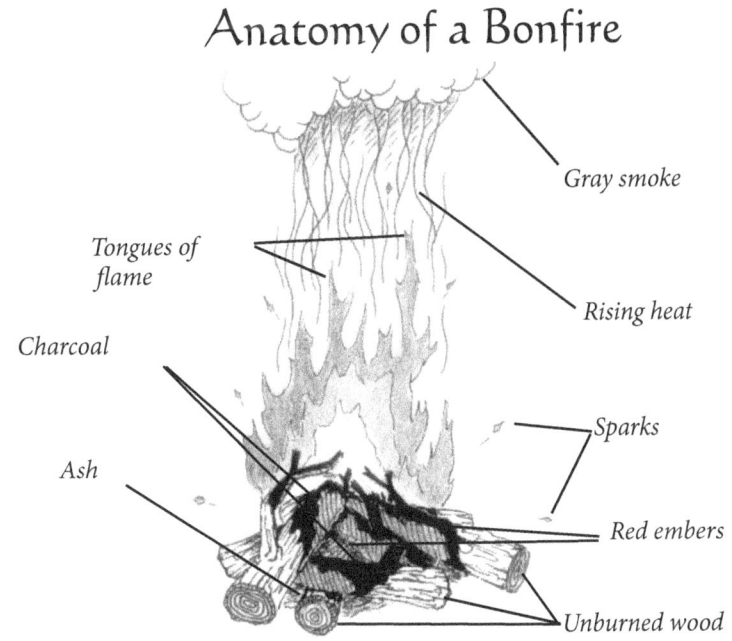

Gray smoke

Tongues of flame

Rising heat

Charcoal

Sparks

Ash

Red embers

Unburned wood

Demonstration #1:

Startle the class by burning a bonfire on a metal trash can lid or a 55-gallon metal drum cut in half. Do this in a sheltered, safe location outdoors so you will not set off the school's fire alarm system. The class should carefully observe and draw what they see as the bonfire burns.

The next morning the bonfire is recalled and the teacher skillfully creates a class consciousness by listing on the blackboard what everyone saw. This accomplished, they are then asked to write on paper their recollection of what they saw.

The metal pan which held the fire has been carefully transported back to the classroom so that the class may draw the "footprint" of the fire the next morning. After it is sketched the class can examine the remains and make further observations such as:

- The center is empty—the fire must have consumed everything there.
- The next layer is soft gray and white ash.
- Then comes black charcoaled wood.
- Finally we have unburned wood on the periphery.

Fire investigators always look for the "hot spot" because it usually indicates where the fire began.

NOTE: Save some of the white ash in a plastic bag for a later demonstration.

Footprint of a Bonfire

Gray ash

Charcoal

Empty—where the fire burned the hottest

Unburned wood

Polarities of Combustion

Upward – flame	*Downward – ash*
Light and movement (flames)	Stillness, heaviness (glowing embers)
Rapid transformation and expansion of all forms which disappear and then new forms appear	General contraction, crumpling, and destruction of all forms
Sparks pop and shoot upward, flame stretches toward the sky.	Charred material collapses into itself and is pulled to earth by gravity.
Bright light with red, yellow, and blue rays out to illuminate the surroundings	Hidden, inward, dull-glowing, throbbing embers only illuminate themselves.
Strives upward and uses lots of air-space	Strives inward to infinity; small particles of dust form which combine with the earth.
The flame is visible and captures our attention.	The ash requires our inner activity to be interested in it and see it.

There is also a tripartite to the polarity and that is the middle zone of the fire. It is less easily observed but here we see the blue flames and what appear to be caves of emptiness. The blue flame is the complementary color to the orange flames on the periphery which demand our attention.

Making Charcoal

Demonstration #2:

Procedure: Find a small, clean metal can with a metal lid. With a nail punch a hole in the center of the lid. With a jackknife slice a small handful of one-inch slivers from a piece of dry pine board. Place the slivers (cellulose) loosely into the can and press the lid on firmly.

Place this on top of a tripod and place a Bunsen burner with a lazy flame underneath. Observe the moisture that will be driven off through the hole in the lid.

When the moisture stops, take a lighted splint and light the gas coming out of the can. Let it burn until it goes out by itself, then remove the flame and allow the can to cool.

When cool, open the can and observe the charcoal. This substance was used for toothpaste in Colonial days. The Egyptians used it to make black eye-shading. Brick charcoal is made the same way and is used by blacksmiths, potters, or anyone needing a controlled, hot, smokeless flame.

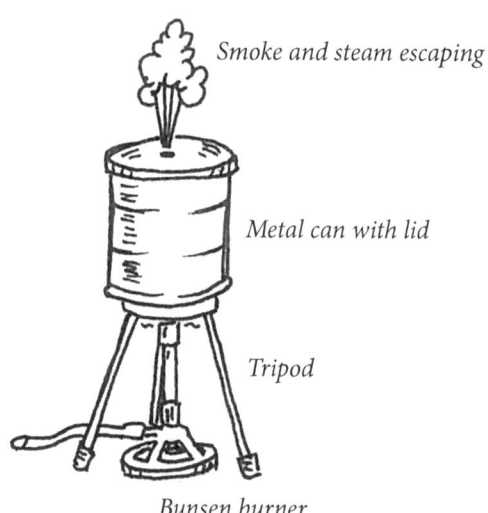

Observation of a Burning Splint

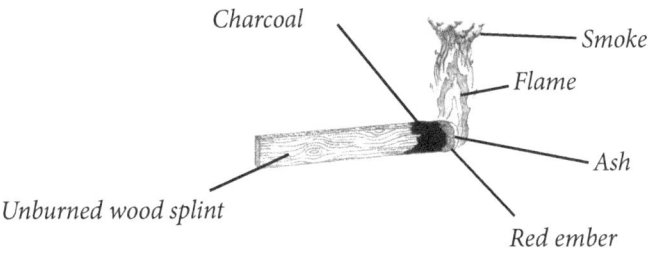

Demonstration #3

Have the students each take a wooden splint and light it from a candle flame. They should observe carefully as the wood burns horizontally as shown in the illustration above. Then they are asked to accurately draw and label what they have seen.

At first the flame makes the splint sizzle, then it turns a charcoal black. This is what we customarily call "burning." But observe carefully and you will see that the charcoal glows bright red/orange at the tip without burning. Then this glowing recedes and is replaced by a gray or white ash. The glow produces more and more ash until gravity pulls it downward to the earth.

Demonstration #4

Place a piece of pine in a Pyrex test tube. With a test tube holder place it over the flame of a Bunsen burner. The wood inside will begin to char and then glow. While still over the flame, tilt the test tube so that the mouth is slightly inclined and watch as a fluid drips out. Catch these few drops of fluid in a watch glass. After it has spilled out you might notice a small flame appear at the mouth of the test tube and a brown-black tar-like fluid appear as droplets on the sides of the test tube.

The clear fluid is water trapped in the wood. The flame at the mouth of the test tube is caused by escaping gases, and the black tar is creosote.

Why didn't the wood itself burn?

The Great Transformation of Substances

Fire has the power to seize upon a heavy oak log and wrap it in leaping flames until it glows through and through like radiant gold, leaving at last only a gray, lifeless ash in its place. Warmth and light have been set free from the substance which held them prisoners. And the unburned lifeless minerals fall to earth once more to become the material for new life. Fire is truly the mighty magician whose process transforms one substance into another.

We burned many different things in class. We found that we could read something about the nature of each substance in the way in which it burned. Here are some of the overall things we noticed about the way things burned:

- Minerals are slow to burn.
- Each burnable substance has a distinct color. Some have ashes, others do not.
- The plant blossom burned quickly and with a clean, light ash.
- The root burned with a high yellow flame and left a coarse ash.
- Animal substances burn less readily. Strong smells accompany the burning, and an ugly heavy ash is left behind.

When we look at fire we feel how it consumes everything and bears it back once more to heaven from whence all things come to earth.

The triangle illustrates the three things which must be present for a fire to burn. Remove any one, and the fire cannot burn.

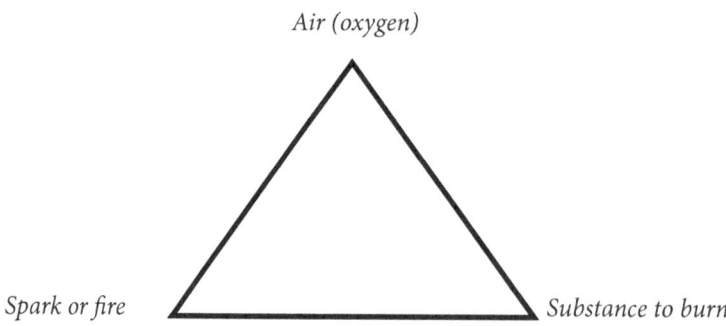

Poetry for the Seventh Grade

Saint Francis

We as human beings are often miserable, heartless,
    small, insignificant.
But within us a flamelike essence drives us ruthlessly upward.
From within this human mire, divine songs well up—
    great ideas—powerful loves—an unsleeping assault
    full of mystery.
                – Nikos Kazantzakis

Fire

And what the might of fire doth seize
No longer monstrous cumbering earth
Is whirling away and vanishing
To hasten up to where it had its birth.
                 – Johann Wolfgang von Goethe

The Candle

Demonstrations #5–8:

Darken the room and have the students paired up in front of the candles. With a taper light each candle and ask the students to accurately draw with their colored pencils a full-page drawing of what they observe.

After this is completed, blow out the candles and conduct the experiments below:

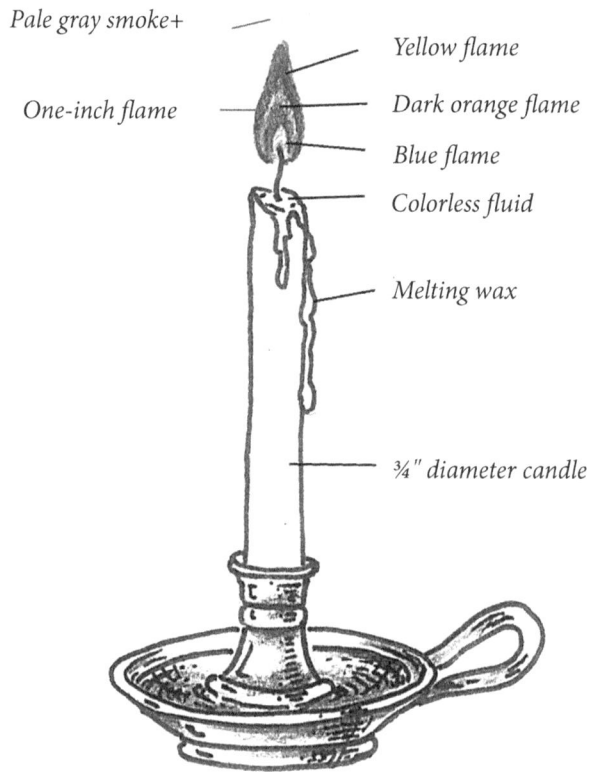

1. With a glass tube carefully blow air into the center of the flame. You will have made a small blow torch.

2. Blow the candle flame out, hold a lit splint above the vapors and watch the flame hop back onto the wick.

NOTE: Also consult *Faraday's Chemical History of a Candle*, Chicago Review Press, 1988.

3. Put a beaker over the candle and observe the flame slowly die out. Without air, fire will not exist. Fire uses up air.

4. Set up a pie pan filled with water. Light a piece of paper, place it in a beaker or glass, invert it and set it in the water. As the paper burns, the water level in the glass rises. Fire consumes air.

5. Carefully place a small glass tube in the center of the candle flame and hold it at approximately a 30° angle to draw off the unburned gases. With care, you should be able to light the gases emitting from the other end of the tube. Fire has unburned gases in it.

6. Take a manila folder or other stiff cardboard and gently lower it horizontally onto the flame until it reaches the inner core.

Hold it there for a second and then observe the footprint of the flame on the cardboard. The pattern of the charring or residue of soot will be clear in the center and dark around the circumference. The flame has solids in it (carbon).

7. Take a cold stainless steel knife or spoon and place it in the center of the candle flame. The black residue left on the knife or spoon is lampblack and was used for making inks in the olden days. Again, fire has solids in it.

8. Darken the room and place a large white posterboard on the blackboard as a screen. In front of it place a lit candle. Slowly approach the candle flame with a lit flashlight until you see a shadow of the flame on the posterboard. Once again, fire has solids in it.

9. Hold a wire screen over the center of a candle flame using pliers. The flame will burn both above and below the wire. By sliding the wire to one side and back again to the center, the flame can be made to burn partly above the screen and partly below. By gently raising and lowering the screen, you can cause the flame to burn entirely above the screen. The small flame above the screen can be made to rise and fall as much as three inches.

10. Observe the burning candle. Ask questions to guide the students into observing that the candle melts, forms a cup, the wax is drawn up the wick, and it is the vapors which combust into a brilliant flame.

Ask the students to share their observations. What do the above experiments tell us about a candle flame? What do we notice about the candle flame?

1. Flammable gases issue from a portion of the candle flame.
2. There are zones within the flame that are hotter or colder.
3. There are three basic regions of a candle flame.
   a. Outer core   – almost invisible
                      – very hot
   b. Middle core – bright yellow
   c. Inner core   – faintly clear region just above the wick
                      – coolest part of the flame
                      – cave of unburned gases

The Plant

1. Take a flowering plant. Carefully lift it out of its pot so you can see the root ball. Snip off a sizeable portion of root and re-pot the plant. Now pluck one blossom and one leaf. Place each in a separate watch glass.

2. Have the students write a paragraph describing each of the three parts of the plant.

3. Darken the room and then take a pair of tongs and successively burn each of the samples, having the students take accurate note of the flame, smoke, ash, sparks and speed of combustion. Take care to catch the ash of each burning in a watch glass for the students to describe. (**NOTE**: If you dry a portion of the root, leaf and blossom for two days beforehand it will ignite faster.)

Plants are like living flames. The roots represent the ash and the blossom the dancing flame. When we burn the blossom not much remains, the stem and the leaves yield a fine ash, and the roots leave a dense coarse ash behind.

The blossom in the human being could be said to be our spirit. It is a controlled fire that is present in all our willed movements. From our spirit a soul light emits. The leaves and stem are like our torso which respires, and our dense bones contain the greatest amount of ash within our body.

Demonstrations #9–11:

Burn separately the blossom, the leaf and the root. Observe and describe: the flame, smoke, sounds, sparks and the ash.

Burning a blossom in a soft flame of a Bunsen burner or an alcohol burner

Combustion

Combustion is the process in which light and warmth which have been imprisoned in the substance are liberated. Freed from constraint, they return to their original states—to their beginnings. Light and warmth strive upward. The dead mineral ash falls to the ground. The watery, in the form of smoke, is wafted round and rises toward the heavens.

What is the difference between a combustible and a non-combustible substance? All combustibles have, at one time, been part of the plant world. Here we find a polarity of upward and downward.

Autumn is nature's time of combustion and this is the best time to teach this main lesson.

Demonstration #12:

Manfred von Mackensen suggests demonstrating the following examples of fire:

Earthy fire: Burn a small pile of charcoal briquettes lit by a Bunsen burner. Fan the fire and observe it as it burns on its own.

Airy fire: Take a long, hole-free, plastic bag such as the bag around the morning newspaper. Flatten it to remove all air and then fill it with propane from a small propane bottle. Close off the end and shut of the propane. Now cross the room to where you have a previously-lit candle. **[CAUTION!]** A foot from the candle quickly squeeze the gas from the bag into the flame. You will get a very dramatic fireball of airy flame which will quickly extinguish.

Fiery fire: Take a small steep-sided bowl of cooking oil and thrust a burning splint into it. It will extinguish. Light another splint and stand it upright in the oil. It will wick up the oil and burn for quite a while.

Watery fire: Take a 50 ml beaker and fill it brimfull of denatured alcohol. With a lit splint ignite the surface and observe the burn. Using tongs or an asbestos glove, pour the burning fluid from waist height into a bucket with an inch of water in the bottom. You will pour liquid fire.

Demonstration #13:

Try to burn water and iodine. Neither will combust and neither will leave an ash.

Demonstration #14:

Ask the students to look around outside and bring to class, in plastic bags, things which will be used to burn. Prepare a rock, a strip of plastic from a gallon milk container, and a piece of animal fat to augment what the class brings.

Materials:

Separate bags containing wood splints, flat pieces of rock, lambs wool, dry leaves, strips of plastic (from a half-gallon milk bottle), pieces of bark, hair, dried dead plants and other samples brought in by the students

Stop watch, metal ruler, watch glass, forceps, Bunsen burner and gas source, safety glasses

Procedure:

Have students carefully burn each item in a relatively dark room. Hold the item with the forceps a foot above the flame and slowly bring each item toward the flame until it combusts. A ruler to measure flame height can be placed in a ring stand by the flame. Students should waft smoke toward their noses by drawing it in a cupped hand. Teams of students should observe different activities, and everyone should record each result. A chart, such as the one below, can be used to note observations.

Flame Observation Chart

Substance	Speed of Burning	Color of Flame	Size of Flame	Description of Smoke	Odor	Description of Ash	Other Comments

NOTE: "Other Comments" can include quality of burning, sparks, sounds, rapid combustion, and so forth.

Student observing the height of the flame with a ruler in the background

After the children have gathered their data, ask them to quietly think about the results. Then ask them which substances burned most readily. They will answer, "The dry, crackly substances from the plant world."

Now compare and discuss the tabulation, noticing which flame was the highest, which ash was the most dense, which smoke was the lightest, which smell was the most pungent, and so forth. Ask them what other observations they made in the "Other Comments" section. Why did certain substances throw sparks? Why did some items emit puffs of smoke? Try to draw out of them as many collective observations as you can. They may now use these collective observations to augment their own notes.

Ignition Variances

Demonstration #15:
- Set a stiff, eight- to ten-inch, metal plate on top of a tripod with a Bunsen burner underneath as shown in the diagram below.
- On each of the four corners of the plate place a different substance.
- Ignite the burner in the exact center of the plate.
- Observe the order in which the substances combust, colors of the flame and smoke, and the nature of the ash.

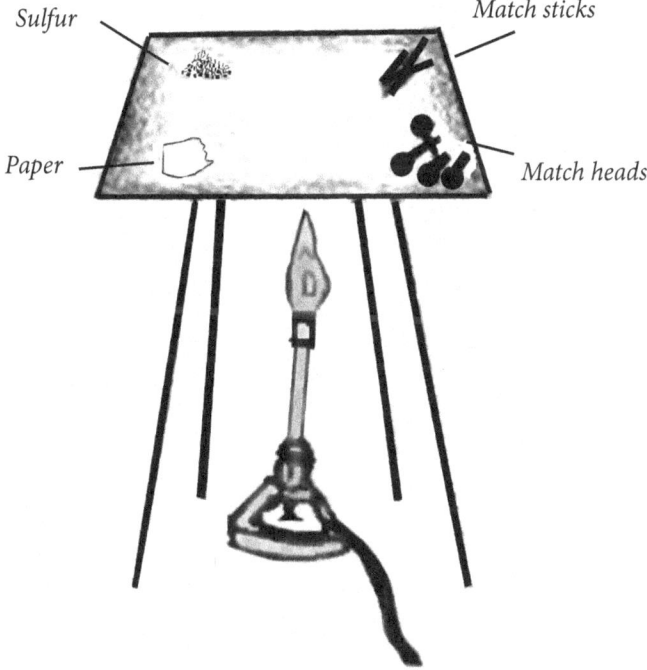

NOTE: Set the above experiment up in a hood, outdoors or an area with adequate ventilation because the sulfur is noxious.

Spontaneous Combustion

Demonstration #16:

Set up a small tin can with a lid as shown in the diagram. Inside the can place 10 ml of dry lycopodium powder or cornstarch and a small, lit birthday-cake candle.

Blow gently on the rubber tube to cause the dry lycopodium powder to puff into the can. The can will explode due to the combustion of the airborne powder, and the lid will fly up to the ceiling with a loud pop.

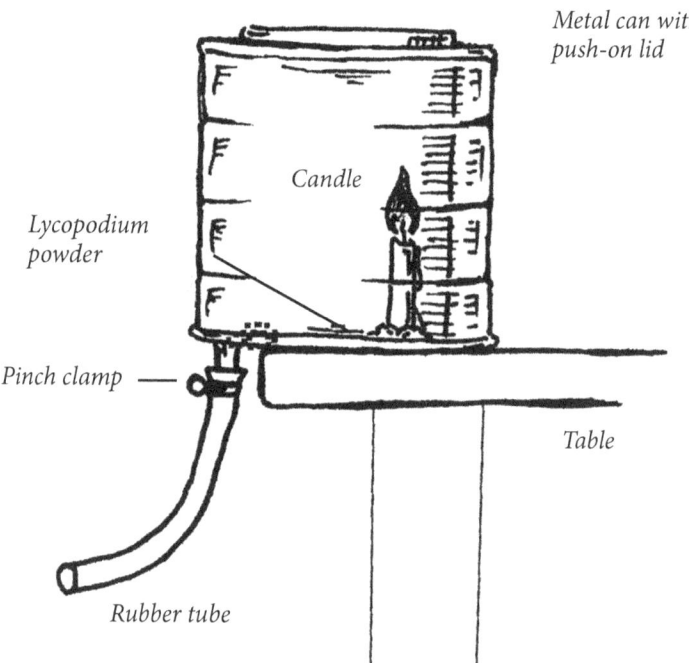

Demonstration #16a:

Dust explosions can be also experienced by placing some dry lycopodium powder or cornstarch on a piece of paper and blowing it into a burning candle or Bunsen burner. Half a teaspoon of powder can be blown with one puff. It will not explode, but you will experience a huge flame.

Spontaneous Fire

Demonstrations #17 and 18:

The students are amazed to see a fire start with no match but just a powder and a liquid. Here are some possibilities.

Experiment A

1. With a mortar and pestle, carefully grind a tablespoon of granulated sugar and place it in a watch glass on a tripod.

2. Do the same with a tablespoon of potassium chlorate and carefully mix it with the sugar in the watch glass.

3. At arm's length, while wearing safety goggles, drop a few drops of concentrated sulfuric acid with a medicine dropper into the center of the powders.

Observation: At first the powders melt into droplets of brown liquid, then they sputter and burst into a bright hot flame. After the flame diminishes you will see a glowing red mass for a moment or two.

Experiment B

1. On a watch glass placed on a tripod, make a cone using one tablespoon of powdered aluminum.

2. Indent the aluminum cone and place a pea-sized portion of sodium peroxide in it.

3. With a medicine dropper, carefully add one drop of water to the sodium peroxide. [Use extreme **CAUTION!**]

Observation: A rapid reaction takes place as the metal combusts with an intense, blinding flash. After the initial flame, the metal glows for several minutes.

NOTE: All chemicals for the above experiments must be kept under lock and key to prevent the students getting into them. They are extremely volatile!

Other Combustion Demonstrations

Demonstration #19:
1. Darken the classroom and take a four-foot board that is about six inches wide.
2. Incline the board at about a 60° angle into a stainless steel sink or a five-gallon pail half filled with water.
3. From a beaker pour some alcohol at the top of the board so that it flows down the board. Put away the alcohol.
4. As the alcohol flows down the board light the stream with a wooden splint at the bottom point of the flow (should be about three quarters of the way down the board).

Observation: What happens? What is the color of the flame? How does the flame move? What does the surface of the board look like afterwards?

Demonstration #20:
This demonstration takes practice and care. It is not for the fainthearted and has elements of danger to it. Warn the students that they must not try this experiment. Nevertheless, it is a perfect demonstration for illustrating how vapors burn and how alcohol has a somewhat cool flame.
1. Darken the classroom.
2. Have a bucket or a large beaker filled with cold water available. Place one hand in the water to get it good and wet.
3. With a medicine dropper take some solution of a previously prepared 3 : 1 alcohol/water mixture.
4. Hold the hand which has been in the water up for the class to see, palm down, with fingers squeezed closely together—this will form a dimple between your pointer and thumb.
5. Into this dimple add the liquid from the medicine dropper and then quickly light it with a wooden splint and a flame borrowed from a candle. The light blue flame will be visible to the class as it dances on your hand. When you begin to feel heat, simply thrust your hand into the bucket of water once again.
6. Fill a watch glass placed on an iron tripod with pure alcohol and light it with a wooden splint. Have the class come forward to look at the flame at eye level. They will notice the flame burns above the alcohol.

Discuss all observations.

Nitrogen Triiodide Explosions

Demonstration #21:

You will need five grams of iodine, three grams of potassium iodide, 20 ml of concentrated ammonium hydroxide, filter paper and a funnel.

Stir the potassium iodide and iodine together in a beaker with 50 ml of water. Add the ammonium hydroxide with a glass stirring rod until no more precipitate forms. Filter and spread a thin layer of the wet solid on several filter papers. [**CAUTION!** Under no circumstances allow any sizeable quantity of the material to dry!] Tear the filter paper into small pieces and allow to dry completely.

Upon drying, the paper is sensitive to touch. You have formed nitrogen triiodide which will explode with the slightest disturbance. It is not a powerful explosive, but it is a very sensitive one.

If you carefully spread wet pieces to dry on the floor of the classroom, they will crackle sharply as the students enter and step on them. (Be sure to warn the janitor so he won't have a heart attack if he enters the room and steps on any undetonated charges.)

If you touch the paper slightly with a yardstick, it will emit a small but sharp explosion.

Other Possible Explosions

Demonstrations #22–25:

Spontaneous delayed combustion/wet and dry

1. On a fire-resistant pad form a small, cone-shaped pile of $KMnO_4$ with a spatula. Then take a medicine dropper and add a few drops of glycerine. Stand back and wait. Within a minute or two, a shower of sparks will startle you and a beautiful lilac-colored flame will shoot up.

Spontaneous combustion started with water

2. On a fire-resistant pad form a small pile of Na_2O_2. Sprinkle aluminum dust on top of the pile. With a medicine dropper about two feet above the pile, release a few drops of water. A violent flash fire will occur.

Cold flame demonstration

3. Prepare 200 ml of solvent consisting of 60 parts methanol and 40 parts water. Add a small amount of NaCl to color the flame. Soak a dollar bill in the solvent for ten minutes, darken the room, remove it from the solvent and ignite it over a candle flame. You will see a luminous blue flame but the dollar bill will not burn up. The flash point for the paper is around 234° and the water will absorb enough of the heat that the temperature of the flame will not get this high.

Solid/solid combustion

4. On a fire-resistant pad form a pile of zinc powder and sulfur powder. Mix the powders together with a dry glass stirring rod or a spatula. Take the handle end of a deflagration spoon or a ten-inch straight length of coat hanger wire and heat it in a Bunsen burner until it glows red. Insert this red-hot metal into the center of the mixture of the zinc powder and sulfur powder. A violent flash and flame will follow.

CAUTION! Use adequate ventilation.

Flame Test

Demonstration #26:

Take a thin wire and make a loop arount the point of a pencil. Wrap the wire around the pencil or a small stick. Dip the loop in water to moisten it and then dip it one at a time into the chemicals below. Darken the room and then burn the chemical in the flame of either an alcohol burner, a candle or a Bunsen burner. Have the students take note of the colors which identify the chemicals.

strontium chloride (tin)	—	bright red flame
potassium nitrate	—	light purple flame
cupric sulfate (copper)	—	green flame
potassium chloride	—	pink/lavender flame
lithium chloride	—	pink to red flame
sodium chloride (salt)	—	bright yellow flame
calcium salts	—	yellow-red flame

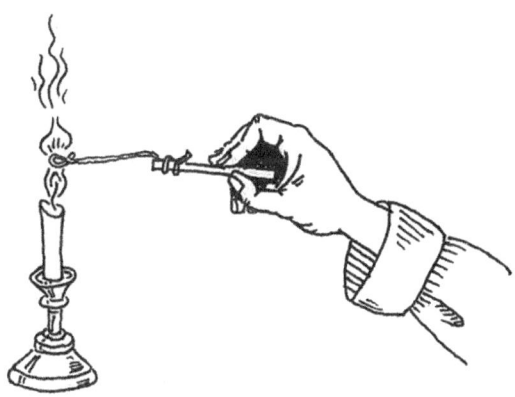

Burning salts with a wire loop

Chemicals in the Home

Common household name	Chemical name
Salt	sodium chloride
Iodized salt	sodium chloride + sodium iodide
Baking soda	sodium bicarbonate
Charcoal	carbon
Cane sugar	sucrose
Vinegar	acetic acid
Ammonia	ammonium hydroxide
Borax	sodium borate
Peroxide	hydrogen peroxide
Eggshells / Oyster shells / Marble chips / Chalk / Limestone	calcium carbonate

The students discuss the chart above and are then asked to look around their homes to find three products with the ingredients listed. They are asked to write them down. The next morning each student slowly reads ingredients while the rest of the class attempts to guess the brand name of the product. (Federal law states that the listings must begin with most abundant ingredient progressing to the least.)

The class can have interesting conversations about processed foods when they realize what they contain. This class is usually a very humorous one, and the reactions of the students are far-ranging.

When asked what they learned, one student told me, "I will never again eat something whose ingredients I cannot pronounce."

Spell of Creation

Within the flower there lies a seed,
Within the seed there springs a tree,
Within the tree there spreads a wood.

In the wood there burns a fire,
And in the fire there melts a stone,
Within the stone a ring of iron.

Within the ring there lies an O,
Within the O there looks an eye,
In the eye there swims a sea.

And in the sea reflected sky,
And in the sky there shines the sun.
Within the sun a bird of gold.

Within the bird there beats a heart,
And from the heart there flows a song,
And in the song there sings a word.

In the word there speaks a world,
A world of JOY, a world of grief,
From joy and grief there springs my love.

Oh love, my love, there—springs a world,
And in the world there shines a sun,
And in the sun there burns a fire.

Within the fire consumes my heart,
And in my heart there beats a bud,
And in the bud there wakes an eye,

Within the eye, earth, sea and sky.
Earth sky and sea within an O,
Lie like the seed within the flower.

– Kathleen Raine

Joseph Priestley
(1733-1804)
and the Discovery of Oxygen

Joseph Priestley lived in Birmingham, England. His ideas on religion and politics were different from other people's, so they thought he was crazy. He sympathized with the ideals of the French Revolution, so his neighbors surrounded his house and burned it to the ground.

Priestley and his family escaped, and he continued his experiments in chemistry. He put some red mercury ash in a tube with a flame under it. The gas that came from the ash was piped into a flask of water. As the gas went in, the water went out and there was nothing but oxygen in the flask. Priestley discovered that if he put a glowing stick in oxygen, it immediately flared into a big flame.

How We Freed Oxygen

Demonstration #27:

We heated a white, salt-like substance called potassium chlorate and found that it melted and then boiled and finally hardened again. Oxygen was released and collected in a flask. When we put a glowing stick into a flask, it flared up in a bright flame. What had taken place can be expressed as follows:

$$\text{Potassium chlorate} \xrightarrow{\text{HEAT}} \text{Potassium chloride} + \text{Oxygen}\uparrow$$

Oxygen Gas Generator

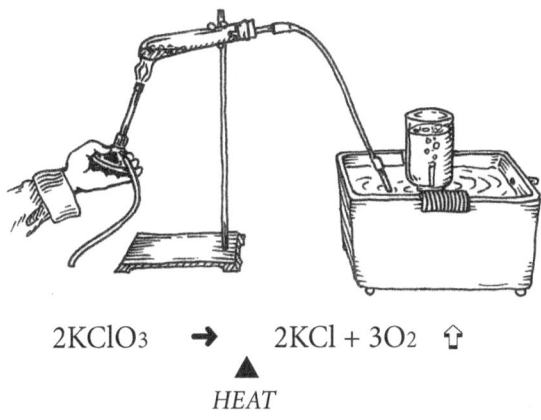

$$2KClO_3 \rightarrow 2KCl + 3O_2 \uparrow$$
▲
HEAT

DANGER! Potassium chlorate is highly explosive!

Oxidation

Oxygen is a very active element which seeks continuously to unite itself with other substances. When, for example, the oxygen in the air unites with iron, rust is formed and heat is released. The chemist would say:

Iron + Oxygen ➜ Iron Oxide (Rust) + Heat

Whenever oxygen unites with another substance in a chemical change, this is called oxidation, and in every oxidation, heat is produced. Rusting of iron and the decay of plant and animal matter are examples of slow oxidation. When oxygen unites very rapidly with a substance, a great deal of heat is produced, and we call such rapid oxidation combustion or burning.

The Nature of Oxygen

Demonstration #28:

If oxygen were not in our bodies, we would be poisoned. Oxygen refreshes our blood, and oxygen is necessary for the digestion of our food.

Oxygen does not smell, it is invisible, and it is a little bit heavier than air. Uses for oxygen include incubators for premature babies, reviving exhausted athletes and reviving drowned people.

Oxygen tanks are an important part of a miner's equipment as well as an astronaut's.

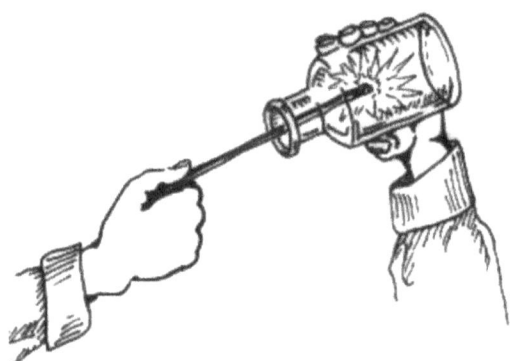

Stick burning vigorously in oxygen

Demonstration #29:

A dramatic, but painfully slow, way to collect oxygen is as follows:
1. Take an aquarium half-filled with pond water. Find some aquatic plants to add to the bottom. Weight them down with stones and place the aquarium in full sun with a fairly constant temperature.
2. Invert two glass funnels over sections of the green plants under water.
3. Fill two large test tubes to the brim with water from the tank. Carefully invert them with your thumb over the openings so that you will lose as little water as possible—then place them over the stem of the funnels.

As the plants go through photosynthesis, the released oxygen will bubble up and displace the water in the test tubes resulting in test tubes of oxygen. This may take several days to accomplish, but it will never be forgotten.

How Calcium Works in the World

In the sixth grade mineralogy we learned that all the calcium rocks, of which the most common are limestone, chalk and marble, were formed on the ocean floor as the shells and bones of myriad sea creatures sank to the ocean's bottom, became mixed with mud and sand, hardened under increasing pressure, and were finally raised above the water in a huge movement of the earth in ages past. The Romans expressed this fact thusly:

Omnius calx e vermibus.
(All lime comes from worms!)

When water into which carbon dioxide has been dissolved runs over limestone (calcium carbonate), it dissolves the limestone and carries it away. The dissolved limestone eventually reaches the ocean where it is absorbed by the tiny sea creatures and is transformed into shell and bone, into coral and even pearls.

When we are young, we need much milk so our bones will grow and harden. When we grow older our bones stop growing, but we still keep on producing calcium. This calcium goes slowly into the blood and the blood flows slower and slower. Finally, the blood cannot do its work and then we die. So calcium can also be seen as a bearer of death.

Class Reading

excerpt from *Ethan Brand: A Chapter from an Abortive Romance*
by Nathaniel Hawthorne (1851)

Bartram, the lime-burner, a rough, heavy-looking man, begrimed with charcoal, sat watching his kiln, at nightfall, while his little son played at building houses with the scattered fragments of marble, when, on the hill-side below them, they heard a roar of laughter, not mirthful, but slow, and even solemn like a wind shaking the boughs of the forest.

"Father, what is that?" asked the little boy, leaving his play and pressing betwixt his father's knees.

"Oh, some drunken man, I suppose," answered the lime-burner. "Some merry fellow from the bar-room in the village, who dared not laugh loud enough within doors, lest he should blow the roof of the house off."

"But, Father," said the child more sensitive than the obtuse, middle-aged clown, "he does not laugh like a man that is glad. So the noise frightens me!"

"Don't be a fool, child!" cried the father, gruffly. "You will never make a man, I do believe; there is too much of your mother in you! I have never known the rustling of a leaf startle you. Hark! Here comes the merry fellow now. You shall see that there is no harm in him."

Bartram and his little son, while they were talking thus, sat watching the same lime-kiln that had been the scene of Ethan Brand's solitary and meditative life, before his search for the Unpardonable Sin. Many years, as we have seen, had now elapsed, since that portentous night when the IDEA was first developed. The kiln, however, on the mountain-side, stood unimpaired, and was in nothing changed since he had thrown his dark thoughts into the intense glow of its furnace and melted them, as it were into the one dark thought that took possession of his life. It was a rude, round, towering hillock of earth heaped about the larger part of its circumference; so that the blocks and fragments of marble might be drawn by cart-loads and thrown in at the top.

There was an opening at the bottom of the tower, like an oven mouth, but large enough to admit a man in a stooping posture, and provided with a massive iron door, which seemed to give admittance into the hill-side. It resembled nothing so much as the private entrance to the infernal regions, which the shepherds of the Delectable Mountains were accustomed to show pilgrims.

There are many such lime-kilns in that tract of country, for the purpose of burning the white marble which composes a large part of the substance of the hills. Some of them, built years ago and long deserted, with weeds growing in the vacant round of the interior, which is open to the sky, and grass and wild-flowers rooting themselves into the chinks of the stones, look already like relics of antiquity, and may yet be overspread with the lichens of centuries to come. Others, where the lime-burner still feeds his daily and night-long fire, afford points of interest to the wanderer among the hills, who seats himself on a log of wood or a fragment of marble, to hold a chat with the solitary man. It is a lonesome, and, when the character is inclined to thought, may be an intensely thoughtful occupation, as it proved in the case of Ethan Brand, who had mused to such a strange purpose, in days gone by, while the fire in this kiln was burning.

The man who now watched the fire was of a different order and troubled himself with no thoughts save the very few that were requisite to his business. At frequent intervals, he flung back the clashing weight of the iron door and, turning his face from the insufferable glare, thrust in huge logs of oak, or stirred the immense brands with a long pole. Within the furnace were seen the curling and riotous flames and the burning marble, almost molten with the intensity of heat; while without, the reflection of the fire quivered on the dark intricacy of the surrounding forest and showed in the foreground a bright and ruddy little picture of the hut, the spring beside its door, the athletic and coal-begrimed figure of the lime-burner, and the half-frightened child, shrinking into the protection of his father's shadow. And when again the iron door was closed, then re-appeared the tender light of the half-full moon, which vainly strove to trace out the indistinct shapes of the neighboring mountains; and, in the upper sky, there was a flitting congregation of clouds, still faintly tinged with the rosy sunset, though thus far down into the valley the sunshine had vanished long and long ago.

The little boy now crept still closer to his father, as footsteps were heard ascending the hill-side, and a human form thrust aside the bushes that clustered the bushes that clustered beneath the trees. …

NOTE: For the complete story refer to: Hawthorne, Nathaniel. *Great Works of Hawthorne.* New York: Harper & Row, 1967, or find a similar collection which includes the short story "Ethan Brand."

Lime(stone)

Demonstration #30:

Calcium carbonate, which we know best in its common form as limestone, has been used from the earliest times as a building stone in the form in which nature presents it to us in the rocks of the earth. The Egyptians built their pyramids out of limestone, and today if we were to walk down State Street in Boston, we would see many high buildings made from limestone.

Burning limestone:

Man has learned to use limestone in other ways too. When we burn it, it is transformed into calcium oxide or quicklime, and a gas is released which we call carbon dioxide.

$$\begin{array}{ccc} \text{Calcium carbonate} & \rightarrow & \text{Calcium oxide} + \text{Carbon dioxide} \uparrow \\ \text{(Limestone)} & \blacktriangle & \text{(quicklime)} \quad \text{("dead air")} \\ & \text{HEAT} & \end{array}$$

Calcium oxide, or quicklime, or burned lime, is used in many ways: in making mortar, refining sugar, softening water, removing hair from leather hides and making glass. It is first, however, generally changed from quicklime into slaked lime.

Investigation of burnt lime:

Now, when water is added to quicklime, clouds of steam arise and it crumbles to a powder we call slaked lime. The quicklime has slaked its thirst.

Slaked lime is combined with sand and water to make mortar. When the mortar dries, it slowly absorbs carbon dioxide from the air and hardens strongly. So the carbon dioxide, which was driven out when calcium carbonate was burned, reunites with the slaked lime to form the rock-like mortar with which bricks in our chimneys are bound together.

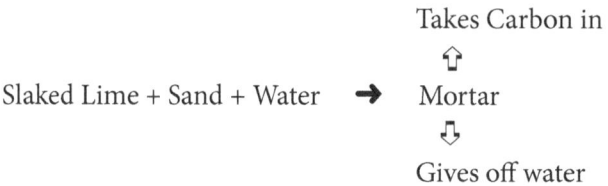

Making Mortar

Assemble 1 teaspoon of calcium hydroxide (slaked lime), 4 teaspoons of sand, a jar and a lid. Place the calcium hydroxide in the jar and make a paste by adding a few drops of water. Stir in the sand a little at a time. Add more water to keep it a stiff paste. Scrape the paste onto the lid, mold it into a brick shape, and allow it to dry for a day or two. This chemical compound is commercially called mortar, and it will set into a hard stone.

Making Quicklime

Demonstration #31:

Marble is composed of calcium carbonate; it can be purchased in rock-sized chunks at a garden supply center. Calcium oxide is called quicklime. They are very different compounds.

Set up the kiln described by John Hoffman at the end of this chapter and proceed as he indicates. If this is not possible then proceed as follows:

1. Take a large lump of white marble and heat it in a solid fuel boiler at 2000°C for 48 hours. Remove it and allow it to cool overnight before you bring it into the classroom. Have the class observe it carefully and compare it with their notes on the original marble. Carefully pour some water on the rock. Patiently observe and in a few minutes, or as long as fifteen minutes, the rock will seem to come alive. It may hiss, sputter and develop fissures reminiscent of primeval geological turbulence. Then it will puff itself up to at least twice its original size, emitting tremendous heat and issuing forth great white clouds of steam.

2. If a solid fuel boiler is not available, I have achieved limited success using a Bunsen burner. Take a thumb-sized piece of white marble, clamp it in a metal screw clamp attached to a ring stand. Place a Bunsen burner underneath. Adjust the screw clamp so that the marble will be in the hottest part of the burner flame. Light the burner and allow it to heat the marble for about twenty minutes while you do other things. The marble should soon glow bright red.

3. Allow the marble to cool completely and place it on a watch glass. Carefully drop one drop of water from a medicine dropper onto the stone. It will pop and sizzle because it is slaking its thirst.

The Lime Cycle

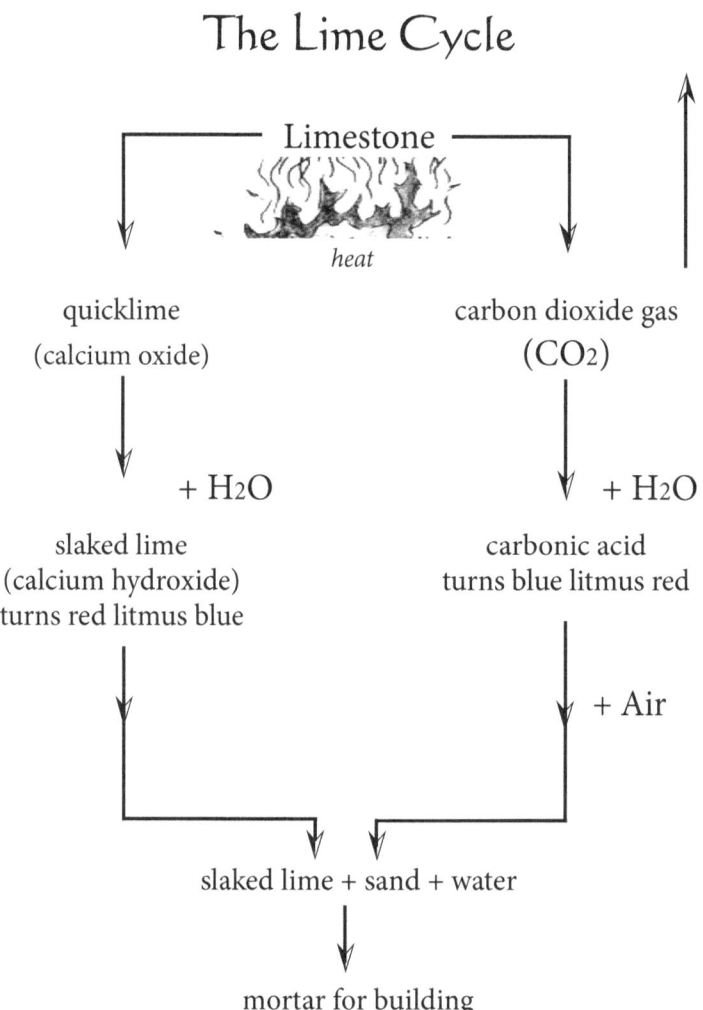

The limestone must burn at 2000° F for four hours.

The three changes are:

Burning: $CaCO_3$ (limestone) $\xrightarrow{HEAT}$ CaO (burned lime) + CO_2

Slaking: CaO (burned lime) + H_2O → $Ca(OH)_2$ (slaked lime)

Building: $Ca(OH)_2$ (slaked lime) + CO → $CaCO_3$ (mortar = limestone)

A substance such as limestone which can crystallize so beautifully and separate into two characteristic substances is called a salt.

A summary of what we have just done can now be placed on the blackboard.

THE LIME CYCLE

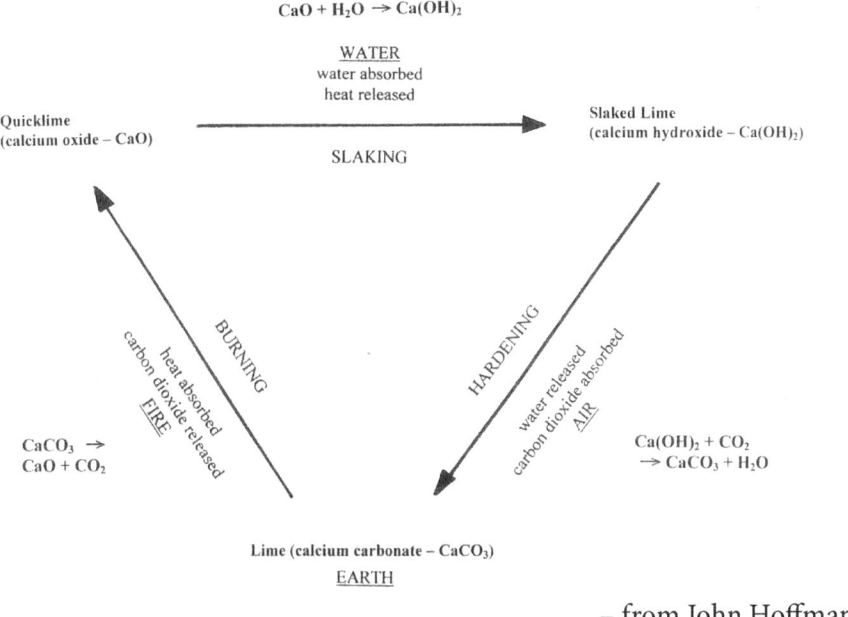

– from John Hoffman

The arrows indicate that something changes into something else.

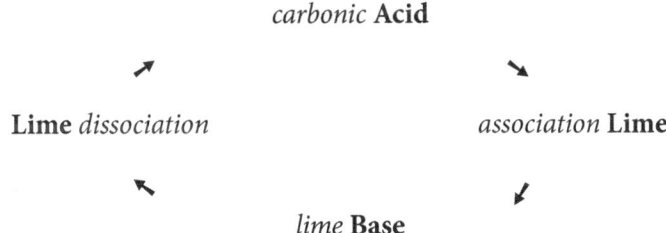

Add a few spatulas of slaked lime to an Erlenmeyer flask and add water. Cork it and shake it until it is throughly mixed. Pour this milky substance through a filter paper in a funnel set in another Erlenmeyer flask. You will now have clear lime water. If not, pour it through another clean filter.

Take a one-foot long piece of fire-polished glass tubing and breathe into the solution through this glass tube. The CO_2 in your breath will turn the lime water milky, and a salty precipitate will fall to the bottom. The lime is basic, the CO_2 in your breath is acidic, and when they mix a salt is formed.

A Lime Kiln

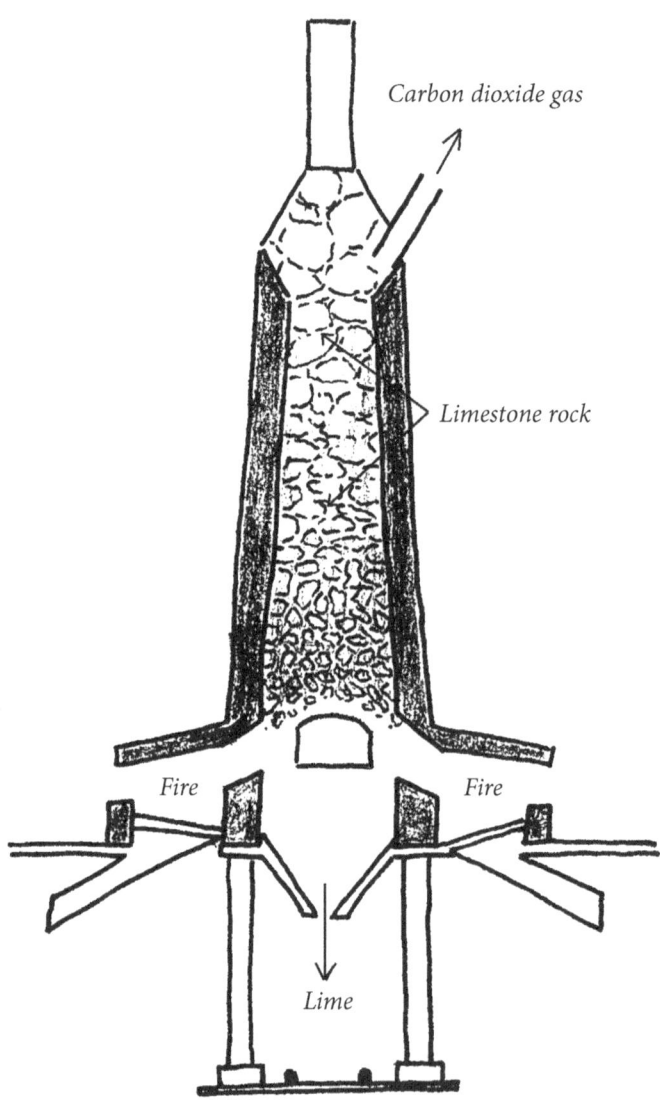

NOTE: To make a class lime kiln outdoors, see the excellent model designed by John C. Hoffman at the conclusion of the chapter on the seventh grade.

Sulfur

Sulfur was known in ancient times. It was called brimstone in the Bible. It is a bright to pale yellow, odorless, brittle solid which has its origin in the bowels of the earth.

It is brought to the surface by hot springs and volcanoes where it can form exquisite crystals. It has a greasy feel, and it exhibits a strong "rotten-egg" odor. It is often found mixed in ores such as pyrites, galena (a prime source for lead) and cinnabar (a prime source for mercury). Sulfur also often occurs within coal, petroleum and natural gas, and is found in the interior of meteorites. It is an element of most proteins and protoplasm in plants and animals.

It has many industrial uses such as in the manufacture of black powder, matches and explosives. It is also used to create rubber, in dyes, in sulfuric acid, and it is used as an insecticide and fungicide.

Most of the world's sulfur comes from Italy, most notably from the volcanic island of Sicily. In the United States sulfur is mined in Texas and Louisiana.

People who have arthritis find relief by bathing in warm sulfur pools because the sulfur softens their bones. During the Plague, sulfur was burned in pots inside of closed houses to kill off the fleas which carried the disease.

Before sulfur burns it melts and then it burns with a soft, steady, blue flame.

Phosphorus

A German alchemist named Henning Brand mixed human urine with sand and then heated the mixture in an oven. When he removed the hot mixture, he found that it glowed intensely in the dark. It was a soft, waxy, off-white material. He named the material phosphorus which means "I bear light." Phosphorus is also made by burning bones, then capturing the gas from the bones and leading it through water, where it hardens. It must be kept in water, otherwise it will smoke and burn with a cold flame. It burns with a shower of clear yellow sparks. It is very dangerous. Phosphorus can be found in the brain, mushrooms, fireflies and rotting wood. It was first used commercially for making the tips of matches which ignite when struck on any rough surface. Unfortunately they could also ignite in the box when they bumped up against each other. In 1845 red phosphorus was discovered and was found to be much safer for making matches.

Demonstration #32:
Burn sulfur and phosphorus in a deflagrating spoon and have the students write down their observations.

Matches
Initially matches were made by placing sulfur and potassium chlorate (an explosive) on the tips of sticks. When rubbed gently the mixture would crackle and then burst into flame with a loud report. These matches were dangerous, and many accidental fires were started with them.

Scientists experimented with using phosphorus which burns at a lower temperature and thus was safer. However, it was discovered that the matches would ignite simply by rubbing against each other. Obviously these were not nice to carry around in your pocket!

Then came the "safety match" which contains manganese dioxide and antimony sulfide. On the side of the match box is painted a mixture containing powdered glass and red phosphorus. Here the match can be struck to be lit. These matches can almost never be ignited by accident.

NOTE: Always cut phosphorus under water. When old it can become brittle and shatter into lots of little pieces when cut. Always use extreme **CAUTION** when handling red or white phosphorus!

Sulfur, Phosphorus and Carbon

In studying how substances burn, we learned that there are three important substances which can be burned which do not come directly from the plant kingdom. They are the minerals sulfur, phosphorus and carbon.

When the earth trembles and rumbles and menacing fire bursts forth from volcanoes, clouds of sulfur fumes are also driven out of the earth. The fire from within the earth lights up once more in the beautiful yellow sulfur crystals. They burn with a dark blue flame. This sulfur fire is also within us, speeding up our digestion, warming our blood and bringing the body juices into circulation. Sulfur enlivens and warms our bodies.

Phosphorus works very differently. It is all light, and its flame is as bright as sunshine. When lightning strikes from the heavens upon the earth, we recognize the smell of phosphorus. We also have phosphorus within us, for it is at work in our brains, so that the light of thought can shine. Phosphorus is also an important element in the formation of our bones.

In the middle, between sulfur and phosphorus, is carbon, which once upon a time was living plant substance. Now it is black and hides its light within itself. The yellow phosphorus flame and the blue sulfur flame are united when carbon, or coal, burns. When we eat plant substance, we burn the carbon within us and breathe out carbon dioxide from our lungs.

Demonstration #33:
Burn charcoal in a deflagrating spoon and have the students write down their observations.

Acids and Bases

Imagine a seesaw. On one end sits "acid" and on the opposite side sits "base." They are of equal weight and will balance the seesaw as long as they remain fixed. However, if one moves toward the center (fulcrum), the equilibrium will be lost and the opposite member will lower to the ground.

The polarity of acids and bases can also be illustrated with regard to their relationship with air and earth. Air is generally measured as a weak acidic gas while the crust of the earth presents a weak base. In the soil we find various clay minerals, iron oxide, manganese dioxide and other similar basic substances.

"Basic" is the description used to describe a moist alkali. The base itself is a solid substance which will, more or less, dissolve in water, or, at least, can be neutralized by a fluid acid. Bases never allow themselves to be volatilized by heating or evaporated in a flame. Usually they remain "ashy" residue and form the "basis" for salts.

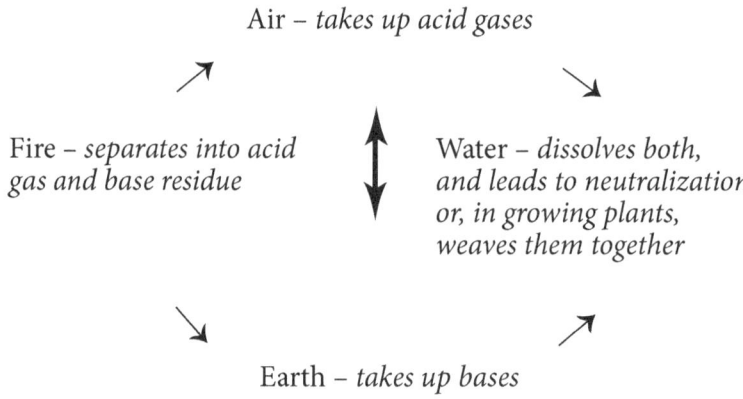

Our bodies need both acids and bases. When we exercise, our muscles stimulate lactic acid. We feel this when we lift weights and feel a burning sensation in our muscles at the end of a repetition or when we run and feel the "runner's stitch" in our abdomen.

When we are still in quiet contemplation, our body creates a "basic" chemistry in our body. To retain optimum health we need to combine activity with stillness in our daily rhythms.

Experiencing Acids and Bases

Demonstration #34:

1. Set up three plastic buckets filled with room-temperature water before class.

In the first add diluted hydrochloric acid until you can feel a prickling, sharp sensation when you stick your hand in and rub your thumb against your forefinger.

In the second add a few crushed pellets of sodium hydroxide, mixing steadily, until you feel a slippery feeling when you rub your thumb against your forefinger.

The third bucket is just pure water and is used as a rinse station. Paper towels and a trash bin are place beside it.

When the children come into class the next morning, ask them to experience the sensations of each, being careful not to spill the beans until everyone has passed the gauntlet. After each has done this, add a small portion of #1 and #2 to test tubes half-filled with red cabbage indicator solution. Again the class should record their observations. The acidic water will turn reddish, and the basic mixture will turn blue/green.

Now, through discussion, they can share their experiences and write them in their notebooks.

2. Ask for three volunteers from the class. Usually the cholerics will jump out of their seats. Have them stand in the front of the classroom with their mouths open and their eyes closed. Onto each tongue place a "pea-sized" portion of baking soda.

Then, with a medicine dropper add several drops of vinegar to all three. Each will foam at the mouth and will have a close encounter with a harmless chemical reaction.

A wash bottle with clean water is handy to rinse their mouths out, and paper towels are available for mopping up. When finished they describe their sensations to their classmates.

The good humor of this experiment is appreciated by all.

Detecting Acids and Bases

Demonstration #35:

Red cabbage makes a wondeful litmus. Boil several red cabbage leaves in a saucepan half-filled with water. Eat the cabbage, strain the water and set it aside in clean bottles to cool.

This liquid can now be used to test for acids and bases. Strong acids will turn the purple liquid scarlet red, and strong bases will turn it yellow/green. Different concentrations will produce different hues of each.

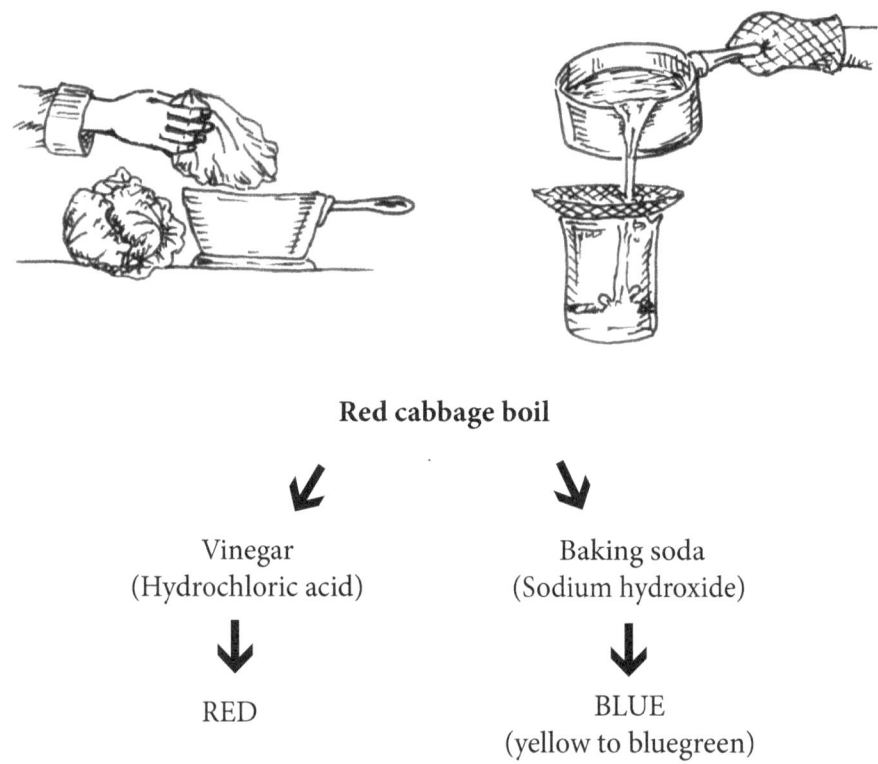

Red cabbage boil

↙ ↘

Vinegar Baking soda
(Hydrochloric acid) (Sodium hydroxide)

↓ ↓

RED BLUE
 (yellow to bluegreen)

Alternating colors by mixing

Three reference colors:

Set up three 250 ml beakers. Fill all four-fifths with cabbage water and line them up on the counter. Leave the central one as a "standard," put a pellet or two of sodium hydroxide in the right beaker and a little hydrochloric acid in the left. These three can be left visible throughout the lessons on acids and bases.

Demonstration #36:

1. Place a piece of wood in a corked Erlenmeyer flask with a glass tube and plastic hose attached and toast it. Capture the smoke in water.

2. Take some of the ash left over from the bonfire which you previously collected in a plastic bag.

3. Set up three beakers half-filled with red cabbage water. One beaker will remain constant with nothing added.

4. Into the first add the ash and stir. Notice the color. It will turn greenish.

5. Into the third add the water with the smoke dissolved in it. Note the color. It will turn pinkish.

The burning wood has emitted an acidic smoke and left an alkaline ash.

Red cabbage water colors:

Green	*Blue*	*Red*
Baking soda water	Cabbage juice	Vinegar
Soap shavings	Alcohol spirits	Lemon juice
Wood ash	Table salt	Sour milk

Acids and Bases

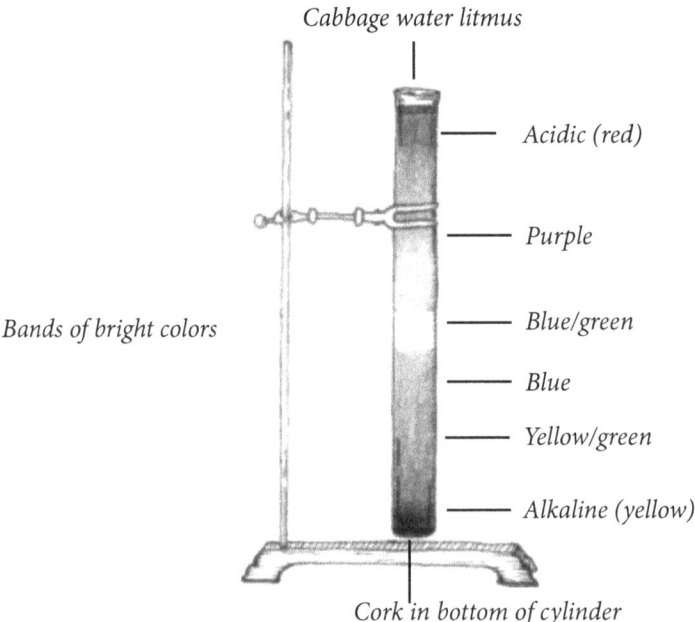

Demonstration #37:

1. Set a long glass tube (three-quarters- to one-inch diameter) in a clamp stand and fill with cold, strained, purple cabbage juice until you come to about two inches from the top.

2. Slowly, with a medicine dropper, add a diluted acid or common vinegar. Watch it turn red and then dissolve. Keep adding slowly until a medium red color appears throughout.

3. Add a tablet of sodium hydroxide and watch it trail a bluish color to the bottom. Add another, and another and another … slowly. You will see a blue or greenish layer form on the bottom. Keep adding the base until this color rises almost to the halfway mark. If you are careful you will get a bright blue/green band between the red and the yellow.

4. Let it set for a few hours and adjust as needed by delicately and gently adding either an acid or base as called for.

5. If you go too far, just slowly add the opposite. Experiment, have fun and you will create amazing balances and color bands if you are patient.

Demonstration #38:
Take a piece each of red and blue litmus paper and press each into a freshly sliced orange, lemon, or grapefruit. The blue litmus will turn red indicating acidity and the red litmus will be unaffected.

Demonstration #39:
Take a small handful of dry straw. Place it on a watch glass and ignite it with a Bunsen burner. Moisten a piece of red and a piece of blue litmus paper with a wash bottle and suspend each in the smoke of the burning straw. The blue litmus will turn red indicating acidity and the red litmus will be unaffected.

Demonstration #40:
Moisten a piece of red and a piece of blue litmus paper with a wash bottle and dip each into the ash of the burned hay. The red litmus will turn blue indicating alkalinity and the blue litmus will be unaffected.

Demonstration #41:
Moisten a piece of red and a piece of blue litmus paper with a wash bottle. Carefully ignite a strip of magnesium held with forceps. Hold the two litmus papers in the fumes. The red litmus will turn blue indicating alkalinity and the blue litmus will be unaffected. Discuss how this is the opposite of what you found in the plant.

Litmus comes from various lichens which grow on trees and rocks. It is used as an acid-base indicator in chemical analyses. Red litmus turns blue when dipped into a moist solution which is basic; blue litmus turns red when dipped into a moist solution which is acidic.

Demonstration #42:
Fill an Erlenmeyer flask half full with lime water. Place a two-hole cork in the opening. In one of the holes place a straight piece of glass tubing which extends to one-inch above the lime water. In the other hole place an L-shaped glass tube so that it penetrates to one-fourth of an inch above the bottom of the flask.

Have a student breathe into the tube. A chemical reaction will take place. The CO_2 in the student's breath will turn the lime water milky.

ACIDS:

1. Taste sour
2. Turn litmus red
3. Neutralize bases
4. Release hydrogen gas when in contact with metals

Some common acids	*Found in*
Acetic	Vinegar
Citric	Lemons, oranges
Tartaric	Grapes
Malic	Apples
Lactic	Sour milk
Boric	Volcanic hot springs

To make	*Chemicals needed*
HCl (hydrochloric)	H_2SO_4 + NaCl chloride
HNO_3 (nitric)	H_2SO_4 + $NaNO_3$ nitrate
$H_2C_2O_4$ (oxalic)	H_2SO_4 + PbC_2O_4 oxalate
$HC_2H_3O_2$ (acetic)	H_2SO_4 + $Ca(C_2H_3O_2)_2$ acetate
$H_2C_3H_4O_6$ (tartaric)	H_2SO_4 + $K_2C_3H_4O_6$ tartrate

NOTE: The information immediately above is for the teacher to help with stock preparations and is not intended for the students.

BASES:

1. Taste soapy
2. Turn litmus blue
3. Feel slippery
4. Neutralize acids

Bases	Formula	Common Name
Sodium hydroxide	NaOH	Lye, caustic soda
Potassium hydroxide	KOH	Potash, potash lye
Magnesium hydroxide	$Mg(OH)_2$	Milk of magnesia
Ammonium hydroxide	NH_4OH	Ammonia water
Calcium hydroxide	$Ca(OH)_2$	Slaked lime, lime water

Strong bases have the ability to dissolve many organic substances such as dirt, grease and food spills, so an important use of bases is in cleaning. Sodium hydroxide will peel and dissolve paint off of wood. Calcium hydroxide is used to soften hair preparatory to its removal from hides before tanning. If your stomach becomes too acidic, Milk of Magnesia (magnesium hydroxide) can be taken to balance your system and ease the burning feeling.

SALTS:

Salts are named after the acids from which they are derived. Some common salts are listed in the table below.

Acid	Name	Salt	Name
H_2SO_4	Sulfuric	Na_2SO_4	Sodium sulfate
HCl	Hydrochloric	KCl	Potassium chloride
HNO_3	Nitric	KNO_3	Potassium nitrate
$HC_2H_3O_2$	Acetic	$Pb(C_2H_3O_2)_2$	Lead acetate

Salts

ACID	FORMULA OF ACID	FORMULA OF SALT	NAME OF SALT
Sulfuric	H_2SO_4	Na_2SO_4	Sodium sulfate
Citric	HNO_3	$NaNO_3$	Sodium nitrate
Carbonic	H_2CO_3	Na_2CO_3	Sodium carbonate
Acetic	$HC_2H_3O_2$	$NaC_2H_3O_2$	Sodium acetate
Hydrochloric	HCl	$NaCl$	Sodium chloride
Hydrosulfuric	H_2S	Na_2S	Sodium sulfide
Sulfurous	H_2SO_3	Na_2SO_3	Sodium sulfite
Nitrous	HNO_2	$NaNO_2$	Sodium nitrite
Chlorous	$HClO_2$	$NaClO_2$	Sodium chlorite

Naming pattern:

> –**ic** acids form –**ate** salts
> **Hydro** + –**ic** acids form –**ide** salts
> –**ous** acids form –**ite** salts

Demonstration #43:

Pour a teaspoon of granulated zinc into an Erlenmeyer flask with a two-hole cork with a glass exhaust tube and a thistle tube. Add concentrated HCl to the thistle tube until the zinc is covered. The reaction will be violent. *Be careful*: the gas is explosive. Take the remaining solution and gently heat it over a Bunsen burner in an exhaust hood until it is almost evaporated. Then pour the last of the solution onto a glass plate and observe as crystals begin to form. These crystals are salt (zinc chloride).

pH

The Danish biochemist Søren Sørensen invented the pH system in 1909. The pH is a number used by scientists to indicate the concentration of hydrogen in a solution. The pH generally ranges from 0 to 14. The letters pH stand for potential hydrogen.

At 77°F (25°C), a pH below 7 indicates that a solution is acidic, and a pH above 7 indicates that a solution is basic (alkaline). A neutral solution, such as distilled water, is neither acidic nor basic and has a pH of 7. Human blood has a pH of about 7.4, milk is 6.5, and battery acid is a little more acidic than the acid in our stomach, which has a pH of about 1.5.

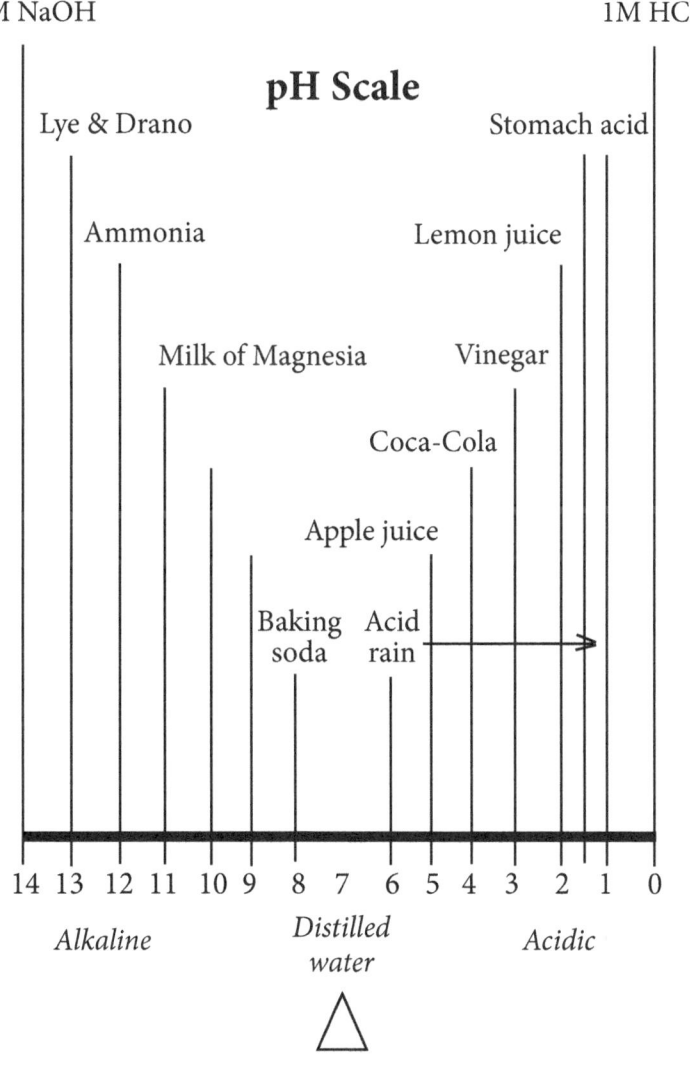

Rock Sugar Crystal

Demonstration #44:

In a clean pan boil three-fourths of a cup of water. While the water is boiling, gently stir in granulated sugar, little by little until no more will dissolve. Continue to stir. It will probably take more than two cupfuls of sugar to make a fully saturated solution.

Be sure to add the sugar slowly while stirring.

Pour the solution into a glass or clean jar. Put a metal spoon in the glass or jar; this will absorb the heat and keep the glass or jar from breaking or cracking. Then remove the spoon.

While the solution is hot, bend a paper clip as shown in the drawing below. Tie a piece of clean cotton string on the end of the bent paper clip. Place the string and the clip into the sugar solution. In order for the string to sink to the bottom, you may have to tie a small, clean metal weight onto it or make a knot at the end of the string.

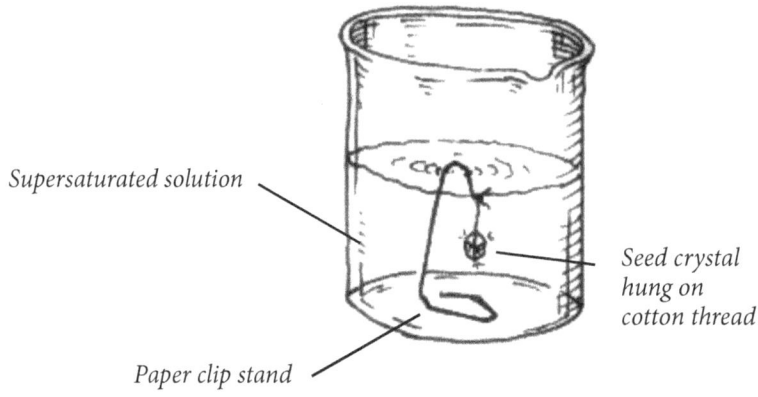

Set the glass or jar in a quiet warm place, where it cannot be moved or in any way disturbed. The solution will cool and then evaporate slowly, leaving behind large crystals of sugar hanging on the string. The crystals will stop growing in two or three days.

Smoking

Cigarette smoke contains 4700 different chemicals, including at least 43 proven carcinogens. A carcinogen is defined as an agent that causes a series of genetic alterations to occur, leading to the formation of cancerous growths.

In the fields, the tobacco is drenched with insecticides and fertilizers. After harvest, it is dried in barns and treated for protection against tobacco beetles. At the factory, tobacco leaves are mixed with stems and scraps and ground into a mash, where artificial flavorings and additives are added. This mixture is then dried and fluffed with freon to look like real tobacco shreds. In addition, cigarette paper is treated with special chemicals so that the paper will burn evenly and the cigarette will continue to burn even if it is not puffed.

Here are a few of the more familiar chemicals found in tobacco smoke: urethane (used to seal paints, etc.), acetone (nail polish and paint remover), ammonia (floor/toilet cleaner), arsenic (poison), butane (cigarette lighter fluid), carbon monoxide (car exhaust fumes), DDT/Dieldrin (pesticides), formaldehyde (body tissue and fabric preserver), hydrogen cyanide (gas chamber poison), nicotine (insecticide and addictive drug), toluene (industrial solvent) and vinyl chloride (used to make PVC piping). Many of the same chemicals are found in cigars and chewing tobacco as well.

Nicotine is present in all tobaccos. It is addictive (causes one to crave more). It can be used as a medicine to calm people down.

Tars are also present in inhaled tobacco smoke. They are black, thick and gooey. They are deposited as a coating over a smoker's lungs and bronchial tubes and inhibits them from functioning properly.

The heat from the smoke that a smoker inhales destroys (burns up) the delicate and tiny cilia that line the nasal passages. These cilia are needed so that we can filter all the bad substances out of the air that we inhale. Once the cilia are destroyed, all sorts of foreign particles can enter the respiratory system and cause illnesses and diseases.

The heat from the smoke also dries up the mucous linings (warm, thick liquid lining our nasal passages and esophagus). The mucous linings are necessary because they help our body to regulate the temperature of the air that we are inhaling; otherwise on a cold day the air would freeze our bronchial tubes.

There are other noticeable conditions that are direct results of cigarette smoking: pre-mature aging of the skin, yellowing of the teeth and fingernails, bad "ashtray" breath, smelly hair, body and clothes, and chronic cough.

Secondary smoke or "passive smoking" is the term used for breathing in other people's tobacco smoke. This form of smoking is usually involuntary and is particularly dangerous because the smoke that drifts from the end of a lit cigarette contains far greater amounts of the cancer-causing chemicals and the other toxic substances than the smoke inhaled by the smoker. The smoke particles involved in passive smoking are also smaller, so they can be inhaled more deeply into the non-smoker's lungs. This is the reason that smoking is being banned in many public places.

Smoking has proved to cause alterations in our biochemistry. It can make cells reproduce rapidly and unguided by our true body design. This rapid buildup of cells in the body is called a tumor. It is a sclerotic (hardening) illness and is also called cancer. Every year many people die from cancer because they have smoked tobacco.

A Skit for an All-School Assembly

I was teaching a seventh grade chemistry class when an assembly was approaching. The class and I wrote the following comic skit about our main lesson, based on Lewis Carroll's poem *Jabberwocky*.

'T was smoky and the seventh grade chemists
    Did combust and explode in their lab.
All dirty were the test tubes,
    And the air smelled pretty bad!

Beware the Carbon atom, my class,
    The molecules that form, the vapors that come to pass.
Beware the mixtures which rumble and grow.
    Observe them in detail and note where they go!

She took her notebook in her hand,
    Eyes open in expectant gaze,
Nose prepared for an unexpected smell
    All ready for Sulfur's noxious ways.

He took his flint and steel in hand.
    Thrice he struck the hissing gas,
Then rested by the Erlenmeyer flask
    And waited for the explosion to pass.

One two! One two! O what a feat!
    The Phosphorus blazed with a white hot heat.
As the energetic chemists made their case,
    The litmus detected the acid from the base.

And, as in ulffish thought he stood
    Carbon, embers and ash appeared from the wood.
Crackle, pop, sizzle, hiss and bang,
    Then came a cheer from the assembled gang.

Organic was the crinkly brown leaf
        And inorganic was the rock.
Oxidation brought an explosive relief
        While Hydroxide cleaned the dirty sock!

And hast thou learned the formula right?
        Come to my arms, my scientific boy!
O Bunsen burner day! Sediment and precipitate,
        He chortled in his joy.

'T was smoky and the seventh grade chemists,
        Did combust and explode in their lab.
All dirty were the test tubes,
        And the air smelled pretty bad!

My students acted out the poem, conducting experiments as they went along. The poem was spoken by the class as a whole and selections by smaller groups. Two students were the teacher and dressed in oversized, white lab coats and safety goggles.

Props included talcum powder, clothespins, confectioners' sugar, sulfuric acid, 2 beakers, 2 stirring rods, 2 test tubes with yellow fluid, and stand, flint and steel, Bunsen burner, 2 litmus in beakers, acid, base, brown leaves, rock, party popper, sock, soapy water in beaker, nerd pen case, bow tie, white shirts or blouses for everyone, table, 2 chairs, safety glasses, 2 white lab coats, Erlenmeyer flask, 2 scrolls with formulas.

Spelling and Vocabulary

Weekly spelling and vocabulary tests should be given. The following words are taken from the main lesson content for each week. The words below are suggestions:

Week #1

- chemistry
- apparatus
- mortar and pestle
- Erlenmeyer flask
- beaker
- forceps
- wire gauze
- Bunsen burner
- watch glass
- funnel
- graduated cylinder
- spatula
- combustion
- Florence flask
- ignite

Week #2

- sulfur
- phosphorus
- deflagrating spoon
- incinerable
- oxygen
- carbon dioxide
- transformation
- metamorphosis
- ash
- embers
- Joseph Priestley
- oxidation
- calcium
- hydroxide
- smoke

Week #3

- acid
- base
- limestone
- organic
- inorganic
- hydrochloric acid
- alkali
- salt
- sediment
- precipitate
- solution
- decomposition
- element
- industry
- ammonia

Building a Portable Lime Kiln

by John C. Hoffman

An important modern industry with a history older than that of the smelting of metals is the heating of lime (calcium carbonate—$CaCO_3$) to produce burned lime or quicklime (calcium oxide—CaO). Quicklime is used in mortars, cements, iron- and glass-making and in neutralizing acid soils. Lime is obtained in the form of limestone, chalk, coral, shells and marble, marble being the least desirable because of impurities.

The chemistry of the lime cycle for mortar is simple. When heated to about 1000°C (1800°F) in a kiln for a period of time, lime breaks down releasing carbonic acid (carbon dioxide—CO_2) leaving quicklime. The quicklime is mixed with sand and water to make a fluid mortar. Quicklime and water produce slaked lime (calcium hydroxide—$Ca(OH)_2$) which hardens by releasing water and re-absorbing carbon dioxide from the air to produce lime. The process comes full circle from lime to quicklime to slaked lime to lime.

Today's students have very little opportunity to observe actual industrial processes. Almost everything comes magically ready-made and packaged. Manufacturers, fearing accidents and lawsuits, have all but closed their doors to public tours. Nevertheless, the lime cycle studied in seventh grade chemistry offers an opportunity for the students not only to observe an important industrial process, but to build and fire a kiln used in the process.

The construction, loading and firing, experimenting with the quicklime, and disassembling of the kiln is a three- to four-day project. It requires firebrick, a metal stack cover, a source of lime (limestone or marble), charcoal, a fan or bellows and some digging. The cost of the metal stack cover and firebricks should be about $110, and the cost of firing and lime about $40. The kiln can be re-fired as many times as desired and then disassembled, the trench filled and the bricks and steel stack cover stored for another class. If the grass at the kiln site is carefully removed, it can be replaced and the site healed.

The kiln is simple to build and has been tested, but the instructions must be carefully followed. You are working with a quarter ton of firebrick

Fig. 1 Lime kiln showing the upper stack and flue opening

and very high temperatures. An unstable structure could be dangerous. An excellent adjunct to the project would be a field trip to collect pieces of limestone or marble.

Figure 1, above, shows an assembled kiln and its flue tunnel opening. Figure 2 shows a cutaway side view of the kiln and flue tunnel. Loose dirt from the trench is packed around the stack and flue tunnel to help hold in heat and reduce air leakage. The kiln stack stands, about 35 inches in height and 20 inches square. It has 14 tiers and requires 110 whole firebricks and 2

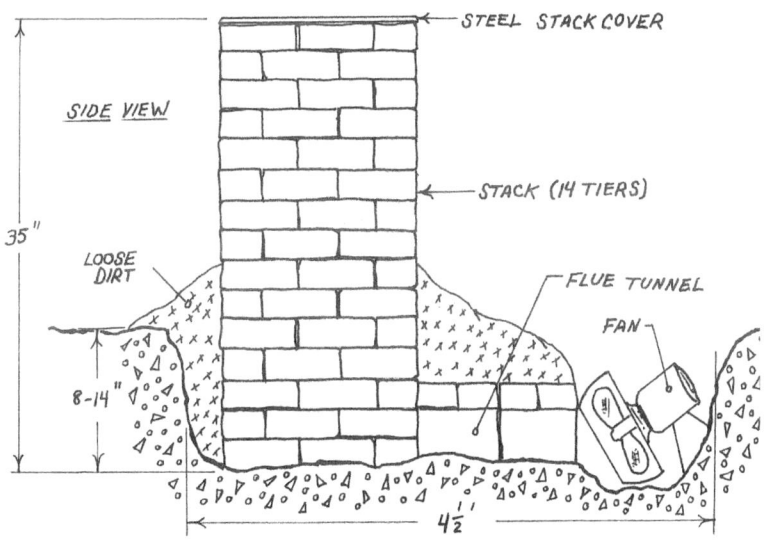

Fig. 2 Lime kiln showing the stack, flue, tunnel and fan

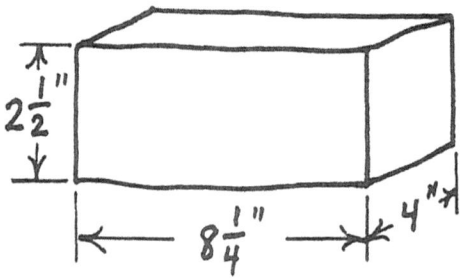

Fig. 3 Firebrick

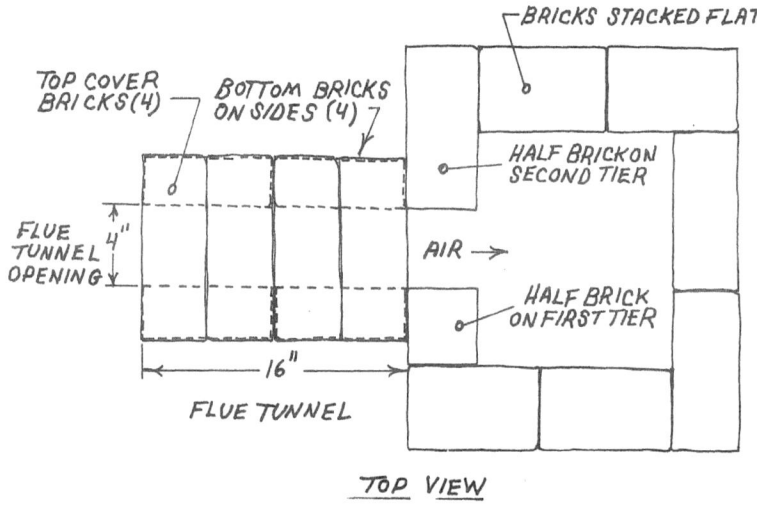

Fig. 4 Brick stacking pattern for the flue tunnel and first two stack tiers

half bricks (see Fig. 3). A brick can be broken in half by striking it along the mid-line of its flat surface with a hammer, but be sure to wear safety glasses.

Figure 4 shows a top view of the flue tunnel and the first tier of the kiln stack. This first tier must be level and tight. The stability of the remaining thirteen tiers depends on the placement of the first tier. Note that the first and second tiers require one half-brick each in order to construct the 4x5 inch opening in the stack for air from the flue tunnel. The remaining twelve tiers are stacked as shown in Figure 5. The only bricks stacked on edge are the four side flue bricks. All other bricks are stacked flat.

Kiln construction should take three to four hours. It begins with the digging of a trench to the approximate dimensions shown in Figure 6. Trench depth depends on how difficult the earth is to dig and how much effort the students are willing to put into digging. After the trench is dug, the bottom needs to be leveled, especially the surface under the stack. It is

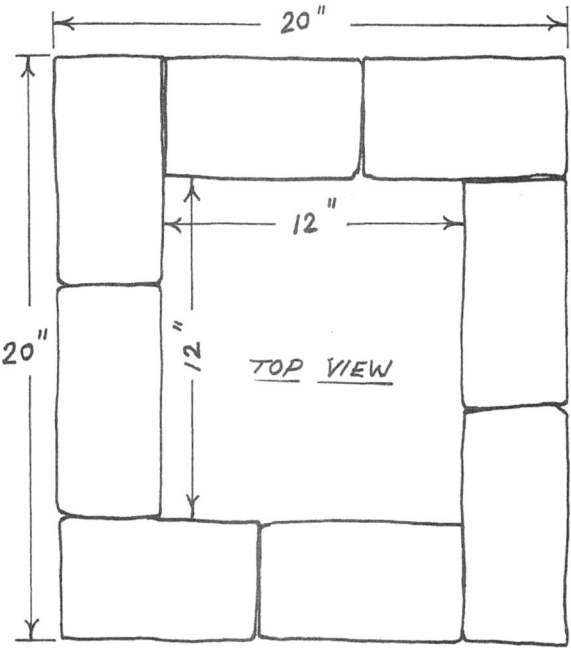

Fig. 5 Stacking pattern for the third through fourteenth tiers

an excellent opportunity to demonstrate the use and importance of a spirit level. Once the trench is level, brick stacking begins with tiers one and two of the stack. The bricks are stacked flat. When these two tiers are in place, the flue tunnel is assembled. Then the remaining twelve tiers of the stack are added, loose dirt is packed around the lower stack and flue tunnel, and the steel stack cover (see Fig. 7) put in place. The first day's work is complete.

Loading and firing of the kiln on the second day begins with the removal of the steel stack cover and the upper six or seven tiers of the stack. This should go quickly and give any students who might have been left out of the first day's activity an opportunity to unstack and restack the bricks. Once the upper stack tiers are removed, one and a half 20-pound bags of charcoal briquettes (30 pounds total) are poured into the stack. Eight pounds of self-starting charcoal are poured on top of this. If the stack is not high enough, then add one or two additional tiers. The pieces of lime are placed on top of the self-starting charcoal. The lime pieces should be about the size of an open hand or smaller and less than one inch in thickness. The pieces should be slightly separated and not stacked. Some lime, marble for example, contains mineral impurities which melt out as slag and can fuse pieces together. Once the lime pieces are placed, add just enough self-starting charcoal to cover them (see Fig. 8).

The upper tiers of the stack are now restacked and the self-starting charcoal lit. Once the self-starting charcoal is burning well, a 20-pound bag of regular charcoal briquettes is poured into the stack on top of the burning charcoal. The steel cover plate is put in place and the fan turned on. **CAUTION**: use safety glasses and shut the fan off when looking into the stack through the cover plate opening. Dust and cinders can be swept up with the hot air flow. Do not remove the steel stack cover when firing. It will be very hot!

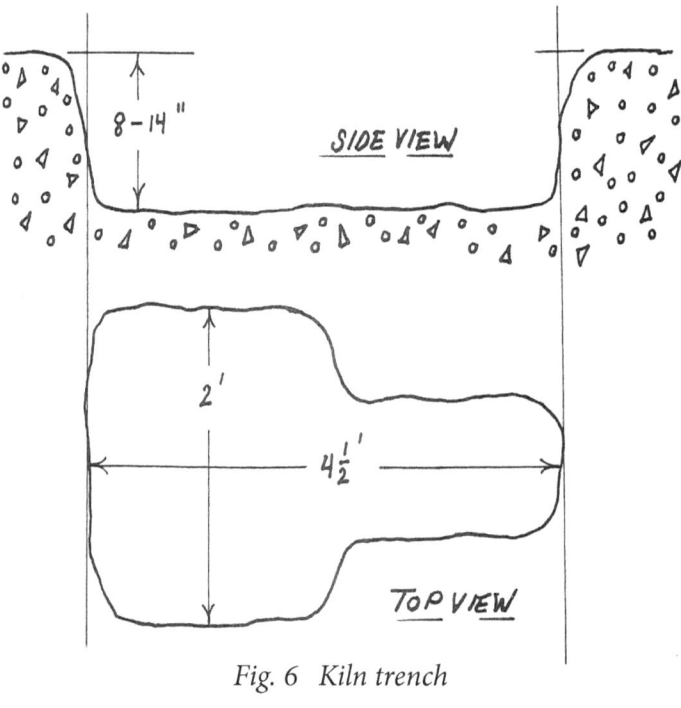

Fig. 6   Kiln trench

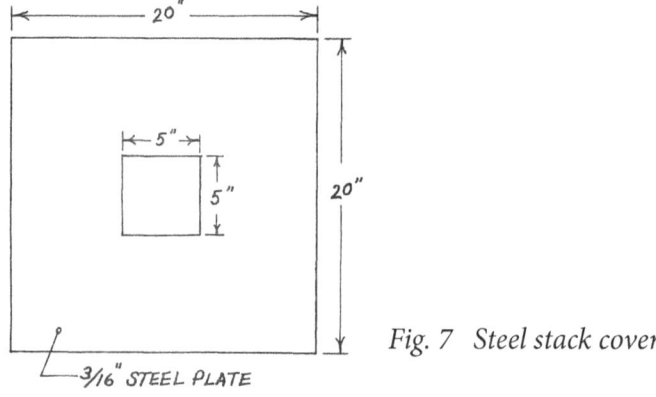

Fig. 7   Steel stack cover

NOTE: The stack heat will cause the cover to warp. This is normal. Do not try to press it down.

The importance of an excess of charcoal in the lower stack (below the lime pieces) is that this charcoal cannot be replenished whereas charcoal can be added to the upper stack (above the lime pieces) through the steel cover plate opening. Throughout the firing an additional 10 to 20 pounds of briquettes should be added as the charcoal burns down.

The firing time for the kiln is five to six hours. If you start firing at 9 a.m., the kiln should be dying down by 2 or 3 p.m. The fan speed should be adjusted for a moderate flow of air. A fan speed too high will cause the charcoal to burn too quickly and will blow off the heat. When the kiln starts dying down, turn the fan off and leave the kiln overnight to cool. Be sure there is no rain in the forecast. If water gets into the kiln, it will start slaking the lime and cause a mess.

The third day's activity begins with the removal of the steel plate cover and the upper six or seven tiers of the stack. The stack should be fairly cool. You will have to feel around in the charcoal ash for the pieces of quicklime. Although the quicklime can be handled with bare hands, gloves are advised. Eye protection is also advised. The quicklime will be about the same size and shape as the original lime pieces, but the appearance will have changed. The once-crystalline lime should now appear dull, dry and flaky. It is important that the students note this change. You may find slag formations around some of the pieces. These should be broken away, although slag will not affect the slaking process.

To demonstrate the slaking process, a piece of quicklime is placed in a Pyrex dish. The students should touch the piece so they can feel that it is not hot. Water is then poured onto the piece. If the mineral is predominately lime, and it has been properly burned, it will suck in the water and begin releasing heat. The students should hold their hands over the quicklime to experience this heat. As more water is added, the quicklime will bloat, hiss and steam. Care should be taken that the students do not get their faces too close. Hot slaking lime will burn. If a student were to get quicklime in his or her eye, the eye should be immediately flushed with water. To emphasize that heat is released, a pea-sized piece of quicklime can be placed in a student's palm and water added. The student will quickly drop the piece. If the slaking lime is held too long, it will burn the skin.

In order to make mortar, enough water is added to the slaked lime to create a paste. Sand is then added to the paste in the ratio of about two parts sand to one part paste, and the two are mixed. The mortar can be used to cement rocks, terra cotta, or bricks together, or it can be spread over wood sticks (lath) or metal screen as plaster. The mortar should set up overnight. The students will find it very fragile, however. It takes weeks and sometimes years for mortar to properly cure or harden back into lime. As water evaporates, microscopic channels are left in the slaked lime through which air can enter. Carbon dioxide in the air slowly reacts with the slaked lime to produce lime. It would be instructive to cement two pieces of terra cotta together and put them aside for a few weeks.

If the slaked lime is tested with a pH-sensitive solution such as cabbage juice, it will test basic like wood ash. Lime water for testing for carbon dioxide is made by stirring a teaspoon of quicklime or fresh slaked lime into a glass of water, then filtering the solution through filter paper or a coffee filter. If you bubble your breath through a few milliliters of this solution using a straw, the solution will gradually turn cloudy. This is a positive test for carbon dioxide. If this cloudy solution is left overnight, a white precipitate will be found at the bottom of the test tube the next day. The precipitate is calcium carbonate.

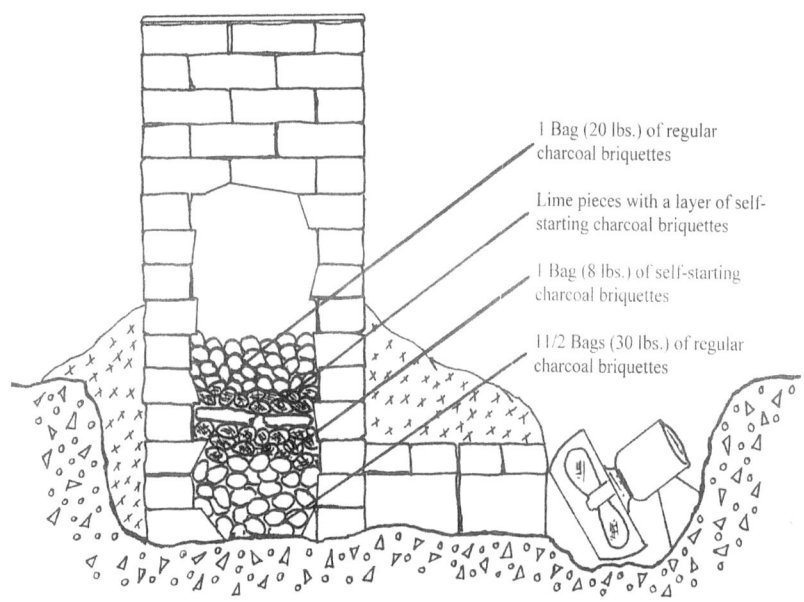

Fig. 8 Loading the stack for firing

Eighth Grade Chemistry

The earth laughs in flowers.
— Ralph Waldo Emerson

Nature is the living, visible garment of God.
— Goethe

Eighth Grade Chemistry

Sample Block Outline *(Three weeks)*

REVIEW
    What is chemistry?
    The three branches of chemistry

COMPLETE (if you were not able to cover them in grade seven)
    Water
        The water cycle, heat convection, solubility study
        Boiling point, freezing point, natures of steam and ice
        Crystallization
    Metals
        The seven metals: gold, silver, copper, iron, mercury, lead and tin—their unique properties
        Origin of metals
        Metals and human beings
        Smelting an ore

NEW
    The distinctions between organic, inorganic and biochemistry
    The plant as a great chemist in nature
    Photosynthesis
    Carbohydrates (their composition and tests for)
    Assimilation of carbohydrate in the human body
    Sugar
    Starch
    Cellulose
    Carbon dioxide gas
    Hydrogen gas
    Alcohol
    Formation of proteins
    Formation of oils

Themes in the Eighth Grade

Stockmeyer indicates that the metals and water should be taught in the seventh grade. As mentioned earlier, I have never been able to do this within the time constraints of the variety of seventh grade blocks, so I have taught them in the eighth grade.

Once completed, the initial focus becomes the production and character of foodstuffs by human beings. This activity necessitates a constant living connection with nature. We immerse ourselves in the environment when we study the plants and their particular landscapes.

Rudolf Steiner commented that one of the teaching goals in the eighth grade is:

> *... you lead the simple chemical concepts (established in the seventh grade) further, so that the students learn to grasp the way industrial processes are connected to chemistry. In connection with the chemical concepts, try to develop an understanding about the substances which build up organic (living) bodies: starch, sugar, protein (albumen) and fats (lipids).* – from *Discussions with Teachers*

It is important that the eighth grader learn that thinking is important and it is thinking which shapes the world. The thinking that is expressed by the discoveries of modern chemistry has made life easier to live.

The themes of photosynthesis, carbohydrates, generating carbon dioxide and oxygen gases, examining alcohol, lipids, oils and proteins are presented and recapitulated in the ninth grade. It is a wise eighth-grade teacher who looks through the ninth grade chemistry curriculum to see what will be coming next.

> *Great men are they who see that spiritual is stronger than any material force—that thoughts rule the world.*
> – Ralph Waldo Emerson

Three Branches of Chemistry

There are three main branches in the science of Chemistry. They are Organic, Inorganic and Biochemistry. Chemistry is a very young science. Nevertheless it has influenced modern civilization more than any other branch of science. In general, chemistry deals with the characteristics of various kinds of matter or substances, with the changes or reactions that they undergo, and how the qualities of the products relate to the character of the path of transformation.

Organic chemistry deals with the substances that include carbon and are formed by living processes. There are hundreds of thousands of these compounds. They greatly outnumber the compounds of all the other elements put together. It is in the field of organic chemistry that man has made rapid progress within the last century, and almost daily new compounds are invented that have never before existed in nature.

Inorganic chemistry is the study of compounds such as acids, bases, salts, metals and do not involve carbon. These compounds are derived from mineral sources.

Biochemistry deals especially with the details of the chemical transformation of compounds within living organisms. It is the chemistry of life, and it is a most intricate, vast and mysterious branch of chemistry.

It is fun to start a main lesson block by startling the children with something they are not expecting to happen. If you begin the eighth grade chemistry block with the study of water, the following demonstration will wake up their senses and anticipation on the first day.

Demonstration:

Prepare steps 1–5 beforehand so that the students will see only the final setup.

1. Set up three 250 ml beakers and one 500 ml beaker on the counter.

2. In the first beaker, fill it three-fourths full with water, add 10 ml of a solution saturated with $NaHCO_3$ and 20% Na_2CO_3 solution, pH 9.

3. In the second beaker, place 10–12 drops of phenolphthalein indicator.

4. In the third beaker, place a 25 ml saturated solution of $BaCl_2$.

5. In the 500 ml beaker, add 5 ml of concentrated HCl plus three dropper squirts of bromthymol blue.

6. In front of the class, empty the clear contents of beaker one into beaker two. It will make a deep wine color.

7. Next empty the combined contents of beaker two into beaker three. It will make a white, milk-colored liquid.

8. Finally empty the contents of beaker three into beaker four. It will foam and make a beer-like frothy liquid.

The teacher can explain that chemistry involves amazing transformations which we will explore in greater detail during their upcoming main lesson and in chemistry classes in the Waldorf high school.

Water

It comes from Heaven, to Heaven it rises, forever changing.
– Goethe

Water ever strives to remain liquid. Its home is therefore the ocean which is the bloodstream of the earth. It must always seek its way back to its liquid state, its home. Water also unites with air and with solid matter. Fish could not live in the sea if it did not have air dissolved in its waters. Sea water, too, has much salt dissolved in it. When sea water is evaporated, the solid salt is left. Water always contains something of earthly origin, i.e., its saltiness, and something of the air. Thus, water unites earth and air and acts as an intermediary between them.

Water is quite special. Without water we could not survive. Taste is made possible by the presence of water. Without water, an acid and a base would not react. Water has three forms: gas (vapor), liquid (water) and solid (ice). Water is always striving for its liquid, whether it is vapor or ice. When it is cold at night and warm during the day, we have dew on the ground. Dew drops form perfect circles, and the drops reflect everything around them. Dew is formed when the thin vapor of water in the air condenses.

When it gets very cold at night, we have hoarfrost. Frost is formed when water vapor first condenses and then freezes. When water is evaporated, it goes up into the sky and makes clouds. When there is mist outside, you could say you were in a cloud. Rain is caused when the water is condensed from the atmospheric vapor in the sky. When it is colder, it either snows, hails, or rains freezing rain (sleet). When it snows, each snowflake is a differently-shaped six-sided crystal, and no one flake is ever exactly the same as another.

When water freezes, it expands, forming ice. Ice is lighter than water, and it will float in it. Pressure melts ice. Because it does, glaciers can move, and we can ice skate because water makes ice slippery.

Seven-tenths of the area of the earth is water. Water is special because it is always giving and receiving (in dissolved substances). It can be mixed with many minerals and substances. Salt in the ocean is an example of this also because it it always giving; it can be very easily polluted. One of the most spectacular things that water can do is to create a rainbow. A rainbow is formed when light shines through water vapor which acts like a prism in the air.

Water boils at 212° F – 100° C
Water freezes at 32° F – 0° C

Four Water Demonstrations:

1. Fill a beaker as full as possible so that the water forms a bubble over the sides of the beaker. Take a steel needle and carefully rub it through your hair so that it will be coated with oil. Gently place it on top of the bubble of water and observe how the surface tension of the water floats the steel needle.

Steel needle floating on surface of water.

2. Take three glass cylinders, each with a different internal diameter. Fill a beaker four-fifths full of water. Add food coloring so that the water is radiant. Set the three cylinders upright in the beaker.

Beaker with three cylinders showing meniscuses and levels of water climb

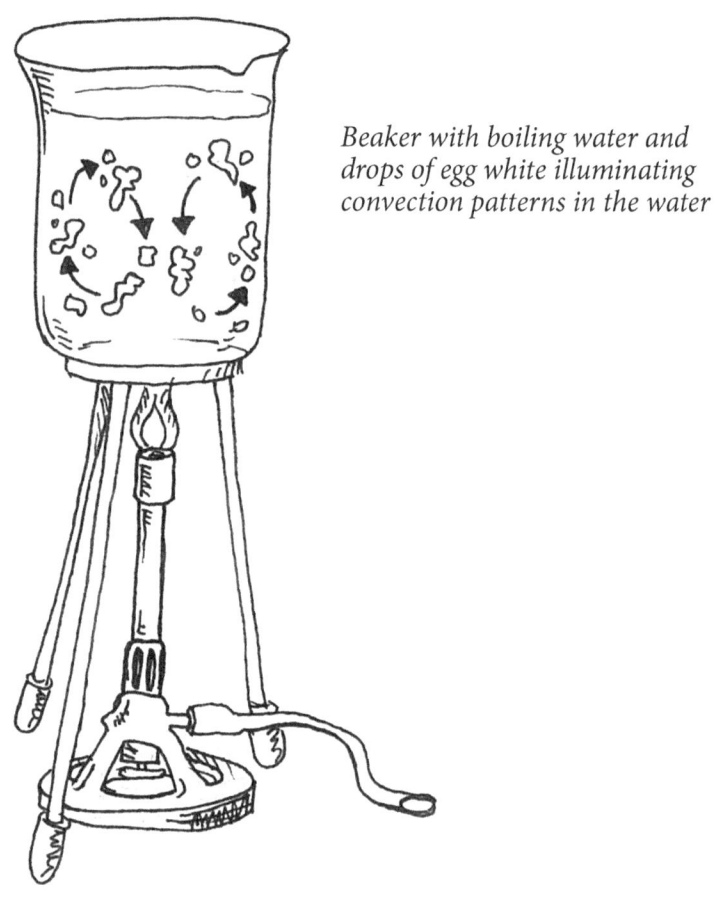

Beaker with boiling water and drops of egg white illuminating convection patterns in the water

3. Fill a 500 ml beaker with water and bring it to a rolling boil with a Bunsen burner. In a 100 ml beaker separate the white from an egg. Fill a medicine dropper with the egg white and carefully add a drop at a time to the controlled boil of the water. Keep adding the egg white slowly until you observe that the pattern of the boil can be seen, as in the illustration above.

4. Carefully, pour 100 ml of mercury into a graduated cylinder.

- Now pour in 100 ml of carbon tetrachloride.

- Next pour in 100 ml of water.

- Finally, add 100 ml of petroleum ether.

- Gently add a piece of cork, a piece of hardwood, a mothball, and a steel screw. Observe upon which fluid each will float.

- Place a cork in the graduated cylinder to prevent evaporation.

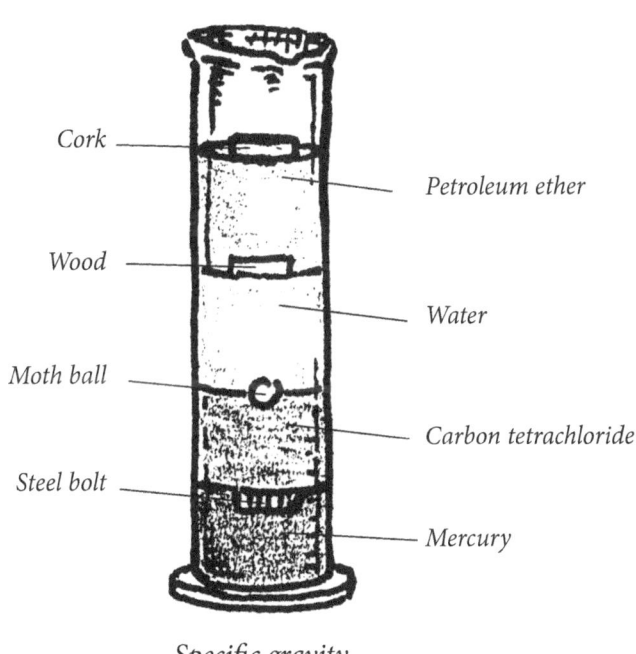

Specific gravity

Crystal Fields

Demonstration:

1. Take a 250 ml beaker and add 3.5 ml of water.

2. Add to this 2 heaping teaspoons of Epsom salts. Stir.

3. Place the beaker with the solution on a tripod and heat it to the point just before it boils.

4. Place a 10-inch pane of clean window glass on the table of an overhead projector. Set up a screen or other white background for projection.

5. Carefully pour the contents of the heated Epsom salt solution in the center of the window glass, turn on the projector and observe the projected image of the crystal fields.

Crystal Garden

Demonstration:

1. In a 1000 ml beaker place 600 ml of water.

2. Add 240 ml of sodium silicate.

3. Add the following crystal salts:

Ferrous sulfate	— mint green
Cupric sulfate	— turquoise
Ferric chloride	— tan
Cobalt chloride	— burgundy

Over time the solution will become cloudy, and the individual salt crystals will grow long, tendril-like "plant" forms from the bottom of the beaker.

Advanced Crystal-Growing Experiment

Procedure:

Obtain several clean jars. Then in a clean pan, boil three-fourths of a cup of water. While the water is boiling, gently stir in the salt or sugar, little by little, until no more will dissolve. *This is a saturated solution.* Remove from the heat. Continue to stir and observe so that you make a fully saturated solution.

Be sure to add the ingredients slowly while stirring!

You will come to a point where one more grain will cause the solid to "snow" out and precipitate to the bottom; *this is a super-saturated solution.*

Put a spoon in the glass or jar. This will absorb the heat and keep the glass or jar from breaking or cracking. Pour in the solution into a glass or clean jar. Then remove the spoon.

While the solution is hot, lay a pencil across the top of the glass or jar. In the middle of the pencil, tie a piece of clean cotton string. Hang the string into the saturated solution. In order for the string to sink to the bottom you may have to tie a small clean metal weight such as a paper clip onto it (Figure A).

Set the glass or jar in a quiet, warm place, where it will not be moved or in any way disturbed. The solution will cool and then evaporate slowly, leaving behind large crystals hanging on the string. When the crystals have stopped growing (two or three days), take the largest to use as a "seed" crystal. Place this crystal carefully back into your saturated solution and it should grow much larger (Figure B).

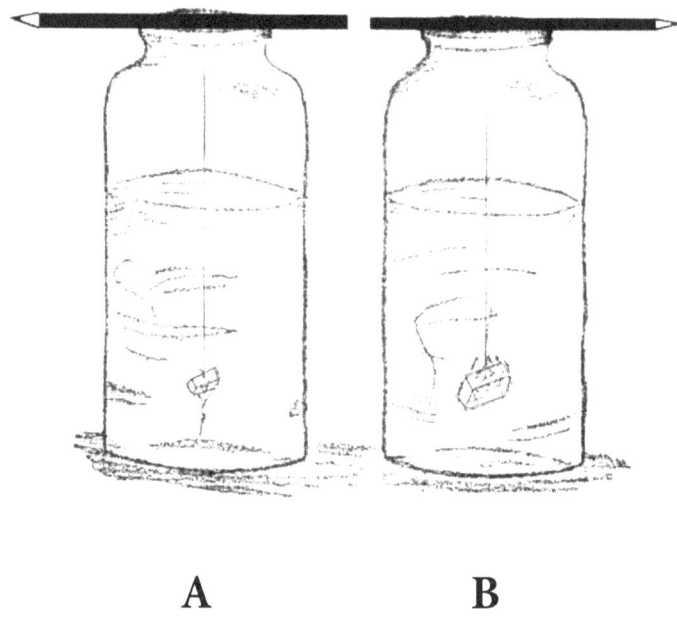

A   **B**

The following salts (available at either a pharmacy, a food store, or from the chemistry lab supply room) can be used:

sugar
table salt
alum
copper sulfate
potassium ferricyanide
strontium formate dihydrate
chrome alum
sodium bromate
Rochelle salt
nickel sulfate hexahydrate
copper acetate monahydrate
alum grown on chrome alum
lithium trisodium chromate hexahydrate

Song of the Spirits over the Water

Gesang der Geister uber den Wasser.
– Goethe

Man's soul is like water:
From heaven it comes,
To heaven it rises,
And to earth again it must descend
Moving to and fro forever.

The pure jet leaps from the lofty precipitous rock-face,
Then rises in cloud-waves of sweet spray against smooth rock,
And streams, veil-like, softly murmurous, down to the depths
    which lightly receive it.

If cliffs project in the path of its fall,
Then angrily foaming it pours stepwise in the abyss.
In its level bed it meanders down the meadowy vale
And on the lake's smooth surface all the stars gaze at their own faces.

Wind is the water's sweet love;
Wind stirs up foaming waves from the deep.
Soul of man, how like the water!
Destiny of man, how like the wind!

Chemical Elements in a 100-pound 8th Grade Student

Oxygen	65 lbs.
Carbon	18 lbs.
Hydrogen	10 lbs.
Calcium	2 lbs.
Phosphorus	14.5 oz.
Sulfur	4.0 oz.
Magnesium	4.0 oz.
Sodium	2.5 oz.
Chlorine	2.5 oz.
Iron	traces
Iodine	traces

The Metals

Here's one way we can imaginatively introduce metals:

The metals came to earth, in gaseous form, from the cosmos. When they came, the earth was still forming, and they mingled with the other gases. When the earth started to cool, the metal gases became trapped inside the rock and earth and slowly cooled, making deposits and veins of metal. Because of this, you have to dig to find them.

There are seven *major* metals. They are: gold, silver, copper, mercury, iron, tin and lead. They are all opaque, and most shine in light, and many are very heavy. Some are very hard (iron) and some are soft (lead). Many are malleable and ductile, and some can be found as crystals. Metals are like the sons of the heavens, and the earth is like the mother.

When we observe the metals we notice the following qualities:
1. Luster or shine
2. Conductivity of heat
3. Heaviness
4. Malleability, plasticity
5. Conductivity of electricity

The use of minerals throughout the ages:

Stone age	–	no use of minerals
Copper age	–	copper
Bronze age	–	tin and copper
Iron age	–	iron
	–	lead and mercury (quicksilver)

Gold is the only mineral which can be found in a readily usable state. This was known to mankind very early. All other minerals cannot be used as found in nature; they have to be taken out of the ore and refined. To do this one needs to use energy. If you leave the minerals out in the open, they revert to the earth (e.g., iron rusts).

Au GOLD

Gold is a noble metal, which means that it does not rust or change under cold or heat. It is the heaviest metal and very malleable. Because it is so soft, other metals are alloyed with it to strengthen it in jewelry and so forth.

Gold can be made into a very thin thread. It is found in veins and in deposits. Gold has a relationship with the sun and was used by Aztecs and the Incas in sun worship. The heart is connected to gold, and all money is based on gold.

Melting gold foil shows its noble characteristics.

Take a piece of gold foil and sandwich it between two three-inch square plates of glass. Use masking tape to seal the edges of the glass plates so they will not slide. Observe it in the shadows with light shining directly on it. It will reflect a strong gold color. Then carry it to the window and look at it from various angles in full light. You will now observe a bluish-green tint because of the incredible thinness of the foil at certain angles. It is this optical quality which allows the malleable gold to be used in such small quantities to cover large areas such as the domes of the Massachusetts State House and the Colorado State capitol building.

Ag SILVER

Silver is noble, and it is white and shining. It is used in medicines and is easy to make into a reflective mirror. Silver is used in photography, and it conducts electricity.

A good experiment is to take a three-foot-tall, three-fourths inch diameter cylinder, insert a cork in the bottom end, and clamp it in a ring stand. Next, fill it with tap water and add 5 ml of chlorine bleach. Then dim the lights and place the cylinder over an illuminated box or shine a flashlight with a black piece of construction paper behind the tube. As you drop in a crystal of silver nitrate, you will observe a silver reflected trail as the crystal sinks.

A variation is to fill a beaker with a dilute silver nitrate solution (one or two crystals in 300 ml of distilled water). Place a crystal of sea salt in the beaker. Observe the white veils as they form. This is an excellent setup for demonstrating the effects of a turbid medium when studying Goethe's color theory.

Another interesting experiment is to place a milky solution of silver chloride in the sunlight. Observe it darken to blackish violet silver oxide. Soak a filter paper in a weak salt (NaCl) solution. Dry it. After it is dry, moisten it with the weak silver nitrate solution. Then place an object like a pencil, a paper clip, or some coins on the piece of paper and place it in direct sunlight. After a while you can observe the darkening of the exposed paper and the light color of the paper under the objects.

Drop .5N sodium hydroxide into a dilute silver nitrate solution. Observe the brown silver oxide precipitate. Dissolve the precipitate with 5% dilute ammonia, warm over a Bunsen burner and you will observe silver as a mirror deposited on the glass.

Cu COPPER

Copper is not noble. It is flexible and somewhat beautiful. Copper conducts electricity. The best faucets are made out of red copper. Copper is often made into pipe and pennies.

Place 1 teaspoon of copper powder or turnings in a 1-liter Erlenmeyer flask. Add 150 ml HNO_3, 2 parts HNO_3, 1 part H_2O. Observe the blue color of the bubbling liquid and the orange smoke. Capture some smoke in another Erlenmeyer flask. Add some H_2O until the flask is three-fourths filled.

The golden oxide and blue precipitate remind one of Botticelli's painting "The Birth of Venus," which was an esoteric study of copper.

NOTE: The nitrogen dioxide produces a biting, noxious vapor. Use care and be sure to have adequate ventilation, preferably a ventilated hood.

Another experiment is to fill a 3-liter beaker with 2 liters of tap water and 50 ml of saturated CuSO₄ solution. Place it on a light box and observe as it gradually becomes turbid and the color becomes blue. Slowly swirl the beaker while adding a few ml of 10% HCl and it will become clear. Slowly add a few drops of NaOH and it will cloud. Play with this a few times by going back and forth.

Hg MERCURY

Mercury is noble. It is in a liquid state most of the time and is very mobile and breaks apart easily. It reminds us of the past when all metals were liquid. Mercury's mobile formlessness breaks through and sets it in motion. It is used in dentistry. Mercury is poisonous and should be handled with **CAUTION**!

When you drop some mercury onto a plate, it breaks into sections, then rapidly reforms itself into a single reflective and dense puddle.

CAUTION! Mercury is a toxic substance and vapors must not be inhaled and the metal must not be allowed to touch the skin.

1. Fill a large Erlenmeyer with distilled water. Add a small amount of HNO₃. Add a crystal of mercuric nitrate and potassium iodide. Observe as a yellow/red precipitate appears and disappears at concentration boundaries.

$$Hg(NO_3) + NaOH \rightarrow HgO \text{ (a yellow precipitate)}$$

2. Mercury was used by the miners in the Rockies. Microscopic gold is often hidden in metal oxides, and mercury has the ability to absorb metals such as gold. The miners would add a few drops of mercury to their gold pans along with the "black sand" after the panning process was complete. They would swirl it around several times and then store the mercury in a bottle and extract the gold later through distillation.

If you place a small piece of tin or zinc in the bottom of a beaker and add a few drops of mercury, over the next few days you will observe the tin or zinc decreasing as it is absorbed into the mercury.

Sn TIN

Tin is brittle and squeaks (cries) when bent. It is very durable and almost noble, but it breaks down and flakes in extreme cold. It has an interior crystalline structure. It is used in making bronze and in tooth filling material. It is also used in making cans.

When you bend a pencil-sized piece of tin, you can hear the "Screech of Tin."

1. Dip a stick of tin in concentrated HCl or H2NO3 to etch the surface and make visible the crystalline structure.

2. Moisten the surface of a piece of tin plate with Aqua Regia. Observe the crystalline structure.

3. Combine SnCl with NaOH and observe the results.

4. Place some tin in a freezer overnight. When you take it out, it will show whitish spots where the tin's inner structure has collapsed and it has become powdery.

NOTE: Tin sticks are hard to find. I make my own by melting small pieces of tin in a plumber's ladle and then carefully pouring it in a test tube the diameter of my little finger. When cool, the test tube is sacrificed to the chemistry gods but you have a wonderful stick of tin which can be bent easily and can be passed on to other teachers who will have this main lesson in the future.

Fe IRON

Iron rusts in water. Without it, we could not breathe. It helps us heal ourselves from its location in the hemoglobin in our blood. Iron is warlike and is found almost everywhere on the earth. There is more iron in the earth than any of the other six major metals. Iron can be magnetized.

1. Blow iron filings across a Bunsen burner with a tall, weak flame, and you will have a fireworks display as illustrated in the diagram above.

2. In a tall cylinder against a white background, add some iron powder to a H_2SO_4 30% solution. Observe the turbidity as H_2 is generated. A greenish $FeSO_4$ (ferrosulphate) is formed. Add HnO_3 at 30% and you will have a brown-colored $Fe(NO_3)_3$.

3. Take a 16d iron nail and place it in a test tube so that it is half covered with water. Let it sit in a sunny location and watch how and where the rust progresses.

4. Obtain a bench grinder with a coarse stone. Find various pieces of scrap iron—a nail, a large spring, an old knife, an old lawn mower blade, and so forth. Most all iron has alloys added—chromium, manganese, silicon, nickel and, most especially, carbon. The carbon content becomes evident when you touch the metal to the grinding wheel. Each will throw off sparks with different star-shaped designs, but the one with the most carbon will throw off the most sparks. This technique is used by the blacksmith to determine the carbon content of a piece of unknown iron. The more carbon the stronger the iron.

Pb LEAD

Lead is found in chalk. It burns and breaks down in water. Lead can be easily polished and tarnished. It is used to stop radiation.

Paints used to have lead in them, but this practice has been discontinued because brain damage resulted when chips of the lead paint were ingested. You can mix a weak solution of lead nitrate and soda to produce lead carbonate—a bright white lead solution.

1. If you mix lead oxide (red lead) with dilute HNO_3 and then heat it, you will produce brown lead dioxide.

Mix a weak solution of orange potassium dichromate with weak solution of cloudy lead nitrate to form lead dichromate which is bright yellow.

2. An old party game can be used to effectively demonstrate the properties of lead. First, over a Bunsen burner heat up a small quantity of lead in a plumber's ladle or old, clean, never-to-be-used-again saucepan. Watch how the lead melts and how shiny it becomes.

Second, into a plastic five-gallon bucket filled with water, carefully pour the lead from a height of two feet above the bucket. It will pop, sizzle loudly and sink. Allow it to cool and take it out of the water and examine it. This was the point where someone at the party would read the pourer's fortune from the shapes that the lead took.

The Seven Metals

Polarities
Silver – Lead
Mercury – Tin
Copper – Iron

Ag = Argentum
Silver ☾
Moon
reflective
memory
makes mirrors
used in photography
(stimulates
nerve-sense activity,
helps memory and
strengthens
reproductive organs)

Au = Aurum
Gold ☉
Sun
heaviest
metal
noble
(strengthens
heart and
circulation as
well as the
eyes and
ears)

Pb = Plumbum
Lead ♄
Saturn
heavy / earthy
blocks radiation
easily tarnished
pliable / soft
(combats destructive
tendencies of the
astral body and brings
alertness to dreamy
children)

Hg = Hydragryum/quicksilver
Mercury / Quicksilver ☿
Mercury
mobility
formlessness
dissolves other metals
(fights inflammation and obsessive
compulsive disorders)

Sn = Stannum
Tin ♃
Jupiter
smooth
tough exterior
crystalline interior
not noble
brittle
(brings inner organization,
formation, into the fluidity of
the organism)

Cu = Cuprum
Copper ♀
Venus
beautiful and flexible
female
colorful
conducts electricity
(fights venous congestion and
strengthens kidney function)

Fe = Ferrum
Iron ♂
Mars
brute force
magnetism
masculine
hard
(speeds healing and strengthens
the nervous system)

The Polarities of the Seven Metals

The resistance to conductivity of heat and electricity increases as follows:
1. lead
2. tin
3. iron
4. gold
5. copper
6. mercury
7. silver

(Mercury is an exception unless it is in a stable frozen form.)

One could say that the first three are *useful* and the last three are *beautiful*—gold is in the middle. We will look at the minerals in pairs.

IRON (Mars) and COPPER (Venus) are polarities.

Iron is used in   – rails, bridges, construction
          – tools (saws, hammers)
          – weapons (formerly a sign of courage)

Iron has the power to give support. Activity and courage are soul qualities with which man connects himself with iron. Iron has "masculine" qualities. Mars was the god of war.

Copper is used for   – roofs of temples, churches
            – electronics, telephone
            – water faucets—they fit well but also break easily and leak.

Copper encloses and surrounds. It is colorful, flexible and enveloping. It conducts electrical current and evenly distributes heat on the bottom of saucepans. Copper has "feminine" qualities. Venus was the goddess of love.

There is a lot of iron in blood—it is found in the hemoglobin in red blood corpuscles. The iron in our blood helps us to fight illness. When we have too little we are anemic and our health is said to be poor. The blood serum contains about 100 millipercent iron and 100 millipercent copper. Men have slightly more iron, women slightly more copper. During pregnancy women have up to three times that amount of copper in the blood serum. The embryo has up to three times the amount of iron (both the male and the female embryos).

Iron is found mostly on the Northern hemisphere, and copper is mostly found in areas around the Pacific Ocean.

LEAD (Saturn) and SILVER (Moon) are polarities.

Lead is mostly found in the Western hemisphere (especially in the Andes Mountains in South America). Silver is found everywhere—it is also abundant in solution (silver salt in sea water), but it is mainly found in lead ore. Saturn is the planetary symbol for lead; it is large and dense.

Lead is used in
- printing (also in pencils)
- roofing
- water pipes
- coffins
- red-lead paint
- protection against x-rays

Lead has a sealing-off, protecting function. This can also be seen in printing—the original type was lead. Also, printing protects ideas from getting lost.

Lead brings an action to a standstill. For instance, lead poisoning makes one age very fast and vitality decreases to zero.

Lead as a mineral usually has a dirty, grey color. If you cut it, it will shine for a moment before oxidizing immediately. (It seals itself off right away.)

Silver is used in
- mirrors
- photographic film
- jewelry

As an analogy one can say silver opens up to the outside world without criticism. It accurately reflects what stands before it. Silver is the world of images and reflections: a mirror image, a photographic image. The interaction of light and darkness makes silver active. A mirror is unthinkable without light, photography is unthinkable without a darkroom.

While mirroring, the silver itself is invisible. When one looks at a mirror one sees oneself. The moon is the planetary symbol of silver; it reflects the light of the sun.

MERCURY (Mercury) and TIN (Jupiter) are polarities.

Mercury is a heavy metal, and at the same time it is a liquid. This goes against one's normal feeling of the way things should be. If one drops (very dangerous) a little ball of mercury, it splatters into many little balls which then can come together again as if sucked back into wholness. It is quick and facile and makes you laugh.

Mercury is used in
- thermometers
- barometers
- blood pressure meters
- quicksilver lamps
- sun lamps
- medicines (formerly more than now)

Alchemists used to especially watch the transitions from solid to liquid, etc. These transitions were called: "sal" (from solid to liquid), "mercur" (from liquid to gaseous) and "sulfur" (from gaseous to a state of heat). So mercury was in the middle area. In plants the alchemists would make the following characterizations: "sal"—roots, "mercur"—the leaves winding around the stem, "sulfur"—the flower.

Mercury is very mobile. It is a liquid that does not wet its surroundings. But all metals dissolve in it except iron and iron-related metals. It has a shiny silver color, and in its liquid state, one never gets to take a look at its interior.

Tin is shiny but solid. Every metal becomes softer through heating, but though tin first does become softer, from 160°C, it becomes much harder, even brittle. In fact it emits a screeching sound when bent. On the contrary, when tin is chilled, it disintegrates into powder. At -50°C, the normal mineral form cannot exist. When one heats tin up to 232°C, it becomes liquid. Tin has the lowest melting point of all heavy metals except mercury. Lead melts at 327°C and boils at 170°C. The boiling point of tin is 230°C. Tin "resists" heating up. Melting always goes together with the losing of form.

While Mercury does not want to be made into a form, tin does not want to lose its form.

Tin is used in
- solder
- bronze (93% copper and 7% tin)
- plates, cups, etc. (formerly)
- tin cans (it provides the lining in steel cans to prevent rusting)

There is just a trace of tin in the human body and it is concentrated. It exists in the muscles and in the mucous membranes of the tongue as well as in the skin. The tongue not only tastes, but investigates the texture of food.

Tin is also used in paper to wrap up chocolate, etc. (wrapper paper = stanniol; tin = *stannum* in Latin). It gives contour to the already existing form. Skin gives contour to the body.

To laugh is quicksilver; to cry is tin (to become rigid).

GOLD (Sun)

Gold is something "to look at." It is beautiful and reflects the sunlight. It used to be a symbol for regal power, and it represents the sun in many religions. We store it in guarded vaults as back-up for national currencies. In a way gold is bound up with the spreading of "culture." Think of the gold rushes to the American West that populated the wilderness.

If you hold gold leaf against the light between two pieces of glass, it has a greenish color. Gold can be used to "intensify" the hue when making color.

The process of manufacturing gold leaf involves inter-weaving the gold between sheets of parchment and pounding it with wooden mallets. The resulting sheets are so thin that it becomes almost translucent if you hold the sheets up to a strong light. Yet when properly applied over sizing (and then polished), the same sheet of gold reflects light so vividly that the object it covers appears to be wrought out of solid gold. Gold is so malleable that ten thousand leaves of gold are less than 1 mm thick. Gold leaf manufacture progresses through five distinct stages: melting, rolling, beating, beating again and packaging. The melting stage involves reducing the gold from a pure 24-karat ingot to an alloy, incorporating silver and copper, which improve the handling characteristic and prevent some problems. Sometimes palladium or platinum is added for obtaining special colors.

The State House in Boston, MA, designed by Charles Bulfinch, had a dome which was coppered by Paul Revere & Sons in 1802. Seventy years later the dome was gilded with 23-karat gold leaf for the first time. The gilding began with several small pieces of 23-karat gold pounded so thin than it was able to cover the 9,100 square feet that make up the gold dome. The cost of the first gilding was $2,862.50; the most recent gilding in 1997 cost $300,000.00.

Though the Boston State House was started after the National Capitol in Washington, it was completed first in 1782, and for many years it was the most important building in the young nation. Indeed, it was hailed as the most beautiful and modern building of its time.

Preparation of a Metal from Ore

Smelting Tin

Procedure:

Grind in a mortar: 1 tsp. charcoal, 2.5 tsp. soda (Na_2CO_3 anhydrous!), 2.5 tsp. potash (K_2CO_3), 1 tsp. tin ore (either stannous oxide from a science supply store or brown fragments of tin graupel from a mineral supplier).

Mix the blackish powder mixture well, half-filling a porcelain or quartz crucible (low form 40–45 mm diameter). Soda and potash serve as "flux" so the metal pearls will melt together. Set the dish slanted in a ring stand; heat with a large propane burner (natural gas is not sufficiently hot); a second hand-held burner with a sharp flame is directed onto the surface. (I use an air-acetylene "Turbo torch" from our jewelry shop.)

Initially some sparks will spiral out of the crucible until the surface layer melts. In a closed "oven" at glowing heat, charcoal reacts with earthy oxide rather than with oxygen from the air.

The upper burner can occasionally be cut back. After a few minutes, peer into the glowing, bubbling mass, and you will see a few tiny, glittering molten metal pearls as they melt out. Allow the students, with safety glasses on, to file past and peek inside the crucible to view them. In about five minutes the small pearls will begin to flow together, while more arise, forming a larger pearl covering the bottom. (If the top flame is hot enough to get the flux fully molten, you will be able to swirl the melt to enhance the merging of the pearls.)

Then rapidly tip over the crucible with the melt (at a low height so you will avoid a splatter) into an iron crucible or onto an iron plate. After a short cooling period where the hoped-for metal pearls solidify and can be seen, we pound the whole mass with a hammer. The slag residue will crack away (clinkers), and the tin will form a lump.

Finely trim out the metal nugget and scrape the surface to a shine with a knife and then pass it around.

The crucible can be soaked in medium concentration hydrochloric acid to clean it.

The Blast Furnace and Industrial Chemistry

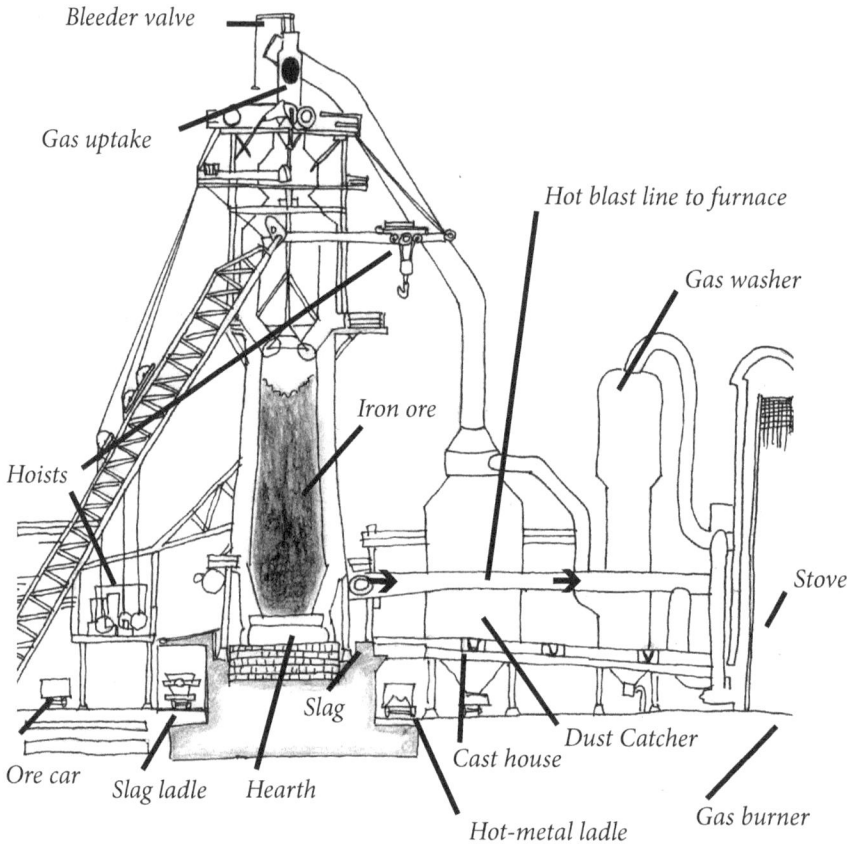

It is important that the students have an inner picture of how this entire operation works from beginning to end. Drawing a picture of a blast furnace helps them internalize the process.

Ore is first mined from the earth and brought to a site where the rock is crushed. Iron is extracted from the ore in a blast furnace like the one pictured above.

The main ore of iron is hematite, iron (III) oxide. The iron is extracted by reduction in the blast furnace. The reducing agent is carbon monoxide. A deposit of iron ore, coke and limestone is put in the top of the furnace. Hot air is blown in near the bottom. The coke burns in the air to form carbon dioxide. This is a strongly exothermic reaction—it gives off heat.

As the carbon dioxide passes up through more hot coke, it is reduced to carbon monoxide. This reaction is endothermic—it takes in heat.

The carbon monoxide reduces the iron oxide to iron. This reaction is slightly exothermic. As the iron moves down the furnace, it melts and runs down to collect in a pool at the bottom. The limestone (calcium carbonate) is put in to remove impurities. It decomposes in the furnace to form calcium oxide which reacts with acidic impurities in the ore such as sand (silicon oxide) to form a slag, which separates from the molten iron at the bottom of the furnace. The molten iron is drawn off in the cast house where it is placed in molds to cool.

What Part of the Earth's Crust Consists of Metals?

Aluminum 8.000%
Iron......................4.500%
Copper.................... 007%
Tungsten.................. .006%
Tin....................... .004%
Lead...................... .013%
Gold, Silver, Mercury .... .001%

Metal	Density (weight in lb. per cubic foot)	Cost per pound (approx.)
Gold	1200	$14,200.00
Silver	655	$198.00
Copper	540	75¢
Iron	440	06¢
Lead	708	35¢
Tin	455	$3.00
Mercury	845	$15.00

Elements in the Earth's Crust

The chart below represents by percentage the amounts of the significant elements in the crust of the earth. Most of these elements are in combination with other elements.

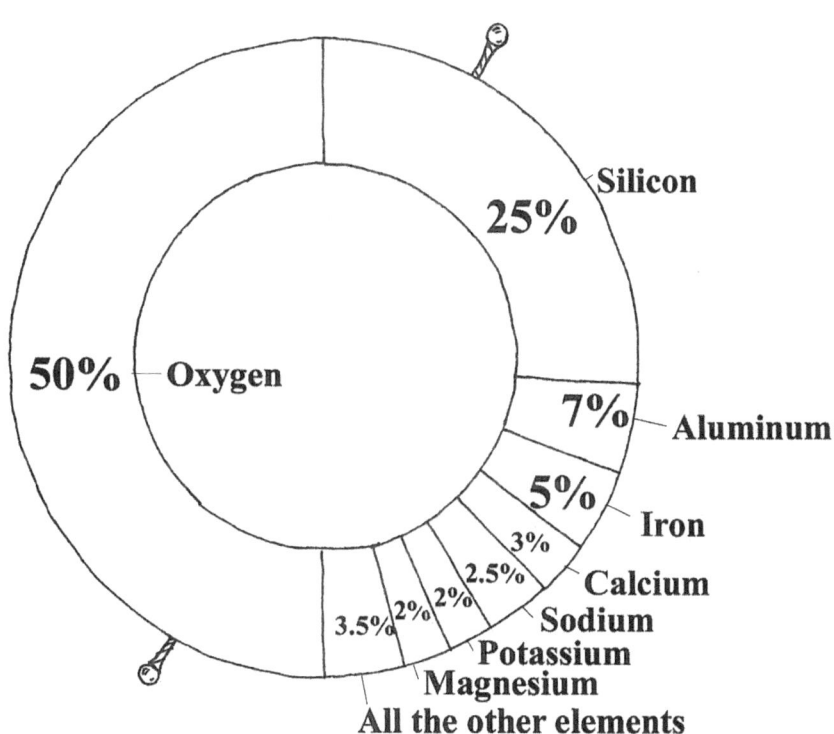

Photosynthesis

The word *photosynthesis* comes from two Greek words, *photo* which means "light" and *synthesis* which means "bringing together." Photosynthesis is a series of complex reactions within the plant. During the daytime, when the sun is shining, the leaves draw in carbon dioxide through their stomas. The sun energy is transformed into chemical energy which in the presence of chlorophyll helps fix the carbon which becomes sugar or glucose. This is called carbon fixation. It takes place in the leaf in organelles called chloroplasts. The sugar is first transformed into starch and then into cellulose which is how the tree grows. Oxygen is released through the leaves when it is dark outside. In a chemical diagram, it can be simplified and written as follows:

$$\text{Carbon dioxide} + H_2O \xrightarrow[\text{chlorophyll}]{\text{light}} \text{Glucose} + \text{Oxygen} \uparrow \text{gas}$$

Each year about eighty billion (80,000,000,000) tons of carbon dioxide is converted by land plants and another six hundred billion tons (600,000,000,000) by marine plants. (Most of this is done by plankton.)

It is estimated that a carbon dioxide molecule spends 120 years in the ocean for every year spent in the atmosphere.

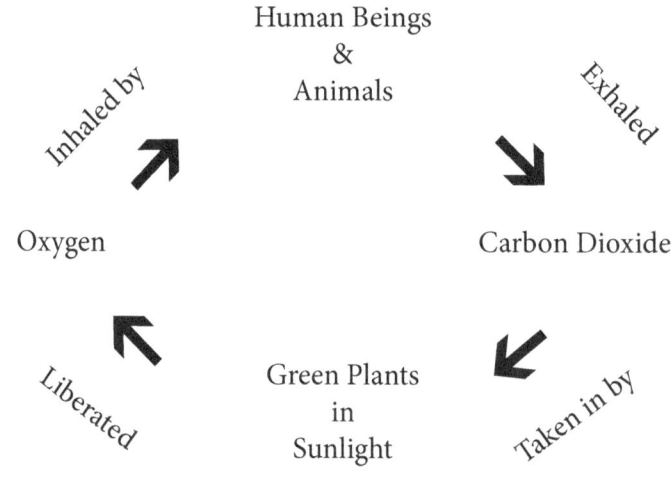

The Process of Photosynthesis

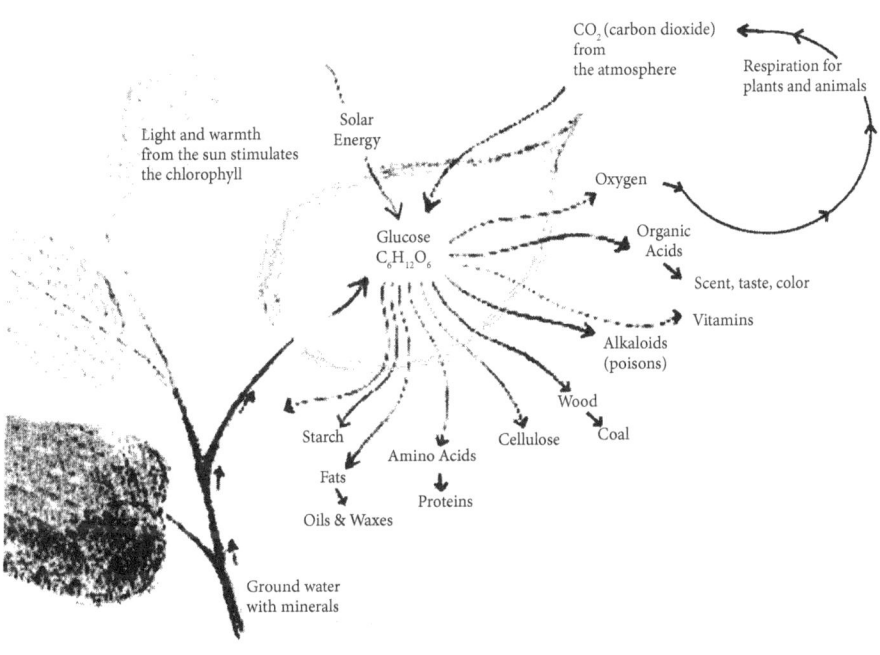

141

Class Reading

THE GREAT AMERICAN FOREST

by
Rutherford Platt

Food in the human menu is hardly recognized as packaged sunlight, but that is exactly what it is. The art of packaging sunlight was originally discovered by plants in the sea, and seaweeds carried the formula for photosynthesis to the water's edge. There they delivered it to ferns and mosses, which in turn bequeathed it to trees.

Growing in the sunlight, trees could make full use of photosynthesis; in fact, their energy factory worked so well that packaged sunlight was not only incorporated into food but into wood, as we have seen. Then wood, in turn, increased the production of packaged sunlight by lifting green needles and leaves high off the ground into more winds, bringing more oxygen and giving more exposure to sunlight. These towering arrangements led to the grand climax of the forest. …

At first glance, a leaf may look as thin as paper; actually it is a spreading one-story factory with ample room between floor and ceiling for sunlight packaging machinery. The standard leaf is designed for utility to present a broad surface to the sunlight. A mature maple tree spreads several hundred thousand leaves with a surface of some two thousand square yards (about half an acre) of chlorophyll.

A square yard of leaf surface in full operation packs about a gram of carbohydrate per hour. This may seem to be a small amount; a gram weighs about as much as the common straight pin. But food production of that half acre of chlorophyll mounts with each hour of every day. There are no Sunday and holiday shutdowns. Photosynthesis does not require a bright sunny day; it works even better when the sky is overcast. Operating an average of ten hours a day during June, July and August, each square yard of maple leaf surface packs a pound and a half of carbohydrate. The seasonal production by the leaves of a single maple tree can total 3630 pounds of packaged sunlight!

The History of Sugar

The first sweetener was honey. Honey needed no processing and was available wherever there were bees. In 330 BC Alexander the Great brought sugar back from India.

At the time of Charlemagne, sugar was totally unknown in Europe. However, in the court of Haroun-al-Rashid many sweet pastries could be had. The Arabs would cut up sugar cane, put it into huge cauldrons with water, and boil it down into a syrup. Then they would pour the syrup into cones made from palm leaves until it hardened and could be pulverized into powdered sugar.

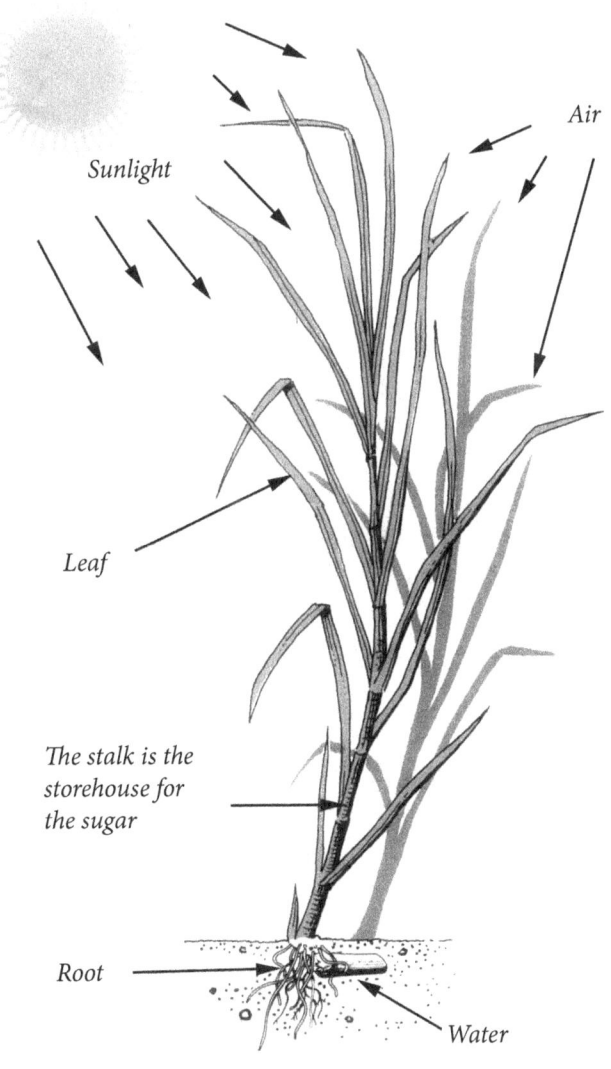

Sunlight

Air

Leaf

The stalk is the storehouse for the sugar

Root

Water

The Venetians planted sugarcane on islands in the Mediterranean Sea. Sugar was so rare that it was presented to royalty in jewel-studded boxes. Sugar was also valued as a medicine.

After America was discovered, Cuba and the Antilles (the West Indies) became the ideal spots for raising sugar. It was introduced to Europe by Christopher Columbus after one of his later voyages. Eventually huge sugar plantations were established with slave labor. The production of sugar for Europe was paid for with human blood.

When a blockade was imposed on Napoleon in 1747 and sugar was not allowed to enter French ports, the French found a way of making sugar out of beets. They would mash the beets and boil them in big pots. Then they would force carbon dioxide gas through the starch water, transforming it into sugar. However, the sugar still had acid in it, so they added lime which neutralized the acid and sank to the bottom as a precipitate while. The sugar water was then skimmed off the top, boiled to a syrup, and hardened into granular sugar. The Germans later developed a substitute for sugar called saccharine by chemically transforming coal.

The production of sugar called forth new machinery and new technology. The first sugar refinery in the United States was built in New York City in 1689, but sugar cane was not successfully grown in the United States until 1751 when a harvest was reported in Louisiana. Today, sugar cane is grown in Florida, Georgia, Texas and Hawaii. These four states produce more than three million tons of sugar cane each year.

All green plants—from grasses to flowers—produce sugar. The giant grass called sugar cane is one of the most efficient sugar producers of all plants. It is the stored sugar in the stalks that is extracted and refined for use as a food for us to eat. The sugar cane cycle takes two years per plant to reach maturity and requires a lot of water; approximately 150 gallons will produce one pound of sugar.

The sugar cane is first cut, then flash-fired to burn off all the leaves in the field. Front-end-loaders scoop up the stalks onto large trucks for transport to the factory where cane cleaners, shredders and mills, pumps, boilers and evaporators, pans and clarifiers process it. Most all of this equipment is controlled by computers today. The aim is simple—to extract as much juice from the cane as possible and transform it into almost-pure crystals of raw sugar. A byproduct of sugar is thick brown molasses. The raw sugar is brownish in color and the crystals are easily defined. It has a strong taste. The raw sugar is further refined by melting it into a syrup and filtering it several times until the liquid is clear. When hardened this is granulated white sugar. Cooks and bakers prefer this white sugar because it does not impart a distinct flavor like the raw sugar and they can, therefore, more easily control the final taste of their product.

The refined sugars have different consistencies. The sugar in most sugar bowls is granulated. Smaller crystals used for baking are called *superfine*, and an even smaller crystal used for icings and candies is called *powdered* or *confectioners'* sugar. Light and dark brown sugars are granulated sugars to which molasses has been added. This sugar is used to make butterscotch, glaze hams, sweeten baked beans and make gingerbread.

World production of sugar exceeds one hundred million tons per year. It is one of the world's most politically-controlled foods. Sugar has been rationed in time of war; it is used as a commodity to earn foreign currency; it is a weapon of international diplomacy, and it is a tool of economic policy-making. There is virtually no free trade or market competition within the world sugar business. Some major importing nations reach trade agreements with exporting nations to buy sugar at set prices to ensure a steady supply regardless of supply shortages or surpluses. The United States has laws to protect its domestic sugar industry and to assure its citizens of ample supplies of sugar at reasonable prices.

An Acre of Sugar Cane Produces

- 100 tons of harvested sugar cane
- 3.5 tons of molasses
- 12 tons of raw sugar
- 11 tons of refined sugar
- 32 tons of bagasse (a type of fuel oil)

and

- Removes 95 tons of carbon dioxide from the air
- Releases 60 tons of pure oxygen

Test for Sugar

Demonstration:

The Fehling test involves two solutions. The first is a blue copper salt solution (copper sulfate) and the other is a clear solution which contains a strong base—lye (sodium hydroxide). By mixing and heating these two substances, they can be used to detect the presence of simple sugars.

When a few drops are added to a solution which has no sugar present and it is heated, the blue color may become a bit darker but otherwise does not change.

When a few drops are added to a solution where sugar is present and it is heated, the color will change from blue to green, to orange and, finally, to a brick red.

1. Mix equal quantities of Fehling "A" solution with Fehling "B" solution. Observe and write the color change.

2. Dissolve some sugar in water and add a few drops to the mixed Fehling solution. Observe and note any color change. Heat the sugar water solution. Observe and note any color change.

3. Now heat the solution (Fehling solution mixed with the sugar in boiling water) for two minutes. Observe and note any color change.

4. Have a volunteer chew a piece of orange for a few minutes without swallowing. Have him carefully expectorate some of his spittle into a test tube. Add the mixed Fehling solution and heat.
Observe and note any color change.

5. Do the same with a soda cracker.

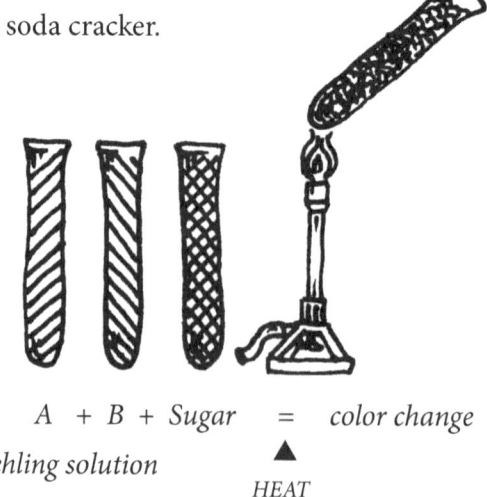

A + B + Sugar = color change
Fehling solution ▲
　　　　　　　HEAT

Starch

During the night, when the sugar production stops in the laboratory of the living plants for lack of sunlight, sugar is transformed into starch. Starch, however, is not soluble in water, and it is deposited in various parts of the plant as minute granules. These granules differ in size and shape depending on the plant in which they are created. In corn they are angular, in wheat round, and in potatoes they themselves look like tiny potatoes. A scientist can tell from which plant a starch granule comes by studying it under a microscope.

Since starch is not soluble in water, it can be separated from the plant such as a potato or grain flour, as we have observed in our experiments. When we put some iodine solution on starch, we discover that it detects the presence of starch—it turns dark bluish-green! In hot water the starch granules swell and form a sticky paste. In this form starch is used in great quantities as an adhesive, and laundry starch is used as a stiffening agent. The greatest and most important use, however, is as food for animal and man. For millennia food prepared from the various grains has been the main source of nourishment.

In order to digest starch it has to be changed back into sugar. When we chew a piece of bread, this process of transforming the starch into sugar starts when the saliva mixes with the bread. When we chew a raw potato, however, this change does not come about. It is necessary that starch be cooked or baked before it is eaten as food by man. The changing of starch into sugar is continued in the stomach and then in the intestines. Starch can also be changed to sugar in the laboratory or factory by heating it in water and adding some acid to the solution. Large quantities of corn syrup or glucose are manufactured in this way.

Take an unsalted box of crackers. Pass them around the class and ask them to chew the crackers but try not to swallow. As they chew ask them to be awake to what is happening in their mouths. They will experience that the dry, starchy crackers become sweet as they mix with their saliva.

Describe the grains which make up the starches and point out how they have geographic significance.

The East – rice
- easily digestible
- grows in water
- little contact with the earth
- ovule granules

Europe/Asia (the middle) – wheat
- sustains life, moderately digestible
- sways in the wind in big fields
- vigorous structure
- large number of grains per plant

North America, the West – corn
- hard to digest
- grows on stalks, on ears
- hard leaves
- swollen kernels

To Look at Anything

To look at any thing,
If you would know that thing,
You must look at it long:
To look at this green and say
'I have seen spring in these
Woods,' will not do—you must
Be the thing you see.
You must be the dark snakes of
Stems and ferny plumes of leaves,
You must enter in
To the small silences between
The leaves,
You must take your time
And touch the very peace
They issue from.

— John Moffitt

Test for Starch

1. Take four different vegetables: potato, carrot, corn and turnip.

2. With a sharp knife cut a thin slice of each (mash several corn kernels into a flat paste) and place each in a separate petri dish.

3. With a medicine dropper place a few drops of tincture of iodine in the center of each vegetable and record your observations.

4. Take three test tubes. Fill each half full with water and add a teaspoon of sugar to one, a teaspoon of corn starch to another, and a teaspoon of cellulose to the third. Place a cork in each and shake vigorously. Add five drops of tincture of iodine to each and record your results.

5. Discuss each and consider a conclusion. Iodine is an indicator for starch.

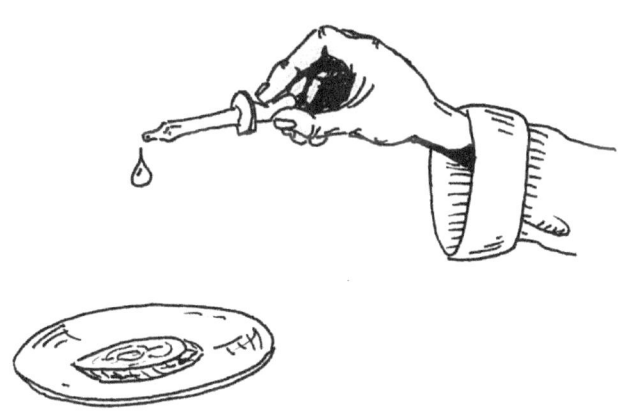

Cellulose

Cellulose is the most abundant naturally occurring organic substance, being found as the principal component of cell walls in higher plants where it provides the main structural feature. Cotton is almost pure cellulose at 98%, flax is 80%, and wood is 40–50%. Chemically, it is a carbohydrate like sugar and starch. Important sources of cellulose are flax, hemp, jute, straw and wood.

Cellulose has been used for the manufacture of paper since the second century. It is insoluble in water and other ordinary solvents, and it exhibits marked properties of absorption.

Cellulose reacts with acids to form esters and with alcohol to form ethers. Cellulose derivatives include guncotton (fully nitrated cellulose), used for explosives; celluloid (the first plastic), the product of cellulose nitrates treated with camphor; collodion, a thickening agent; and cellulose acetate, used for plastics, lacquers and fibers such as rayon.

Nutritionally, cellulose provides fiber to help our food pass through our digestive system. It scours our intestines and helps to keep them clean. We are not, however, able to digest cellulose and gain any nutritional benefit from it. Termites have special enzymes which allow them to digest cellulose.

Because cellulose has no form of its own, it is built into the whole of the plant and serves it as a structural material. In modern chemistry cellulose is one of the most important substances in the creation of new products; thus it serves us in the same manner it serves the plant.

Experiments with Sugar, Starch and Cellulose

1. Have two volunteers come forward. With a clean spatula place a small amount of granulated sugar on their tongues. Ask them to describe the taste, using only adjectives, to their classmates who record what they report. Rinse their tongues off with a wash bottle and clean water. Have the students then daub their own tongues with a clean piece of paper towel.

Repeat the above with starch (corn starch).

Repeat the above with purified cellulose.

2. Have the students take a small portion of granulated sugar between their forefinger and thumb and rub. Have them describe the texture to their classmates.

Repeat with starch.

Repeat with cellulose.

3. Fill a Pyrex test tube half full with water. Add a teaspoon of granulated sugar. Cork the test tube and shake it vigorously. Observe whether or not it dissolves. Place it in a test tube rack to observe later after it has time to settle.

Repeat with starch.

Repeat with cellulose.

4. Repeat #3, only this time carefully heat each substance and note your observations.

NOTE: *Use **CAUTION** with the starch because it can shoot out a hot glob of paste like a cannon.*

5. Place each substance in a clean teaspoon and heat it over a Bunsen burner until it ignites. Observe it burn. Notice any smoke, sparks, pooling, and so forth and record your observations.

Have the students construct a grid so that they can easily compare their results and discuss the nature of each substance.

Alcohol

We have all seen a grape vine. It is a climbing plant and is very exuberant. As it grows it shoots out tendrils which can grab onto trees, fences or houses. It appears to constantly pull itself closer to the sun. Its roots go deep into the soil and exert great pressure to draw as much water up as possible. If you cut a vine in the spring, you could have a six-foot column of sap squirt out!

The grape plant likes water and sunshine and lots of time to grow. This water and sunshine create a powerful interplay of fire and water within the clusters of succulent grapes which form as fruit. We see the water in the swelling of the grape. We taste the fire (sunlight) in the grape's sweetness. The more southern the location of the grape plant, the more sun it gets, and the sweeter the grape becomes.

After the grape has achieved ripeness, a bacteria on its skin causes it to change. This change is called fermentation. As the grape ferments CO_2 escapes. The sweet taste is replaced by a fiery one. What was formerly calm and nourishing now whips up the senses and overheats us in the form of alcohol.

Sugar from the grape is taken immediately into the blood stream. Alcohol enters still faster—not even the liver acts as a barrier. When we drink the alcohol it spreads immediately and unhindered throughout our whole system and has an effect on our thinking and motor skills.

The gift from the grape as sugar is real. That received as alcohol is an illusion. Sugar furnishes a basis for our willing which gives us mastery over our body. Alcohol creates only the feeling that we can do anything we like, although it does not increase our capacities.

Sugar develops warmth in our stomachs. Alcohol overheats us. Instead of stimulating our forces, it creates a desire to bluff and make exaggerated demands.

Alcohol remains within our body for two weeks after we have tasted it. It stimulates us and makes us want to drink more. Anyone who drinks more than once in a two-week period over an extended period of time is called an alcoholic. One out of every five teenagers who drink is an alcoholic. Alcoholism is considered a disease. It will slowly destroy the liver, and the activities of a drunk ruin many families and friendships.

NOTE: *Alcohol is studied more completely in the ninth grade. However, I like to create the mental picture of alcohol in the human body in a non-preaching manner while the students are still open to hearing it in the eighth grade.*

Carbon Dioxide Generator

Demonstration:

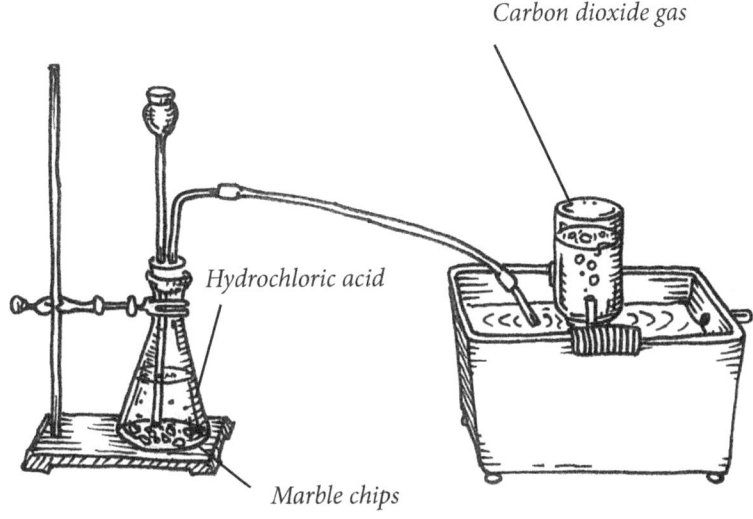

Carbon dioxide gas

Hydrochloric acid

Marble chips

$$CaCO_3 + 2HCl \rightarrow CaCl_2 + H_2O + CO_2 \uparrow$$

Set up your apparatus like the diagram above. Cover the bottom of a Florence flask with marble chips. Carefully add dilute hydrochloric acid through the thistle tube. You will observe a brisk bubbling action. The gas released will egress through the tube and displace the water in the wide-mouthed bottle. Collect three or four bottles and stand them upright on the counter with a small glass plate over each so that the gas will not escape. (It is heavier than the air, and you can actually pour it out by inverting the wide-mouthed bottle.)

1. Light a wooden splint on fire and insert it into the gas-filled bottle. The gas will extinguish the flame. Have the students record their observations.

2. Add a medicine dropper-full of distilled water to the wide-mouthed bottle, shake it vigorously, and then test the water with litmus.

3. Have a volunteer smell the gas and describe it to the class. Then ask her to pour some into her mouth and taste it.

The Production of Hydrogen

Demonstration:

Put ten to twenty small pieces of zinc into a Florence flask and pour hydrochloric acid over them. Add water and observe the bubbles that begin to rise immediately. The flask will become very hot! Lead off the gas with a tube, as in the diagram below. Light the gas and observe it burn with a hot, blue flame at the center. Fill a balloon with the gas and watch it rise to the ceiling. Then add oxygen (from a small oxygen tank) and explode the balloon by touching it with the long end of a deflagrating spoon which has been heated to a red heat in a Bunsen burner. There will follow a strong, bright flash, and you will find traces of moisture on the pieces of the exploded balloon.

You will find that hydrogen is highly flammable, it is colorless, and it is lighter than air. When the elements hydrogen and oxygen are mixed and ignited, they explode and form the compound water. The chemist would express this in the following way:

Dilute Hydrochloric Acid + Zinc ➡ Zinc Sulfate + Hydrogen ⇧

Hydrogen + Oxygen ➡ Water (H_2O)
▲
HEAT

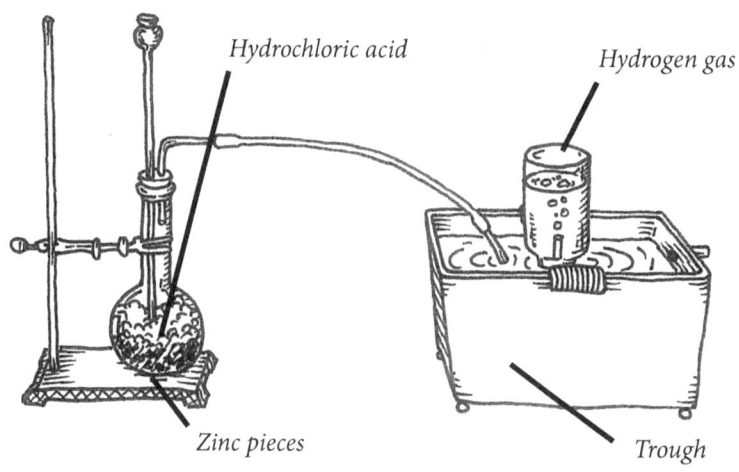

Proteins

While the plants are composed of carbohydrates, the bodies of animals and men consist of proteins. There are many different kinds of proteins, and they all are rather complex compounds. In addition to the elements of the carbohydrate, C, O and H, proteins contain nitrogen (N). There are some plants that are much richer in protein content than others. These are the legumes (peas, beans, lentils). These plants are able to capture nitrogen from the air with acids made from special bacteria in the soil. They build grape-like clusters of root material around the bacteria where the proteins are formed.

To obtain a bountiful harvest, the farmer fertilizes his clover with nitrogen-rich fertilizer such as cow manure. He also knows that clover and alfalfa are rich in proteins which help the cow produce rich milk, or when plowed under as a "green manure," the nitrogen which was absorbed into the clover or alfalfa goes into the soil as nitrogen salts. When dissolved in the water of the soil, they are drawn up by new growing plants which in turn are able to combine the nitrogen with C, O and H to build up new proteins. The plants, through their roots, are able to extract other minerals, such as sulfur and phosphorus, from the soil to form the very life-fluid of the plant—protoplasm.

Protein does not burn easily and it gives off a stench. It dissolves in water forming a cloudy solution or colloid. When we digest protein, it is reduced to simpler substances from which we form our own body tissue. All other protein disintegration outside of the body (putrefaction and decay) leads to strong toxins. In digestion the liver collects the used protein and forms non-toxic urea, which is eliminated through the kidneys and the skin.

Demonstration:

1. Take some hard cheese (protein) and grind it with a mortar and pestle; add water and 1 gram (or ten pellets) of sodium hydroxide followed by the same amount of copper sulfate powder. You will observe a purple color appearing first on the protein and then staining the entire solution.

2. Try the above experiment with egg white.

Bluret Test for Protein

Demonstration:

1. Place a small piece of white wool and a piece of white silk on a watch glass or petri dish.

2. Using a medicine dropper, add several drops of concentrated nitric acid (HNO_3). **CAUTION!** nitric acid will burn your skin.
Observe any change in color. If a yellow color is present, this is an indication of protein.

3. It is possible that the yellow color may be due to the presence of some other chemical in the material so we must confirm the test for protein by using a base.
Carefully rinse off the nitric acid with a plastic wash bottle and water. Use care not to splash the acid on your clothes or hands. When complete add a few drops of 25% ammonium hydroxide (NH_4OH), a base. If protein is present, this reaction will result in an orange color appearing.

4. If time permits try this test on a piece of white cotton or linen (both carbohydrate fibers) and note your results.

Oils and Fats

We receive a final gift from the plant kingdom in the form of fats and oils. We extract large quantities of oil from flaxseed which we call linseed oil. Oil is also taken from cotton seeds and peanuts, as well as many other seeds and nuts. Aromatic oils are formed in the blossoms and in the leaves of some plants, such as the eucalyptus plant. In some trees the wood and bark are saturated with oils which we extract to make turpentine.

If we call sugar "crystallized sunshine," then we might call the plant oils "liquified sunshine." It is here where we have the greatest concentration of sun energy stored in the plant. When we burn oil, we release the sun energy in the form of heat and light, and we can readily understand why people all over the world, ever since man has known fire, have used plant oils for acts of consecration.

Oils and fats are also very complicated in their chemical composition, consisting mainly of various proportions of carbon and hydrogen. They are lighter than water and are not soluble in water. When burned they leave no residue. As a food they give man and animal long-lasting energy, but fats are not easily digested. It is only in the small intestine that fats are finally transformed into human nourishment.

Demonstration:

1. Fill a 500 ml beaker nearly full with water. Warm it gently over a Bunsen burner until it is warm to the wrist (about 50°C).

2. With a medicine dropper, drop individual droplets of corn, peanut, olive, or safflower oil onto the surface. Observe. Then release some oil droplets beneath the surface. Observe. Stir the water. Observe again.

3. Add oil to a watch glass which has a small amount of water in it. Add some propanol which will act as a solvent and dissolve the oil. Add a few drops of liquid dishwashing solution to this mixture and observe.

4. Try the above experiments once again substituting butter or animal fat (bacon, beef fat, etc.).

Spelling and Vocabulary

Weekly spelling and vocabulary tests should be given. The following words are taken from the main lesson content for the week. The words below are suggestions:

Week #1

    meniscus   noble metal
    condensed   bronze
    evaporated   meander
    pollution   surface tension
    metallurgy   chemical compound
    mineral   electrical
    malleable   biochemistry
    ductile

Week #2

    fermentation   carbohydrate
    alcohol   cellulose
    ethanol   Fehling solution
    methanol   starch
    crucible   sugar
    dissolve   glucose
    precipitate   fructose
    denatured alcohol

Week #3

    protein   aromatic oil
    nitrogen   crystallization
    nutrition   chlorophyll
    photosynthesis   pigments
    synthetic   distillation
    legumes   albumin
    protoplasm   esters
    fertilizer

Ninth Grade

Chemistry

What is not fully understood is not possessed.
— Goethe

If a man's eye is on the Eternal, his intellect will grow.
— Ralph Waldo Emerson

Thinking is the talking of the soul with itself.
— Plato

Ninth Grade Chemistry

Introduction
    Bunsen burner observation and experiments
    Glass bending
    Oxidation and reduction flame

Photosynthesis
    Leaf structure
    Sugar   Digestion of sugar
                 Properties of sugar
    Starch   Properties of starch
                 Test for starches in vegetables
    Cellulose
                 Properties of cellulose
    Carbohydrate lab

Transforming cotton to nitro-cellulose and plastic

Commercial use of plants

Rarefaction/solidification
    Chlorophyll
    Chromatography
    Historical reading: Ingenhousz on photosynthesis
    Gases   Phlogiston theory
                 Carbon dioxide   Carbon tower
                                       Reading on carbon
                                       Carbon dioxide cycle
                 Hydrogen
    Alcohol   Fermentation
                 Distillation experiment
    Esters
    Fats, oils and waxes
                 Saponification experiment
    Textiles
                 Synthetic textiles
    Plastics
    Rubber
    Hydrocarbons
    Making aspirin
    Drugs

Themes in the Ninth Grade

Organic Chemistry and the Ninth Grader

The fifteen-year-old ninth graders stand before us. When we observe them, what is it that we notice? Quite readily we may see that they are filled with emotional energy. They do not seem to think, but rather they "do" things and then watch the results. They are passionate, irascible, apt to be carried away by their own impulses, and yet they have high aspirations. At this point in their lives they have met few humiliations and can be brazen and all-knowing. They can carry everything too far whether it be their love or hatred or anything else. They are compassionate and suppose all people to be virtuous, or at least better than they really are.

Riding the waves of advancing adolescence, they can at any given moment be lonely, moody, argumentative, depressed, ecstatic and challenging to all authority. Adolescence is a time of tremendous physical and chemical change. The body is in revolution, and the soul is in conflict. Rudolf Steiner refers to the onset of adolescence as "a gentle sprinkling of pain that never goes away!"

What is going on inside ninth graders? Physically their heart is doubling its density. Their blood pressure is increasing. Their lymphatic system is shrinking which may open up the body to infections in the throat area. Boys' voices are changing. (They drop a full octave while the girls' drop only one tone.) The limbs, starting with the feet and legs, are beginning to elongate. (This can cause pain and restlessness.) The lungs are increasing in size and the breathing is changing—costal for the girls and a deeper diaphragm breathing for the boys. Two dozen different hormones are being released leading to the emergence of individual sexual characteristics. Fat becomes distributed over the body, lips thicken, thighs firm up, and the hips take on adult curves. There is rapid acceleration and deceleration of the skeletal growth, and there is a need for lots and lots of sleep—especially on Saturday and Sunday mornings!

The alpha waves of the adult are added to the low frequency waves of the young child as the brain experiences change. The child feels alone, restless, sometimes angry and begins to formulate questions for his/her teachers, such as, "What really matters? What is the point of it all? Who am I?" It is a difficult passage in life and calls for a lot of compassion from adults.

The end of the fourteenth year is that point in time when the intellect is being born and the individual begins to find enjoyment in logic. Teachers and other adults become the whetstones upon which the teenagers can sharpen this newfound ability to reason. They must be met in their school experience with subjects and teachers who challenge them.

The curriculum of the Waldorf school attempts to meet and exercise these forces. For the ninth grader, the "what" has become the significant question, and properly directed, concrete and practical activities such as a phenomenological, or sense-based, approach to science is one of the answers.

Rudolf Steiner organized the Waldorf curriculum so that the chemistry in the ninth grade should be carried forward from what was done by the class teacher in the eighth grade. This recapitulation and extension involve direct experience and prepare for an intellectual grasping of the subject in a way which is not abstract. It becomes then a living knowledge.

This age group benefits from a study of contrasts: black with white, inhaling with exhaling, heat with cold, anabolic with catabolic, and acidic with basic. A key to working with this age is to have them summarize as much as possible. This helps to center and pull the pupils in.

Organic chemistry is one of the ninth grade main lesson blocks. Chemistry is the study of the inner nature of substances. The organic is the world of the living. Everything we refer to as organic has carbon in it and has had to be living substance at one time. As said before, the ninth graders are confronted by the task of maturing not only with regard to sex but also readiness for earth-life. Organic chemistry is placed at this point in their blossoming self-knowledge for very specific reasons. The teacher must invigorate their awakening to their surroundings in order to help them retain their health. This will help to regulate their impulsive jumping into activity. Kolisko said that the themes for this main lesson are to "connect the students with substances which form the living body and to show how chemistry is involved in the industrial processes."

The ninth graders' thinking is a "willed thinking." They learn by doing. Science is filled with activities which, when structured properly, lead the students into discrimination in their thinking.

The material covered should include the symbolic relationship between man and the plant world and a deep understanding of photosynthesis, the assimilation of carbon dioxide, the carbohydrates, and their dual directions toward solidification on the one hand (cellulose/diamonds) and toward rarefaction (alcohol/esters) on the other.

The contents of this block should be discussed in relation to the physiological processes going on in the students' bodies. They should experience the respiration of the plant in photosynthesis and contemplate nature's manufacturing factory for making carbohydrates. The technological processes of making paper and artificial silk (rayon) can be demonstrated. Finally vegetable and animal fats can be examined as well as mineral oils, rubber and petroleum. Joseph Priestley's achievements and studies of phlogiston are studied as well as the natures of oxygen and carbon dioxide. Van Helmondt's observation of the plant and Ingenhousz's discovery of the oxygen-carbon dioxide respiration cycle in plants can be read to the class.

Waldorf chemistry teachers have wonderful resources in the works and indications of Rudolf Steiner, Karl Stockmeyer, Eugen Kolisko, Frits Julius, Gerhard Ott, Wolfgang Schad and Manfred von Mackensen. Their writings can be referred to for specific experiments and direction in Waldorf science teaching.

In my class I like to keep the students actively involved in the experimental process. Besides demonstrations I involved them in nineteen different experiments over a three-week main lesson block. These experiments involved chromatography, the making of synthetic rubber, the fermentation and distillation of alcohol, the making of rayon, the creation of esters, saponification, the chemical identification of sugars (both monosaccharides and disaccharides), starches, cellulose and photosynthesis, to name a few. The starches corn, wheat and rice as representatives of the West, Europe and the East, were discussed. We did solubility tests, density tests, flame tests, fractional distillations, and so forth. We did microscopic tests, distinguishing between vegetable, animal, mineral and synthetic fibers after our study of rubber. Every student concocted a synthetic rubber ball of his own. The students were asked to write reports in their main lesson books on these experiments to include: a list of apparatus, a sketch of the setup, the procedure, their observations, and whatever questions (at least two) that the particular experiment awoke in them in the evening, as they reviewed their main lesson work.

The next day in class we reviewed the experiment and tried to evolve any conclusions, which were then written down in their block books. The conclusions, concepts and questions were drawn from the experiments. The rarefied side of the carbohydrates (alcohol and esters) were, after a night of contemplation, contrasted with the earthy side (starch and cellulose).

One assignment I like to do with my students is to have them research a biography of a modern scientist for both oral and written reports. In the oral report I ask them to include where the scientist lived, what his or her upbringing was like, what his or her physical appearance was like, how he or she became interested in science; to give an explanation of his or her most significant discovery and what it meant to the development of science; and to describe what difficulties he or she encountered in life and how he or she overcame them. I also ask them to include one humorous anecdote from the life of the individual they research. Scientists included have been Nobel, Boyle, Newton, Cavendish, Priestley, Dalton, Pasteur, Curie, Einstein and others. I first contemplate each child and then assign a specific biography that I imagine will enkindle his or her interest. Then I hand them a photocopy of a brief biography and sketch I have prepared to help them get started. They are required to write notes from each other's reports.

It is beneficial for the teacher to plan one or two field trips during the block so that the students can have a first-hand experience of an industrial process created by human thinking and borrowed from man's observations of the activities of the plant world. I like to visit a local distillery and schedule a brewmaster to give a talk on fermentation some days after we have studied it in class.

The ninth grader needs to experience the world as his own and should feel that the world is an important and fine place to be. The task of the teacher is to bring the students of this age down into their physical bodies, to plant them firmly on the earth. We must invigorate their awakening in their surroundings in order to help them find their own personal health and balance which they will need in their adult lives.

As described above, the building up and the breaking down of the natural world is experienced through ninth grade organic chemistry. By describing physiological processes, one can come to questions such as alcoholism from an objective point of view at a time when the students are still open to such observations. They can see how sugar develops warmth in us while alcohol overheats us. Instead of stimulating our forces, the alcohol creates a bluff and develops exaggeration and illusion. When they meet these realities through their own observations and experiments within the chemistry lab, then they have learned objective lessons for life.

The fifteen-year-olds entering the ninth grade should be taught in such a way that they are led to the feeling that everything in the world is important. They must learn to trust human thinking, and they should experience that thinking is capable of dealing with inner as well as outer problems. In their science courses, in particular, they should realize that it is human consciousness which awakens technology and that a proper, moral technology can provide us with a better world in which to live.

NOTE: This article was first published in *Child and Man*, January 1988, Vol. 22, No. 1; subsequently published in *Waldorf Curriculum Studies – Volume 1, Science in Education*, Callington, Cornwall, UK: Langthorne Press, 1992, pp. 120–123.

For clarity on the first day of class I always hand students, a sheet showing my grading criteria and expectations. An example is below:

CHEMISTRY 9
GRADING AND EXPECTATIONS

1. It is expected that everyone will be on time at the start of the class.
2. If you miss a class, it is your responsibility to ask a fellow classmate for notes, but you must give him or her credit for what you copy.
3. If you miss a quiz, lab, or test, it is your responsibility to ask me for a makeup time.

Your grade will be based on the following:

Classroom notes & illustrations	35
Laboratory work	30
Oral report	10
Biographical essay	10
Quizzes	5
Final exam	10
Total	100%

What I am looking for in your laboratory work is careful, attentive and accurate observations. If you are asked to write down what you see, you should be as detailed as you are able.

Unless special consideration is given by me, all assignments are due on the date listed. Late assignments will result in a lowering of your grade.

All oral reports are due on the date assigned.

Biographical essays are due on _____

All main lesson books are due on the final day of the main lesson block.

Lab Sheet

Lab Report – Chemistry 9

        Student name: _____

        Experiment # _____

Name of Experiment: _____

List all apparatus used in experiment:

Draw a sketch of the setup:

Describe the procedure:

List all your observations:

What conclusions can you make?

Write at least one question that this experiment brought to your mind.

☐ Teacher's approval

The Carbon Tower

In a 200 ml beaker, place 1 inch of confectioners' sugar. In a second 200 ml beaker, place 10 ml of concentrated sulfuric acid (DANGER!).

Ask the students to observe the two substances. One will be seen as white and powdery, while the other will be seen as a viscous, slightly yellowish fluid. Both substances are cool when the bottom of the 200 ml beaker is touched.

Pour the acid in the sugar and stir with a glass stirring rod. Then stand back and observe. The solution will start to bubble and a black froth will form. Slowly, a column of carbon will rise up the sides of the beaker and will project five or six inches above it like a black tower.

The beaker will be too hot to touch, indicating an exothermic reaction (gives off heat).

The sulfuric acid has "dehydrated" the carbohydrate, and black carbon remains. The gases formed cause the material to foam and rise. The purpose of this experiment is to show the presence of the element carbon at the beginning of the main lesson block on organic chemistry.

Carbon

Carbon is the common element upon which organic chemistry is based. There are three common forms of carbon—coal, graphite and diamond.

Coal is peat that was placed under enormous pressure by debris which settled on top of it. Peat deposits are actually quite varied and contain everything from pristine plant parts (roots, bark, spores, etc.) to decayed plants, decay products, and even to charcoal if the peat caught fire at some time. Peat deposits typically form in waterlogged environments where plant debris accumulates; peat bogs and peat swamps are examples. In such environments, the accumulation of plant debris exceeds the rate of bacterial decay of the debris. The bacterial decay rate is reduced because the available oxygen in organic-rich water is completely used up by the decay process. Anaerobic (without oxygen) decay is much slower than aerobic decay. Burial causes compaction of the peat, and, consequently, much water is squeezed out during the first stages of burial.

Coal is a readily combustible rock containing more than fifty percent of carbonaceous material by weight, formed from compaction and induration of variously altered plant remains. Most coal is fossil peat. Peat is an unconsolidated deposit of plant remains from a water-saturated environment such as a bog or mire.

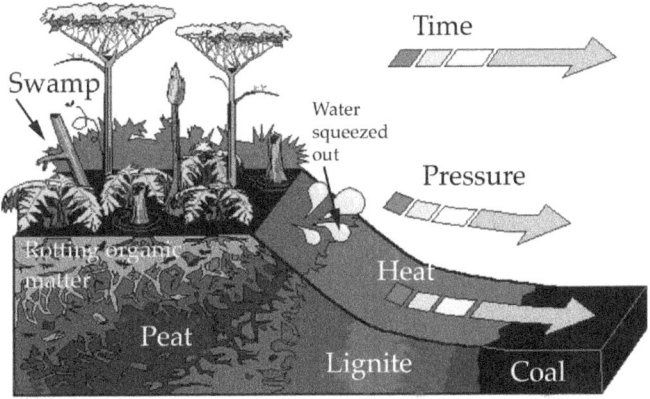

There are three basic types of coal: lignite (brown coal), bituminous (soft coal) which is approximately 85% carbon, and anthracite (hard coal) which is 95% carbon. Bituminous is a dense coal, either black or dark brown in color, often with well-defined bands of bright and dull material, used primarily as fuel in steam-electric power generation, with substantial quantities also used to make coke. Bituminous coal is the most abundant coal in active U.S. mining regions.

Anthracite is the highest grade of coal; it is used primarily for residential and commercial heating. It is a hard, brittle and black, lustrous coal, often referred to as hard coal, containing a high percentage of fixed carbon and a low percentage of volatile matter. The moisture content of fresh-mined anthracite generally is less than fifteen percent.

Coal tar is a thick, black, sticky liquid obtained as a byproduct in the manufacture of coke and coke oven gas from soft coal. Much coal tar is produced by the steel industry as it produces millions of tons of coke each year to fuel the furnaces used in separating iron from its ores. Various grades of tar are recovered by condensing (changing to liquid) hot vapors from a coke oven or a coal gas producer. Manufacturers heat coal tar and condense its vapors to produce light oils, such as benzene and toluene. Benzene is used as a solvent and in the production of perfumes and some gasolines, and toluene is used in the manufacture of dyes, paints, explosives and antiseptics.

Tar acids, such as carbolic acid, and tar bases, such as aniline, are other coal tar products. Carbolic acid and aniline are used to make dyes. Creosote and pitch are heavy liquid coal tar products. Creosote is used to preserve wood because it is toxic to bugs and bacteria. Pitch is used in the manufacture of roofing materials and paint. Sir William H. Perkin, an English chemist, pioneered in coal tar chemistry by making mauve, the first synthetic dye. Petrochemicals (chemicals made from petroleum) are increasingly supplementing coal tar chemicals for use in industry and chemistry.

Chemists have derived thousands of compounds from coal tar such as artificial vanilla flavoring, medicines, anti-dandruff shampoos, explosives and perfumes. The principal compounds in coal tar are benzene, tolulene, phenol, napthalene and anthracene.

Diamonds also come from compressed carbon and are usually found in three types of deposits: alluvial gravels, glacial tills and kimberlite pipes (dikes of former volcanoes). Diamonds are amongst the hardest of materials. Large stones are faceted to scatter light and are the most prized stones in jewelry. Small diamonds and diamond dust are bonded to steel to create grinding wheels that can wear away most every other material.

The Carbon Dioxide Cycle

Carbon dioxide makes up about 0.033 percent (or 330 ppm) of our atmosphere. It is critically important to all life on earth. The cycling of carbon dioxide between the oceans, the atmosphere and the landmasses is a key regulator of the climate of the Earth. The cycle taken by carbon dioxide is illustrated below.

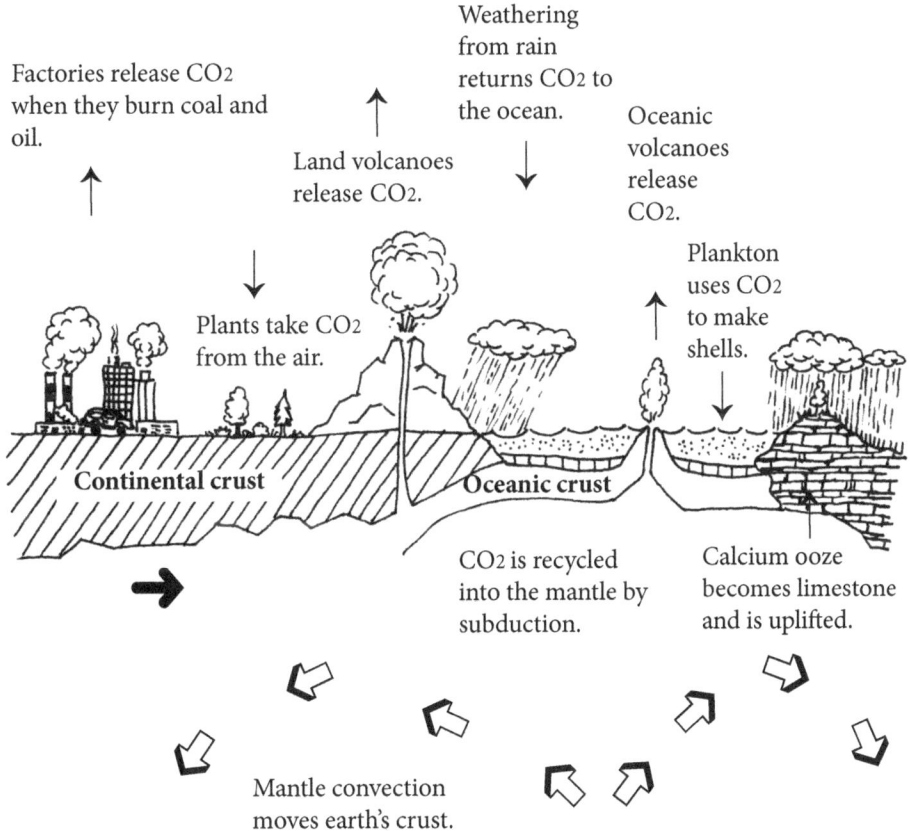

Properties of Carbon Dioxide

The gas carbon dioxide was discovered by Joseph Black in 1754. He noticed that upon heating magnesium carbonate, a gas was given off which he named "fixed air." Today we call it carbon dioxide.

Lab Report – Chemistry 9
        Student name: _____
        Experiment # _____

Name of Experiment: _____

1. Take a piece of charcoal and heat it. Capture the "smoke" in an inverted Erlenmeyer flask. Cork it. Add distilled water, shake, and check the acid-base balance with litmus paper.

Record the results:

2. Repeat number 1. This time insert a burning splint into the Erlenmeyer. Notice the condensation inside the flask.

Record the results:

3. Compare the results of the experiment above with the experiment you did with a glowing splint into the bottle containing oxygen.

☐ Teacher's approval

The Bunsen Burner

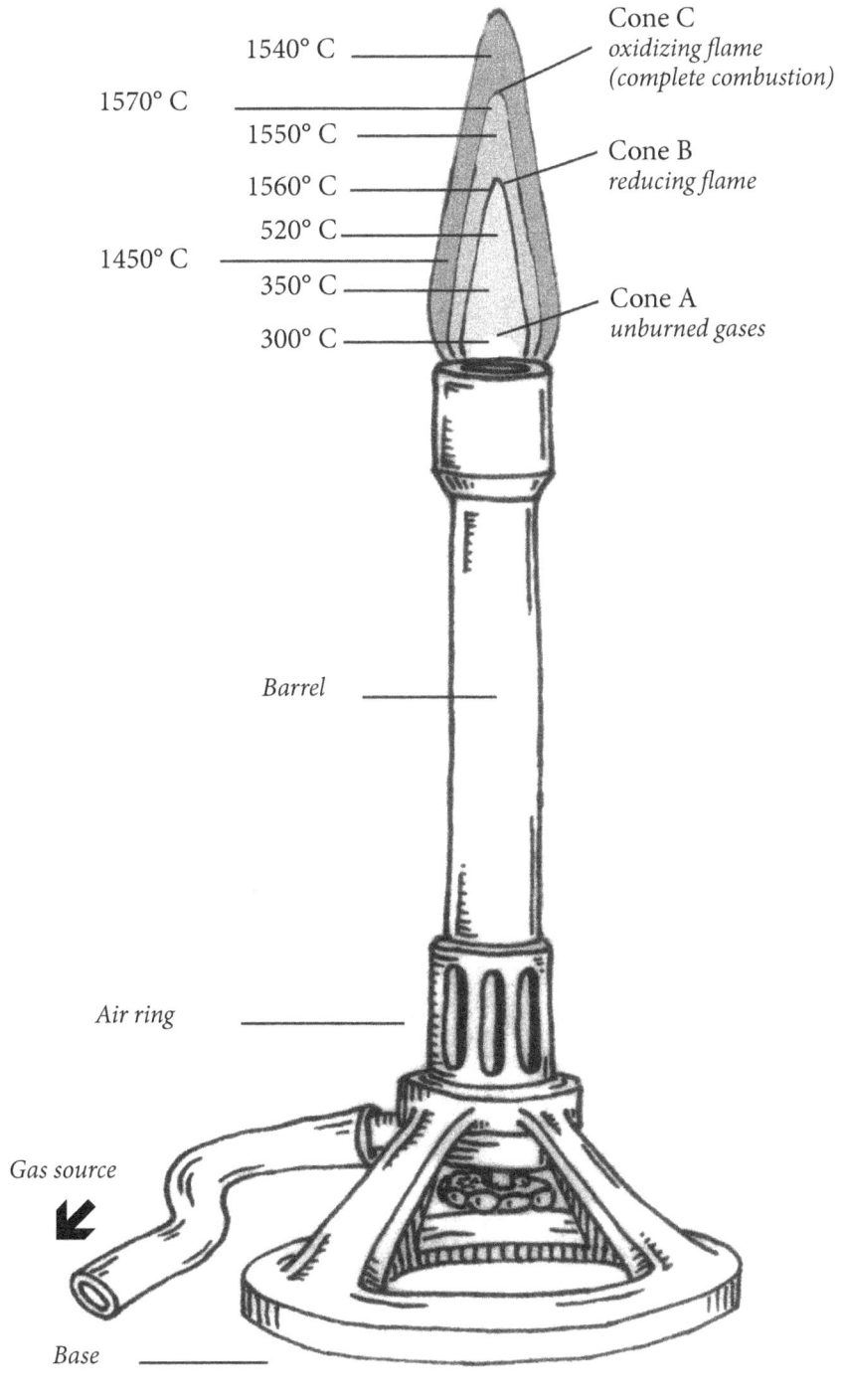

Bunsen Burner Experiments

Lab Report – Chemistry 9

        Student name: _____

        Experiment # _____

Name of Experiment: _____

1. Examine the construction of the Bunsen burner. Note the location of the air inlet.

2. Using a flint, light your burner.

3. Close the air inlet and note below the effect on the flame.

4. How do you think that it is possible for the gas to burn with the air inlet completely closed?

5. Hold a spoon or a cold porcelain dish above the luminous gas flame and examine the solid deposit. Describe it.

6. Push a pin crosswise through a match, just below the head of the match. Turn the burner off, and hang the match exactly in the center of the burner barrel, with the head pointing up. Now turn on the gas, and ignite it at a point 8–10 cm above the burner. Write down your observations.

7. Check your results of #6 above with the lab team next to you to see if their results correspond to yours. If they do, give an explanation of why you think what happened did happen with yours. If their results are not the same as yours, check to see if someone else in the class has the same results as you. If not, check with the teacher.

8. As accurately as possible draw a picture of your Bunsen burner showing all the working parts. Make the burner barrel five inches high so that you will be able to show the details of your flame.

                                                     ☐ Teacher's approval

Bending Glass

The first exercise with glass is for each student to make a stirring rod.

1. Take a long tube of glass and a triangular file. Measure off seven inches and mark it with a black indelible pen. With one smooth stroke of the triangular file, scratch the glass. (Do not allow them to "saw" with the file.) Place thumbs on either side of the scratch, lift it to chin height and pull it apart while exerting a slight outward force. This will break off the glass.
2. Fire polish one end by holding it at the top of Cone B and constantly rotating it. The flame should become bright orange, and the edges of the glass will be noticeably rounded. Allow this to cool and then polish the other side.
3. When cool repeat with the other end, but hold in the heat longer so that the walls will collapse and a blunt end will result. Allow to cool and you have a stirring rod.

The second exercise is to create an "S" tube for fermentation.
1. Cut a fourteen-inch length of tubing and fire polish each end as in the exercise above.
2. Create bends as shown in the diagram below. Be sure to rotate the tube in the flame to spread the heat around. When bending, bend slowly and evenly so the bend is not crimped or flattened. Always allow sufficient time to cool before proceeding with the next bend. When finished store in a drawer or cabinet until the alcohol and balloon fermentation experiment.

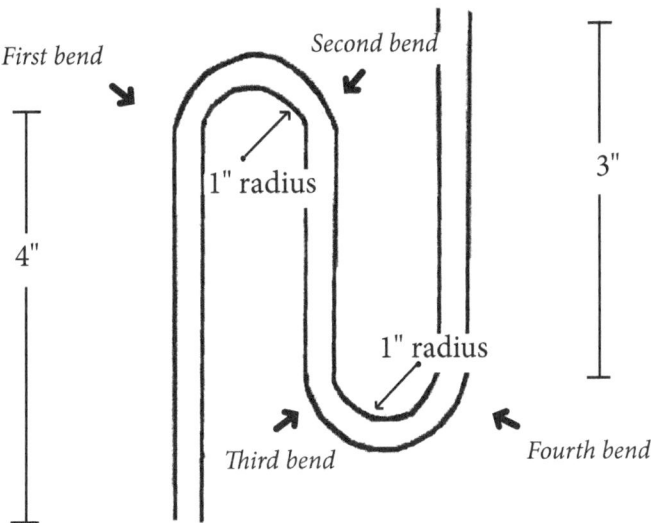

Oxidation and Reduction Flame as Seen in a Copper Wire

Lab Report – Chemistry 9
    Student name: _____
    Experiment # _____

Name of Experiment: _____

List all apparatus used in experiment:

1. Obtain a three- to four-inch piece of copper wire from the front desk. Light and adjust your Bunsen burner.

2. Hold the wire at each end and place the middle of the wire one-half inch down from the tip of the Bunsen burner flame in Cone C. Watch the wire carefully and draw below what you see. (The drawings included below are for the teacher—the students would draw them from their observations.)

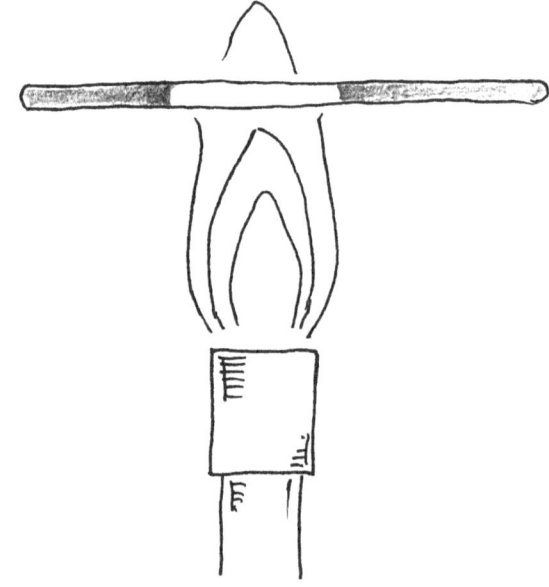

3. Hold the wire at each end and place the middle of the wire just into Cone B. Watch the wire carefully and draw what you see below.

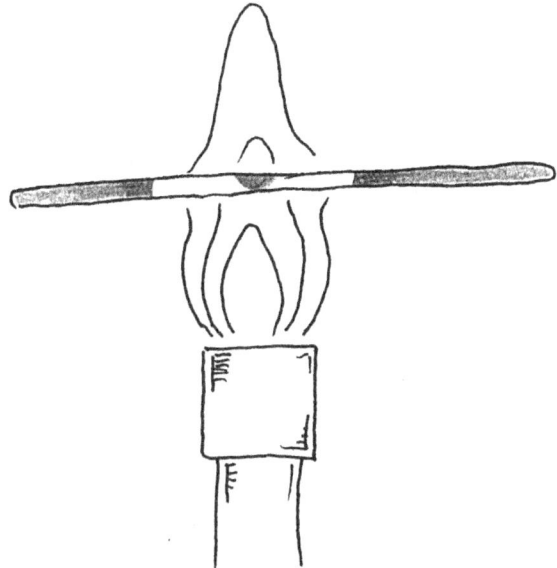

4. Hold the wire at each end and place the middle of the wire in Cone A approximately one-fourth of an inch above the barrel of the Bunsen burner. Watch the wire carefully and draw below what you see.

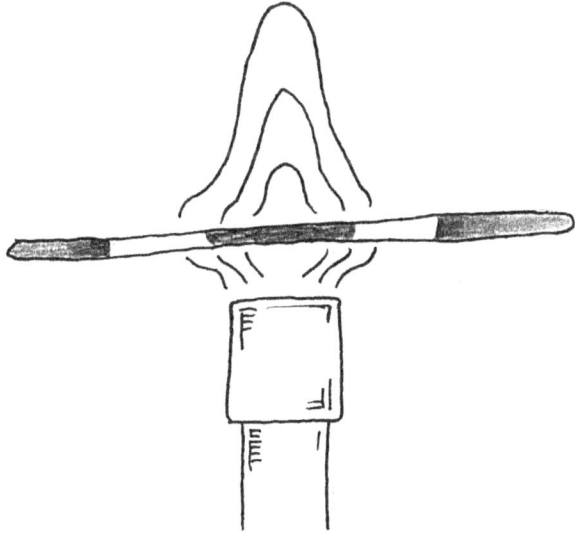

What conclusions can you make?

☐ Teacher's approval

Phlogiston

The phlogiston theory was developed in the early 1700s by a German chemist and physician named Georg Ernst Stahl. Stahl observed materials as they were burning and surmised that all flammable materials give off phlogiston as they burn. He recognized that air was necessary for combustion but believed that the air absorbed the phlogiston that was released. He speculated that plants remove phlogiston from the air and store it and that is why dry leaves burn.

The phlogiston theory provided an explanation for the results of a number of contemporary experiments and offered clues to areas of study in which new discoveries could be made. For that reason the theory was widely accepted in the 1700s and led to many discoveries in chemistry.

Around 1750 chemists developed ways to isolate and study gases and made many related discoveries. In the 1750s, the Scottish chemist and physician Joseph Black identified carbon dioxide, the first gas recognized to have properties different from those of air. In 1766 Henry Cavendish, an English chemist and physicist, discovered important properties of hydrogen and identified it as an element. Because hydrogen is very flammable, he believed it was pure phlogiston. Oxygen was discovered independently by the Swedish chemist Karl Scheele in the early 1770s and by the English chemist Joseph Priestley in 1774. A wooden splint burns stronger in oxygen than in air. Thus, Priestley believed oxygen could absorb great quantities of phlogiston. He called oxygen dephlogisticated air (air without phlogiston).

Photosynthesis

One of the most amazing chemical reactions which makes life on our planet possible is photosynthesis. Photosynthesis is a series of complex chemical reactions by which plants produce sugar which cellular respiration then converts into ATP (adenosine triphosphate), an energy source used by all living things.

Photosynthesis occurs in the plant organelles called chloroplasts. It requires the energy, light and warmth from the sun, water drawn up into the plant from the earth, and carbon dioxide absorbed from the atmosphere.

Technically speaking the plant requires six parts of carbon dioxide to react with six parts of water under the influence of 670 kilo-calories of sunlight energy in order to produce one part of simple sugar. (A kilo-calorie is the quantity of energy required to raise the temperature of 1000 grams of water 1°C.)

Carbon dioxide enters the plant through stomata, tiny mouths or valves on the underside of the leaf. It enters through a process called diffusion and it immediately dissolves in water. Something quite unusual now happens in fluid dynamics. As carbon dioxide dissolves, there is a lower concentration of carbon in the intercellular spaces. This creates a suction which helps draw water up from the roots through the xylem in the vascular bundle.

The plant's green pigment is called chlorophyll. It is the chlorophyll which transforms the light energy into chemical energy. The light and chlorophyll now essentially decompose the water, and the oxygen held in the water is released through the stomata into the atmosphere. The leftover hydrogen from the water then reacts to form 3-phosphoglyceric acid which in turn reacts with three parts of the carbon to become a simple sugar.

The first product produced by photosynthesis in most plants is therefore, sugar (glucose). When the light diminishes, the sugar is transformed to starch. The starch further transforms into cellulose which the plant uses to build itself into a larger and stronger plant.

- The process of photosynthesis produces carbohydrates which humans, animals, birds and fish need for food.

- The process of photosynthesis produces oxygen which humans, animals, birds and fish need for respiration.
- Our fuel is traceable to the process of photosynthesis. When we burn wood, we are deriving energy from the sun, "captured" by the cellulose and lignin.

Cellulose is a complex carbohydrate consisting of repeating sub-units of glucose. Lignin is the non-cellulose part of cell walls. Coal, natural gas, oil and peat are all end products of mineralized cellulose which has been buried under the earth's surface.

In summary photosynthesis:
- occurs only in the presence of chlorophyll and light
- stores energy in sugars
- CO_2 and H_2O are raw materials
- Glucose and O_2 are products

Humans and animals receive energy when eating carbohydrates in a similar manner. They break down the organic compounds by digestion, consuming the oxygen and giving off carbon dioxide as a byproduct.

Composition and Structure of a Leaf

Chlorophyll is the green pigment in plants that acts as the light receptor for the process of photosynthesis. In this process, the elements of water and air are combined and transformed with sun energy into carbohydrates such as sugar and starch. Since plants provide nourishment for man and animal, chlorophyll can be considered as the key to life on earth.

As a substance, it is closely related to hemoglobin in the blood. The chief difference is that in blood the elements are arranged around a nucleus of iron, while in chlorophyll they are arranged around a nucleus of magnesium. Chlorophyll could be described as the originator of food, while hemoglobin helps in the carrying of life-giving oxygen into every living cells of animal and man.

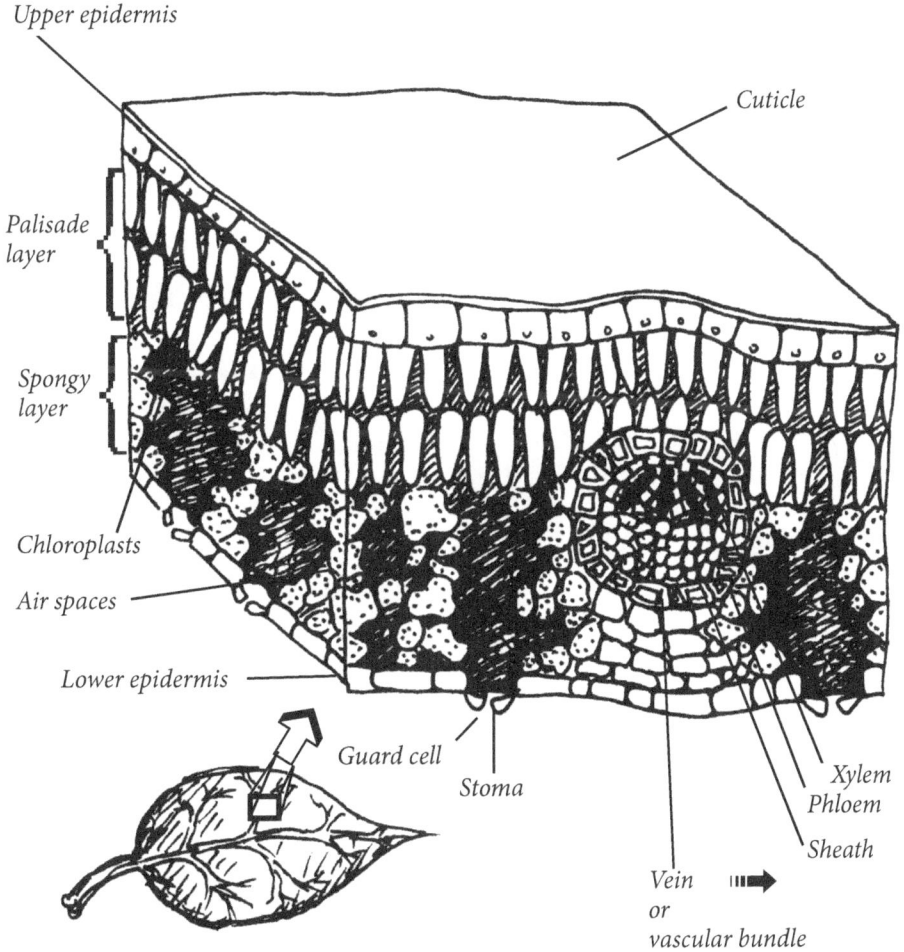

When we look at the cross-section of a leaf through a microscope, we notice that the side turned toward the sun is a thin, transparent, air- and water-proofed layer. Below this roof of the leaf are long cells arranged in a horizontal layer. These are called palisades. They are arranged this way so that they will absorb the maximum amount of sunlight. Through these cells flows a liquid which is called protoplasm, and in it flow countless specks of chloroplasts filled with green chlorophyll.

Below the chloroplasts we find irregular cells called spongy cells. They are designed to promote the exchange of air and water. The bottom layer or the floor of the leaf is similar to the roof with the exception that it is perforated with tiny air valves which open and close systematically to control the flow of air and water vapor. These valves are shaped like mouths and are called stomata. In every leaf there are tens of thousands of stomata.

The leaf has pigmentation which gives it color. The green comes from chlorophyll, the orange from carotene, and the yellow from xanthophyll.

It has been estimated that a square yard of leaf surface is needed to produce one gram of carbohydrate per hour. A large maple tree has several hundred thousand leaves and produces several thousand pounds of carbohydrates each growing season.

Class Reading

Jan Ingenhousz
(1730–1799)

Jan Ingenhousz was born in the Netherlands in the town of Breda. He studied medicine, chemistry and physics at the Universities of Louvain and Leiden, receiving his medical degree from Louvain in 1752. In 1765 he visited London and became expert at administering smallpox inoculations. News of his expertise spread and he was invited to Vienna in 1768 by the Empress Maria Theresa to inoculate her family and to become her court physician.

In 1779 Ingenhousz returned to England and published his work on the gas exchange between plants and the atmosphere. His experiments demonstrated that plants absorb carbon dioxide and give off oxygen (in his words, "purify the air") only in the light, and that the reverse process occurs in the dark. The light process later became known as photosynthesis. Ingenhousz also conducted research on soils and plant nutrition, improved apparatus for generating static electricity, and studied heat conduction in metals.

excerpts from

Experiments upon Vegetables, Discovering Their great Power of purifying the Common Air in the Sunshine, and of Injuring it in the Shade and at Night.
To Which is Joined, A new Method of examining the accurate Degree of Salubrity of the Atmosphere

London, 1779

SECTION I.

Some General Remarks on the Nature of the Leaves of Plants and Their Uses.

It seems to be more than probable, that the leaves, with which the most part of plants are furnished during the summer in temperate climates and perpetually in hot countries, are destined to more than one purpose. Such a great apparatus, which nature displays as soon as the sun begins to afford a certain degree of warmth upon the surface of the earth, can scarcely be considered as solely destined either to ornament, to nourishment of the plant, to its growth, to ripen its fruit, or for any other peculiar and single use. It seems probable, that they are useful to the growth of the tree; for, by depriving the tree of all its leaves, it is in danger of decay. By taking a considerable part of the leaves from a fruit tree, the fruit is less perfect; and by taking them all away, the fruit decays and falls before its maturity. It is also probable, that the tree receives some advantage from the leaves absorbing, by their means, moisture from the air, from rain and from dew; for it has been found a considerable advantage to the growth of a tree, to water the stem and the leaves now and then. But I leave the discussion of those articles to others, who have made these considerations an object of their pursuits. The late Mr. Baker has published to the world his microscopical observations on the subject. Mr. Bonnet, of Geneva, has published a very elaborate work upon the same, entitled, "Recherches sur l' usage des Feuilles dans les Plantes, et sur quelques autres Sujets relatif l'Histoire de la Végétation, par Charles Bonnet, à Gottingen et Leiden, 1754." This work contains a great deal of interesting inquiries upon the nature, properties and utilities of those wonderful organs; all of which have been treated with the greatest attention, and have thrown much light upon this subject.

This celebrated author has taken a great deal of notice of those air bubbles which cover the leaves when plunged under water. He says that the leaves draw these bubbles from the water. He is the more persuaded that this is the case, because he found these bubbles did not appear when the water had been boiled some time, and appeared more when the water is impregnated with air, by blowing in it. He had also observed, that they did not appear after sunset. He explains his opinion farther upon this head: he says, that these air bubbles are produced by common air adhering to the external surface of the leaves, which swells up into bubbles by the heat of the sun; and that the cold of the night is the reason why these air bubbles do not make their appearance at that time. As he found that dry leaves put under water gather such bubbles also upon their surface, he concludes, that the appearance of these bubbles cannot be owing to any vital action in the leaves.

I took some pains to disclose the cause of these bubbles, which, I think, are of more importance than Mr. Bonnet at that time imagined them to be; and found the fact to be generally this:

The most part of leaves gather these bubbles upon their surface, when plunged in any water in the sun-shine or by day-time in the open air; but infinitely more in fresh pump water than in any other. In clear river water they appear later, less in number and in size; less so in rain water, and the least of all in boiled water, in stagnating, and in distilled water.

They are not produced by the warmth of the sun rarifying the air adhering to the leaves; for many kinds of leaves produce them almost as soon as plunged under water, though the water be very cold, and the leaves warm from the sun-shine be plunged in it.

They do not appear after sun-set, at least not in any considerable number; but those that already exist do not shrink in or disappear by the cold of the night.

As soon as the sun begins to diffuse its warmth over the surface of the earth in the spring, and to promote that general tendency to corruption which all dead bodies of the animal and vegetable kingdom, and many other substances, are so liable to, the trees display in a few days, the most wonderful scene that can be imagined. Contracted as they were in the state of stupor and inactivity in which they remain during the winter, exposing to the air no other surface than that of their trunk and branches, as if they wanted to have as little to do as possible with the external air, they all at once increase, perhaps more than a thousand times, their surface by displaying those kind of numberless fans which we call leaves. Some of them produce their leaves a long while before any flowers appear upon them; others a good while after the flowers are formed, and the fructification is already in an advanced state; and keep their leaves in the best condition, and even push out continually new ones, long after the whole fructification is finished; which seems to indicate, that the chief use of these fans is not to assist the fructification and propagation of their species. These fans, when compleated, seem to compose or arrange themselves in such a manner as to expose their upper and varnished surface to the direct influence of the sun, and to hide as much as they can their under surface from the direct influence of this luminary. It seems as if they required rather the light of the sun than the influence of its heat, as their polished surfaces must reflect some of the rays of the sun, and thus moderate the degree of heat.

It will, perhaps, appear probable, that one of the great laboratories of nature for cleansing and purifying the air of our atmosphere is placed in the substance of the leaves, and put in action by the influence of the light, and that the air thus purified, but in this state grown useless or noxious to the plant, is thrown out for the greatest part by the excretory ducts, placed chiefly, at least in far the most part of plants, on the under side of the leaf.

Is there not some probability that the under part of the leaves may have been chiefly destined for this purpose; because in this way the dephlogisticated air, gushing continually out of this surface, is inclined to fall rather downwards, as a beneficial shower for the use of the animals who all breathe in a region of the air inferior to the leaves of trees? Does not this conjecture get some weight, if we consider that dephlogisticated air is in reality specifically heavier than common air, and thus tends rather to fall downwards?

If we add to these reflexions another of no less importance, viz. that most sorts of foul air are specifically lighter than common air, we shall be inclined to believe that the difference of the specifical gravity of that beneficial air of which I treat, and that which is become hurtful to our constitution by corruption, breathing and other causes, indicates one of those special blessings designed by the hand of God: for by this arrangement we get soon rid, in a great measure, of that air which is become hurtful to us, as it rises soon up out of our reach; whereas the dephlogisticated air, being heavier than common air, is rather inclined to settle on the surface of the earth among animal creation.

But, as animals spoil equally as much air in the winter as in the summer by the act of respiration, it might seem somewhat surprizing, that this great laboratory ceases entirely by the decay of the leaves. Is this defect supplied by some other means equally powerful? Though we are very far from being able to trace all the active causes which contribute their share in keeping up the wholesomeness of our atmosphere, yet we have already traced some of them, and therefore must not despair of discovering some more. The shaking of foul air in water will in great measure correct it. Water itself has a power of yielding dephlogisticated air, as Dr. Priestley discovered. Plants have a power to correct bad air and to improve good air. Winds will blow away the noxious particles of the air and bring on air corrected by the waters of the seas, lakes, rivers and forests. All these causes exist equally in the winter as in the summer, or at least nearly so. The influence of the vegetable creation alone ceases in the winter: but the loss of this influence is, perhaps, more than amply counterbalanced by the diminution of the general promoting cause of corruption, viz. heat. Every body knows, that warm weather hastens in a great degree putrefaction. In the summer time numberless insects are produced, which did not exist in the winter: these insects infect the air by the corruption of their bodies. That immense quantity of animal substances and many others, which undergo a putrefaction by the warmth of the weather, seems to require an additional power or agent to counter-act it; and this office is destined to the leaves. In frosty weather no animal substance is subject to putrefaction, which cannot go on without a proper degree of heat. The perspiration of animals is less offensive in the winter than in the summer and, of consequence, must corrupt the atmosphere less. It seems therefore probable, that, if we are deprived of one way by which air is corrected in the winter, we have also at that time less causes which tend to contaminate our element.

SECTION II.

On the Manner in Which the Dephlogisticated Air Is Obtained from the Leaves of Plants.

As the leaves of plants yield dephlogisticated air only in the clear daylight, or in the sun-shine, and begin their operation only after they have been in a certain manner prepared, by the influence of the same light, for beginning it; they are to be put in a very transparent glass vessel, or jar, filled with fresh pump water (which seems the most adapted to promote this operation of the leaves, or at least not to obstruct it); which, being inverted in a tub full of the same water, is to be immediately exposed to the open air, or rather to the sun-shine: thus the leaves continuing to live, continue also to perform the office they performed out of the water, as far as the water does not obstruct it. The water prevents only new atmospheric air being absorbed by the leaves, but does not prevent that air, which already existed in the leaves in different forms, most generally in the form of round bubbles, which, increasing gradually in size and, detaching themselves from the leaves, rise up and settle at the inverted bottom of the jar: they are succeeded by new bubbles, till the leaves, not being in the way of supplying themselves with new atmospheric air, become exhausted. This air, gathered in the manner, is really dephlogisticated air, of a more or less good quality, according to the nature of the plant from which the leaves are taken and the clearness of the day-light to which they were exposed.

It is not very rare to see these bubbles so quickly succeeding one another, that they rise from the same spot almost in a continual stream: I saw this more that once, principally in the *nymphaea alba*. …

SECTION IV.

The Dephlogisticated Air Oozing Out of the Leaves in the Water Is Not Air from the Water Itself.

The reverend Dr. Priestley found, that water, chiefly pump water, standing some days by itself, forms at the bottom and sides of the vessel a kind of green matter, seemingly vegetable, from which air bubbles rise continually to the top of the jar, if exposed to the sunshine: that this air is fine dephlogisticated air, which shews that there is a faculty in water to produce by itself this beneficial fluid; and thus, that the mass of the waters of the seas, lakes and rivers, have their share in purifying the atmosphere.

But as this dephlogisticated air is not produced immediately from the pump water, but only when this green matter is formed, it is clear, that the air obtained from the leaves, as soon as they are put in the water, is by no means air from the water, but air continuing to be produced by a special operation carried on in a living leaf exposed to the day-light, and forming bubbles, because the surrounding water prevents this air from being diffused through the atmosphere.

It is true, that pump water, placed in the sun-shine, will soon yield some small air bubbles, settling at the bottom of the jar, and every where at the sides; but this air is very far from being the same as that contained in the air bubbles of the leaves.

I placed, in a warm sun-shine, a great number of inverted jars, full of pump water, and collected carefully from them all the air yielded by these bubbles, which proved to be much worse than the common air.

I boiled some pump water in a pot, in which I had placed a long cylindrical jar, quite full of the same water: a good deal of air was collected at the top of the inverted jar, which was by the heat disengaged from the water. This air proved to be much worse than common air and entirely unfit for respiration.

Abbé Fontana has made, some years ago, a great many experiments, tending to investigate the nature of air contained in different waters.

SECTION V.

The Dephlogisticated Air Oozing out of the Leaves in the Water Is Not Existing in the Substance of the Leaves in This Pure State, but Is Only Secreted out of the Leaves When It Has Undergone a Purification, or a Kind of Transmutation.

If the dephlogisticated air collected from the leaves in the sun existed in them in its pure state, it must appear as such when squeezed out of the leaves under water; or, at least, if the leaves are only shook gently under water, without hurting their organization, or when they are put in warm or in boiling water.

I squeezed a handful or two of potatoe leaves under water and kept an inverted jar full of water above it, to receive the air. A great deal of it was instantly obtained, which proved to be nearly as good as common air.

I squeezed, in the same way, some air out of leaves of sage, salvia, which proved to be somewhat worse than the former. A potatoe plant was shook under water, so as not to hurt it: a good deal of air was immediately disengaged, which, by the nitrous test, proved to be worse than common air.

A plant of lamium album was treated in the same way, and in like manner a good deal of air was obtained, which was nearly of the same quality with the former.

Some leaves of an apple tree were put in a cylindrical jar full of pump water. The jar was then inverted in a vessel full of the same water and placed upon the fire. As soon as the water grew warm, the leaves were covered with air bubbles, just as in the sun. After the water had boiled a little while, it was put by to cool. A great deal of air was obtained, which proved to be so bad as to extinguish flame.

Some of the same leaves were put into a jar, inverted in a pot full of water, and only placed near the fire: a great deal of air was obtained, but as poisonous as the former.

SECTION VI.

The Production of the Dephlogisticated Air from the Leaves Is Not Owing to the Warmth of the Sun, but Chiefly, if Not Only, to the Light.

If the sun caused this air to ooze out of the leaves by rarifying the air in heating the water, it would follow that, if a leaf, warmed in the middle of the sun-shine upon the tree, was immediately placed in water drawn directly from the pump, and thus being very cold, the air bubbles would not appear till, at least, some degree of warmth was communicated to the water; but quite the contrary happens. The leaves taken from trees or plants the midst of a warm day, and plunged immediately into cold water, are remarkably quick in forming air bubbles, and yielding the best dephlogisticated air.

If it was the warmth of the sun, and not its light, that produced this operation, it would follow, that, by warming the water near the fire about as much as it would have been in the sun, this very air would be produced; but this is far from being the case.

I placed some leaves in pump water, inverted the jar, and kept it near the fire as was required to received [sic] a moderate warmth, near as much as a similar jar, filled with leaves of the same plant, and placed in the open air, at the same time received from the sun. The result was, that the air obtained by the fire was very bad, and that obtained in the sun was dephlogisticated air.

A jar full of walnut tree leaves was placed under the shade of other plants, and near a wall, so that no rays of the sun could reach it. It stood there the whole day, so that the water in the jar had received there about the same degree of warmth as the surrounding air (the thermometer being then at 76°); the air obtained was worse than common air, whereas the air obtained from other jars kept in the sun-shine during such a little time that the water had by no means received a degree of warmth approaching that of the atmosphere, was fine dephlogisticated air.

No dephlogisticated air is obtained in a warm room, if the sun does not shine upon the jar containing the leaves. …

SECTION VII.

Reflections.

It might, perhaps, be objected, that the leaves of the plants are never in a natural state when surrounded by pump water; and that thus there may, perhaps, remain some degree of doubt, whether the same operation of the leaves in their natural situation takes place.

I cannot consider the plants kept thus under water to be in a situation so contrary to their nature as to derange their usual operation. Water, even more than they want, is not hurtful to plants, if it is not applied too considerable a time. The water only cuts off the communication with the external air; and we know, that plants may live a long while without this free communication. Besides, water plants, as *persicaria urens, beca bunga* and others, which I have employed in my experiments, are often found a long while quite covered by the water in which they grow.

By bending a living plant (the root remaining in its own earth) in an inverted jar full of water, you only surprize nature upon the fact in the middle of its operation, by shutting at once all communication with the free air. In such a situation no air can be absorbed by the leaves, or by any parts of the plant under water; but any air may freely come out of it.

Without covering the leaves or the plant entirely with water, it is impossible to know what quantity of air oozes out of the plant and of what quality this air is; for any air issuing out of a plant incorporates immediately with the surrounding air and makes a compound whose constituent parts are an intimate mixture of air from the plant and common air; and it would be as difficult to judge accurately how much dephlogisticated air such a plant has communicated to the ordinary air which was already in the jar, as it would be for a chymist to judge accurately what quantity of distilled water was mixed with a certain quantity of common water, if some of it was really added to it on purpose to puzzle him. It may, however, be ascertained, in an inaccurate way, what quantity of this beneficial air a plant, placed in a jar full of common air, has communicated to it, by computing the degree of superior goodness the air is found to possess.

As plants yield in a few hours such a considerable quantity of dephlogisticated air, though their situation seems rather unfavourable for it when they are kept under water; may it not with some degree of probability be conjectured, that they yield much more of it when remaining in their natural situation; for then, being continually supplied by new common air, their stock of dephlogisticated air cannot be exhausted. It is an unfavourable circumstance, that air is not an object of our sight; if it was, we should perhaps see that plants have a kind of respiration as animals have; that leaves are the organs of it; that, perhaps, they have pores which absorb air, and others which throw it out by way of excretion, as are the excretory ducts of animals; that the air secreted, being dephlogisticated air, is thrown out as noxious to the plant (which article is clearly demonstrated by Dr. Priestley and Mr. Scheele); that in the most part of plants, principally trees, the greatest part of inhaling pores are placed upon the upper side of the leaf and the excretory ducts principally on the under side.

If these conjectures were well grounded, it would throw a great deal of new light upon the arrangement of the different parts of the globe, and the harmony between all its parts would become more conspicuous. We might find, that partial tempests and hurricanes, by shaking the air and the waters, produce some partial evils for the universal benefit of nature; that, by these powerful agitations, the septic and noxious particles of the air are blown away and rendered of no effect, by being thus diluted with the body of air and partly buried in the waters. We might conceive a little more of the deep designs of the Supreme Wisdom in the different arrangement of sublunary beings. The stubborn atheist would, perhaps, find reason to humiliate himself before that Almighty Being, whose existence he denies because his limited senses represent to him nothing but a confused chaos of miseries and disorders in this world.

Note: This reading is taken from "Selected Classic Papers from the History of Chemistry" on the web at:
    http://webserver.lemoyne.edu/faculty/giunta/paperabc.html
This is a source for many original papers that can be shared with the students.

Sugar

CRYSTALLIZED SUNLIGHT

Sugar is the simplest, purest and most important of all energy foods. It is produced in every green plant. In the presence of sunlight the leaves of the plants develop chlorophyll. This green substance is essential in this greatest of Nature's laboratories where sugar is produced as a result of a working together of sun forces with the substances of the earth. The plant, rooted in the dark soil of the earth, draws water and minerals from the soil. The green leaves breathe and absorb CO_2 (carbon dioxide) from the surrounding air, and with the help of the sun's light and warmth, a chemical synthesis (or uniting) of carbon, hydrogen and oxygen results in the creation of sugar. This building process through the help of sunlight is called photosynthesis. In the process of creating sugar, the plant releases oxygen into the air.

$$6\ CO_2 + 6\ H_2O + \text{Sunlight} \rightarrow C_6H_{12}O_6 + 6\ O_2 \uparrow$$

| Carbon dioxide from the air | Water from the soil | ▲ Heat or energy | Sugar (carbohydrate) | Oxygen released |

The sugar is the solution in the sap of the plant and is the fundamental building material in the structure of the plant. Within the life process of the plant, sugar is transformed into starch $C_6H_{10}O_5$ and cellulose (beta glucose) $C_6H_{10}O_6$. Some plants maintain more sugar than others, and these are the main source of sugar for mankind. They are sugar cane, grapes and sugar beets.

The Digestion of Sugar

Common table sugar is sucrose. Sucrose occurs in sugar cane, sugar beets, a number of vegetables and fruits, and in the sap from certain trees like the maple. Today about one-third of the world's sugar supply comes from sugar beets.

The process the body uses to extract the substances it needs for living is called *digestion*. The human being takes in water, sugar, proteins, carbohydrates and oxygen and puts out carbon dioxide, urine and fecal waste.

There are two main types of sugars: *monosaccharides* (one unit simple sugars) and *disaccharides* (complex sugars). The monosaccharides are glucose or dextrose, galactose and fructose. Disaccharides are carbohydrates composed of two monosaccharide molecules. They are created through dehydration synthesis (removal of water) and broken apart through hydrolysis (addition of water). Some disaccharides are sucrose (which is a combination of glucose and fructose), lactose (which is glucose and galactose) and maltose (which is made of two parts of glucose). Sucrose is found in cane sugar; lactose is found in milk; and maltose is found in beer.

Diabetes occurs when the body does not have enough insulin to break down the sugars it takes in. It is one of the fastest growing diseases in the United States. The normal content of sugar in the body is 0.1%. In the body of a diabetic, it can be anywhere from 3% to 10%. Many diabetics must monitor their sugar intake. Some need injections of insulin to help their bodies to digest sugar.

If you eat too much sugar your body can go into toxic shock, or you can lapse into a coma.

The Properties of Sugar

Lab Report – Chemistry 9

        Student name: _____
        Experiment # _____

Name of Experiment: _____

List all apparatus used in experiment:

      A. glucose   B. fructose   C. galactose

1. Place a spatula-tip of the three sugars each in a test tube half filled with water. Observe them settle. Shake and record observations.

A.
B.
C.

2. Place each of the three powders, separately into an old spoon. Place a gentle Bunsen burner flame under each and watch it melt and ignite. Describe what you observed.
(Suggestions: How did it melt? How fast did it melt? Did it smell? How did it burn? What kind of ash was left?)

A.
B.
C.

3. Make a "saturated" solution of each (add enough powder to 10–20 ml of water so that a small amount of it is left undissolved) and allow each to crystallize overnight in its own individual watch glass. Describe the crystals.

A.
B.
C.

☐   Teacher's approval

The Major Sugars

Monosaccharides

Chemical name	Commercial name	Source
Fructose	levulose	honey, plant juices, sap (used by our metabolism)
Glucose	dextrose	grapes, blood sugar (used by our blood and heart)
Galactose	hydrolyzed lactose	milk sugar (used by our brain and nerves)

Disaccharides

Chemical name	Commercial name	Source
Maltose	malt sugar	sprouted barley
Sucrose	cane sugar	sugar cane, beets
Lactose	milk sugar	milk from mammals

A sugar called *ribose* (from a chemical group called phosphate sugars) forms the helix backbone of the structure which is the bearer of the life pattern of our bodily tissue, our DNA (deoxy-*ribos*-nucleic acid).

An oxygen-rich product of glucose is glucuronic acid, which becomes ascorbic acid or vitamin C.

When glucose is woven together with other substances in the plant, it forms the plant dyes which give color to the flowers or the dyes anthoxanthin and anthocyanin which give color to the autumn leaves.

Sugar is woven into the antibiotic substance made by nature. Galactose is essential in forming the cerebrosides which build up our nerve tissue.

Polysaccharides

Polymers of carbohydrates are called polysaccharides. They make up some of the most biologically and economically important naturally occurring compounds. Polysaccharides include starch, glycogen and cellulose, all three of which yield only glucose when completely hydrolyzed by acid. Hydrolysis is a chemical reaction in which a substance reacts with water and is changed into another substance. For example, starch changes into glucose, natural fats into glycerol and fatty acids.

Starch

Starch occurs naturally in plants, which use it to store glucose units for energy. It is often found in seeds and tubers (e.g., potatoes). It consists of two kinds of polymers of glucose. The simpler kind is called amylose, and it makes up about 20% of starch. The average amylose molecule has over a thousand units. During digestion the glucose units are broken up.

A significant fraction of starch is amylopectin. Its structure is more complicated, with as many as a million glucose subunits in a single unit of this starch. Studies have shown it is randomly branched every 20–25 glucose units and is not just a long single chain polymer as with amylose.

Cellulose

Cellulose makes up almost half of the material of wood. Important fibers such as cotton and flax are almost pure cellulose and thus show its properties clearly.

Like amylose, it appears to be a linear polymer of glucose units, but they are chemically bonded in a different way than amylose. Thus, cellulose is not digestible by our stomach's enzymes.

The Properties of Starch

Lab Report – Chemistry 9
        Student name: _____
        Experiment # _____

Name of Experiment: _____

List all apparatus used in experiment:

1. Place a spatula-tip of cornstarch in a test tube half filled with water. Observe it settle. Shake and record observations.

2. In an old spoon place some cornstarch. Place a gentle Bunsen burner flame under it and watch to see if it will melt and ignite. Apply the flame directly to the cornstarch. Describe what you observed.

3. Make a supersaturated solution of the cornstarch and see if it will crystallize in a watch glass. Describe the crystals.

        ☐ Teacher's approval

Tests for Starch in Vegetables

Lab Report – Chemistry 9

        Student name: _____

        Experiment # _____

Name of Experiment:_____

List all apparatus used in experiment:

Place three drops of tincture of iodine onto the cut surfaces of the four vegetables below. Observe carefully and write what you see happening (if anything).

potato	onion
hubbard squash	turnip

What are your conclusions?

☐   Teacher's approval

Cellulose

Cellulose is the third of the important carbohydrates formed in the plant. In this form it no longer serves as a nourishment to man. Cellulose hardens into solid fibers and, thus, gives the plant structure the strength to grow into long stalks, branches or trunks. This substance becomes man's basic substance for clothing and shelter. We use the fibers of the flax plant to spin and weave linen. We weave cloth from the seed fiber of cotton. We build many of our houses with wood which is the most solidified cellulose in the plant kingdom. In terms of human diets, cellulose is indigestible and thus forms an important, easily obtained part of dietary fiber.

In modern chemistry, cellulose is one of the most important substances in the creation of new materials. Scientists observing the silkworm spinning silk wondered if they could produce silk synthetically. They bleached wood pulp (cellulose), mercerized it by treating it with sodium hydroxide, and then dissolved it in carbon disulfide. This straw-colored solution is called *viscose*. The viscose is forced through an apparatus that looks like a shower-head and is called a *spinneret*. When the viscose goes through the tiny holes and meets a hardening solution of sulfuric acid and sodium sulfate, it becomes fine threads. The threads are cleaned of chemicals, dried and spooled to be woven into cloth. This thread is called *rayon* or "artificial silk."

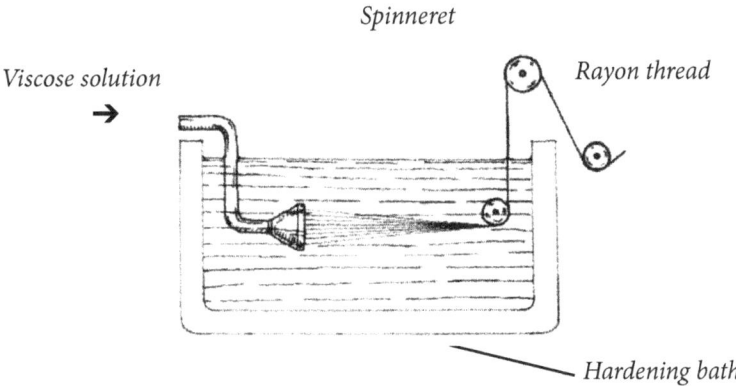

If the cellulose syrup is forced through narrow slits, you have cellophane.

The Properties of Cellulose

Lab Report – Chemistry 9

        Student name: _____

        Experiment # _____

Name of Experiment: _____

List all apparatus used in experiment:

1. Place a spatula-tip of chemical-grade powdered cellulose in a test tube half filled with water. Observe it settle. Shake and record observations.

2. In an old spoon place some cellulose. Place a gentle Bunsen burner flame under it and watch it. Apply the flame directly to the cellulose. Describe what you observed.

3. Make a supersaturated solution of the cellulose and see if it will crystallize in a watch glass. Describe the crystals.

☐ Teacher's approval

Microscopic Lab on Carbohydrates

Lab Report – Chemistry 9

        Student name: _____

        Experiment # _____

Name of Experiment: _____

List all apparatus used in experiment:

1. Obtain a microscope, adjust the light source, and set the cylinder at the lowest setting. (This will be the shortest objective.)

2. Obtain a few granules of sugar and place them on the glass slide which you will then place on the microscope stage. Focus first on a grain of sugar and then change the cylinder so that you increase the magnification.

3. Draw the sugar at the highest magnification that you are able to focus on. Repeat the above for starch and cellulose.

+   ◯   ◯   ◯

    Sugar   Starch   Cellulose

Observations:

Sugar —

Starch —

Cellulose —

What questions do the above observations bring to your mind?

What conclusions can you make?

☐   Teacher's approval

The Transformation of Cotton into Nitro-Plastic

Lab Report – Chemistry 9

        Student name: _____

        Experiment # _____

Name of Experiment: _____

List all apparatus used in experiment:

The cotton you are receiving has been chemically treated. I took 10 ml of concentrated HNO_3 (nitric acid) and put it into a 250 ml beaker. To this I carefully added 20 ml of concentrated H_2SO_4 (sulfuric acid). I mixed the two acids and then placed the cotton in the mixture, leaving it there for about three minutes. Next I poured off the acid and rinsed the cotton with plenty of cold water. Gently, I patted the cotton with absorbant paper towels. I tested with litmus to make sure it was neutral. If it was not, I washed and dried the cotton again and then allowed it to dry overnight.

1. Secure a piece of the treated cotton from the front desk and put it onto a watch glass.

2. Dissolve the cotton with 5 ml of acetone (or ethyl acetone) in a watch glass; stir with a glass rod into a smooth mass and then spread out evenly. Put it on the window ledge to evaporate overnight.
Observations:

3. Watch as your teacher ignites a piece of the treated cotton.
Observations:

4. After your sample has dried, examine it and note your observations.
Observations:

                                      ☐   Teacher's approval

Commercial Use of Plants
Natural Products Chemistry

Different parts of the plant are used for a wide variety of products, some of which are listed below:

Roots

Medicines, dyes and soft drink flavorings

Carrots, beets, potatoes and yams

Stems

Celery, asparagus, sugar cane

Wood for houses and furniture, quinine for tires, linen for shirts

Leaves

Cabbages, lettuce, spinach, herbs

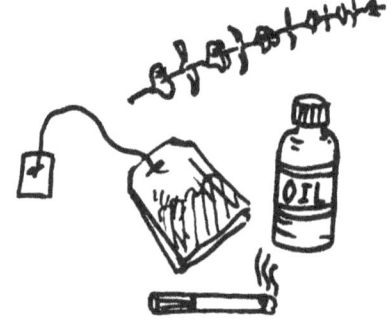

Teas, aromatic oils, cigars, thatched roofs

Flowers

Cauliflower, broccoli

Essential oils for perfumes, honey

Seeds

Corn, peas, beans

Linseed oil (basis for oil paints) mustard, pepper

The Metamorphosis of Plants

by Johann Wolfgang von Goethe

Every form has a likeness and none resembles another
Therefore it is that their chorus points to mysterious laws.
Closely observe how the plant, by little and little progressing,
Step by step guided on, changes to blossom and fruit.

First from the seed it unravels itself, as soon as the silent
Fructifying earth allows it to spring into life.
And to the charms of the light, the holy, the ever-in-motion,
Trusts the delicate leaves feebly beginning to shoot.
Leaf and root and germ, still void of color and shapeless,
Onward they strive and swell, in gentle moisture confiding,
Yet one simple form it remains when first thus appearing.

Soon a shoot, succeeding it, rises on high, and renews,
Piling up node upon node, ever the primitive form.
Truly not always the same, for the following leaf, as you see it,
Ever produces itself, fashioned in manifold ways,
More expanded, indented, in points and in parts more divided.

Yet here Nature with powerful hands restrains its growth,
Leading it tenderly on toward a higher completion,
So that the structure ere long gentler effects will disclose.

Soon and in silence is checked the growth of the vigorous branches,
And the rib of the stalk develops perfecting its shape.
Ranged in a circle, in numbers that now are few and now countless.
Gather the smaller-sized leaves, close by the side of their like.

Round the axis compressed the sheltering calyx, unfolding,
Frees the highest forms of manifold colored coronas.
Yes, the new, colorful leaf feels the heavenly hand;
And, on sudden contracting itself, the tenderest figures
Twofold as yet, hasten on, destined to blend into one.

How confidingly the lovely pairs stand together.
Gathered in countless array there where the altar is raised!
Now, here and there unnumbered germs spring swelling to life,
Gently concealed in the womb of their mother, the ripening fruit.
And here Nature closes the ring of her forces eternal;
Yet a new one joins, at once, the one that preceded.

Rarefaction / Solidification

In sugar there is a balance of carbon and water, $C_6H_{12}O_6$. Life processes transform sugar in two directions, one goes toward starch and cellulose, and the other toward alcohol. In the first we observe a solidifying process: starch, wood, cellulose, coal, diamond. While water is separated off from the sugar, the proportion of carbon to hydrogen and oxygen increases. This causes a loss of mobility and a loss of a readiness to undergo chemical change.

In the other direction, the process is of increasing rarefaction (less density) which takes place when glucose is decayed through fermentation to become alcohol. In this process CO_2 is released. If we took some yeast and added corn syrup to it, bubbles would form and a process called fermentation would take place.

$$C_6H_{12}O_6 \rightarrow 2C_2H_5OH + 2CO_2 \uparrow$$
Glucose & yeast   alcohol   gas

Alcohol is made by the fermentation of fruit (glucose) or grain (starch) and is called ethanol (ethyl alcohol) or C_2H_5OH. There are many other kinds of alcohol which can be produced. Methanol (methyl alcohol) or CH_3O_4 is called wood alcohol because it is obtained from the distillation of wood. It is extremely poisonous but is used as a solvent for shellac, lacquer, resins and dyes. Ethanol (or grain alcohol) is used extensively as an antifreeze. Rubbing alcohol is ethanol or isopropyl alcohol. Denatured alcohol is a mixture of methanol and ethanol and is, therefore, poisonous.

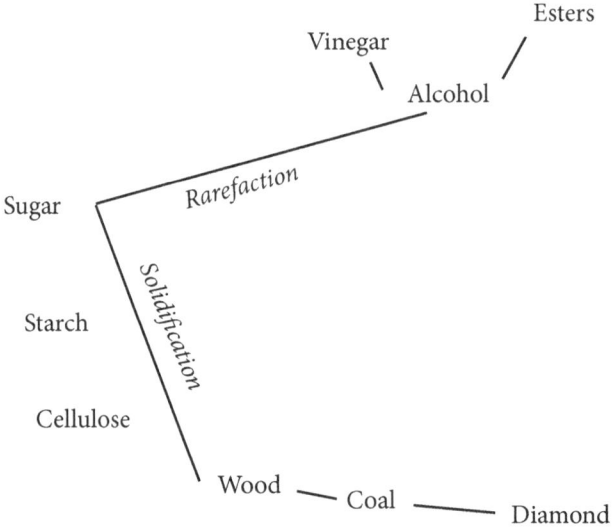

Chromatography

Chromatography is used to separate, but not isolate, different liquids. There are three kinds of chromatography: paper chromatography, liquid column chromatography and gas chromatography.

Paper chromatography is used to find out how many different dyes are in a certain color and to identify them. A small amount of color is placed on the paper, and the paper is then placed vertically in a jar of solvent. As the solvent is absorbed by and rises up the paper, the color is drawn up with it. Because different dyes move at different rates, they become separated.

Liquid column chromatography is much the same except that a liquid is poured into a glass tube containing silica powder. Different liquids move at different rates through the powder, and the colors are separated.

With gas chromatography, the sample is introduced into a stream of an inert gas, commonly helium or argon, that acts as carrier. Liquid samples are vaporized before injection into the carrier stream. Because of its simplicity, sensitivity, and effectiveness in separating components of mixtures, gas chromatography is one of the most important tools in chemistry.

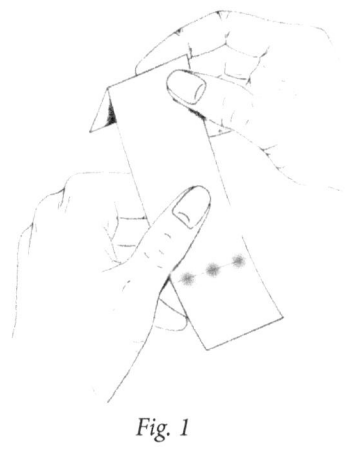

Fig. 1

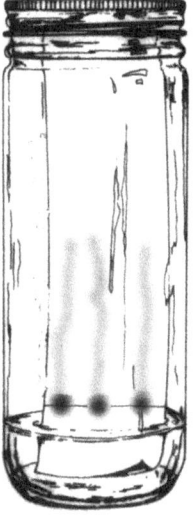

Fig. 2

Chromatography

Lab Report – Chemistry 9

        Student name: _____

        Experiment # _____

Name of Experiment: _____

List all apparatus used in experiment:

TLC or thin layer chromatography is a testing of plant pigments to show the colors present. Chlorophyll is the principal photosynthetic pigment found in green plants, giving them their characteristic green color. Since chlorophyll is insoluble in water, other solvents must be used to extract the chlorophyll and any other photosynthetic pigments. In addition to chlorophyll, carotenoids are present in plants. These may be of two types: carotenes and xanthophylls, both of which are yellow, red, or orange.

1. Place 20 drops of iso-octane-acetone solvent into the glass jar and place the cap on top.

2. Place 3 spots (see Fig. 1, previous page) along the same horizontal plane about 1 cm (three-eighths of an inch) from the bottom on the TLC strip with a thin glass capillary tube. (Be sure to keep your finger on the end of the capillary tube to control the size of the drop. The smaller the drop, the better the result.) Repeat the spotting five more times or until the spot is dark-green or orange, making sure to allow each spot to dry before adding the next. Using this technique, bands will be produced. Be sure to work on a scrap piece of paper.

3. Place the strip into the glass jar and cover. (See Fig. 2, previous page)

4. Allow the strip to develop until the solvent has migrated to within 1 cm of the top, then remove the strip and mark the front edge containing the solvent with a pencil. It will air dry within a few minutes. Paste or tape the strip on this page below.

                                        ☐   Teacher's approval

Table 1: Summary of Chlorophyll Chromatography

Spot #	Pigment type	Visible color	Rf
1.	Carotene	yellow	.98
2.	Xanthophyll-11	yellow	.86
3.	Xanthophyll	red	.80
4.	Phaeophytin a	dark gray	.67
5.	Phseophytin 1	light gray	.60
6.	Xanthophyll	yellow	.50
7.	Chlorophyll a1	light blue green	.48
8.	Chlorophyll a	dark blue green	.46
9.	Chlorophyll b1	light yellow green	.30
10.	Chlorophyll 11 b	dark yellow green	.25
11.	Xanthophyll	yellow	.15

Table 2: Summary of Carotenoid Chromatography Rfs

Pigment type	Rf
Alpha Carotene	.97
Beta Carotene	.94
Lycopene	.81
Leutein	.75
Violaxathin	.66
Neoxathin	.28

$$Rf = \frac{\text{pigment distance}}{\text{solvent stance}}$$

What pigments were present in your sample?

The Discovery of Hydrogen

Henry Cavendish was a wealthy, eccentric Englishman. He had been left a large inheritance so he never had to earn a living and could devote his life to experimentation. He had a difficult time interacting with other human beings, so he lived in isolation and even had an extra set of stairs build on his house so that he would not have to meet any of his servants face-to-face. Whenever he wanted anything, he would leave a note for them.

He discovered hydrogen gas by pouring dilute sulfuric acid over zinc. The gas that emitted from this reaction was explosive, much lighter than air, and when mixed with oxygen it would explode leaving a residue of water.

Hydrogen Bubbles

Lab Report – Chemistry 9
    Student name: _____
    Experiment # _____

List all apparatus used in experiment:

1. In a plastic basin mix together 1 cup of commercial dishwashing liquid with 10 cups of distilled or deionized water and 4 tablespoons of glycerin. This solution will make wonderful bubbles and works best if it is allowed to sit in a sealed container for a day or two.

2. Assemble your gas generator and insert one end of the right-angle bend through a two-holed rubber stopper. Attach clear plastic tubing to the free end of the glass bend. Insert the stem of the thistle tube through the other hole in the stopper so the tip of the stem is 1/4" from the bottom of the flask when the stopper is inserted in the flask.

3. Place 50 grams of mossy zinc in the bottom of the flask and then insert the stopper.

4. Pour 15 ml of 6 M HCl through the thistle tube onto the zinc in the flask. The stem of the thistle tube will become submerged under the HCl. You will notice that the HCl starts to fizz and bubble as the chemical reaction

commences. The bubbling is producing hydrogen gas. Allow the process to work for a couple of minutes. You can add more HCl if the reaction slows down.

5. Take the clear plastic tubing and insert the loose end into the soap mixture in the basin. Immediately large bubbles filled with hydrogen will rise.

6. Carefully take a candle which has been taped to a two-three foot stick, light the candle well away from the gas generator, and then torch the bubbles. Be sure to have on an apron and safety goggles as the bubbles will explode with a vigorous pop.

SAFETY PRECAUTIONS: The HCl is toxic, corrosive and will burn you if it touches your skin. The hydrogen gas is highly explosive. Do not do this experiment in a room with low ceilings. Instead, take it outdoors. There should be no open flames, sparks, or other flammables around as you are preparing this experiment.

Fermentation

Fermentation is the process in which fungi, bacteria, or yeast is added to a sugar solution; the solution releases carbon dioxide and becomes alcohol. From the processing of corn kernels comes corn syrup which, when added to yeast and allowed to sit for awhile, becomes ethyl alcohol or ethanol. This alcohol is used for human consumption.

Another process of fermentation uses grapes. The red grapes are mashed together, allowing the natural yeasts on the skins to mix with the liquid and inner contents of the grapes. This mixture is allowed to sit and ferment. Finally, as the alcohol content builds, the bacteria is killed off, and the solution is filtered and then bottled as red wine.

The Indians of Peru made a sacred drink called *chicha*. Sitting in a circle, the women would chew raw corn kernels. The saliva would break the starch down into sugars. They would spit the liquid saliva and pulp into a clay pot. When the pot was filled, it was allowed to ferment. After several weeks it was filtered and they had a strong liquor.

Wood alcohol, or methyl alcohol, is made from distilling wood. This type of alcohol is used as a solvent. It is poisonous, and drinking it can cause blindness.

Fermenting Alcohol

Lab Report – Chemistry 9

        Student name: _____

        Experiment # _____

List all apparatus used in experiment:

1. Take an Erlenmeyer flask and place the grain or fruit you have brought from home.

2. Add 150 ml of the warm yeast mixture from the front desk.

3. Place a balloon over the mouth and place your apparatus in an area in the lab where the temperature will remain constant. Leave it for seven days, making notes of the transformation, if any.

4. Strain off the liquid into a clean Erlenmeyer flask, attach to the distillation apparatus, and distill a small amount of the liquid. Save as much of the first "fraction" as you are able.

5. Add the liquid saved from above to a watch glass and ignite it.
Observations:

What conclusions can you make?

        ☐   Teacher's approval

Distillation

Distillation was discovered in the 18th century when scientists were trying to separate and organize chemicals. During distillation there are no chemical changes, only physical separation.

There are two types of distillation—destructive and fractional. Destructive distillation produces methyl alchohol, or methanol, and is produced when you put some wood chips in a flask and heat it. The gases flow out through a tube and are cooled by water where they condense and drip into a beaker. This process destroys the wood chips and creates methanol.

Fractional distillation separates liquids with different boiling points, for example, water and ethanol. If you start out with a solution of 50% ethanol and 50% water in a beaker, you will end up with an 80% alcohol and 20% water mixture in the beaker. Since the boiling point of alcohol is much lower than water, the alcohol evaporates, condenses on the sides of the tube, and runs into a beaker.

The alcohol content of something is measured by "proof," and the proof is always twice the percent. So 50% is 100 proof, 60% is 120 proof, 70% is 140 proof, and so on.

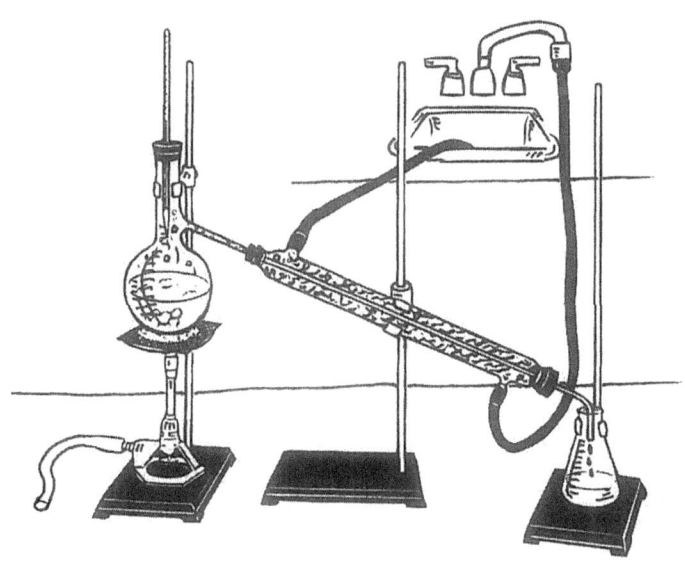

Setup for distillation

Esters

Esters contribute to the flavor and smell of most fruits and flowers. All these oils are immiscible in water, flammable and evaporate easily.

Esters form when acids and alcohol are combined. They produce fragrances used for artificially scenting and flavoring. The following esters can easily be made in class. Place a drop on a piece of paper or cotton to capture the smell.

1. Into a test tube put 5 ml of acetic acid. Add 5–6 drops of H_2SO_4 and 3 ml of ethanol. Heat gently. You will have an odor like vinegar at first, but then a "fruity" odor will emerge.

$$CH_3COOH + C_2H_6O \rightarrow CH_3COOC_2H_5 + H_2O$$
acetic acid   ethanol   ethyl acetate   water

2. Into an evaporating dish put 1 gram salicylic acid. Add 1 ml of methanol. Add 3 drops of concentrated H_2SO_4. Heat it gently. You will have an odor like wintergreen.

$$C_6H_4(OH)COOH + CH_3OH \rightarrow C_6H_4OHCOOCH_3 + H_2O$$
salicylic acid   methanol   methyl salicytate   water

3. Into a test tube put 10 ml of acetic acid. Add 5 ml of amyl alcohol and 2 ml of H_2SO_4. Gently heat the solution. You will have an odor like bananas.

$$CH_3COOH + C_5H_{11}OH + H_2SO_4 \rightarrow CH_3COOCH_{11} + H_2O$$
acetic acid   amyl alcohol   methyl acetate   water

4. Into a test tube put 2 ml of butyric acid. Add 2 ml of ethanol and 2 ml of concentrated H_2SO_4. Heat the solution gently. You will have an odor like pineapple.

$$C_3H_7COOH + C_2H_6O + H_2SO_4 \rightarrow C_3H_7COOC_2H_5 + H_2O$$
butyric acid   ethanol   ethyl buterate   water

Some synthetic equivalents of various natural smells are listed below:

Acid + Alcohol	Smell
Butyric acid + methanol	apples
Butyric acid + ethanol	pineapple
Acetic acid + isobutanol	banana
Benzoic acid + ethanol	cloves
Butyric acid + isoamyl alcohol	pear
Isobutyric acid + octyl alcohol	parsnip
Isobutyric acid + methyl alcohol	apricot
Propionic acid + benzyl alcohol	jasmine
Isobutyric acid + propyl alcohol	strawberry
Formic acid + ethanol	rum

Other fragrances are:

Benzal-stearate	cherry almond
Benzal-citrate	pineapple
Ethyl-salicilate	fruity
Ethyl-butrate	cheesy
Methyl-benzate	wintergreen
3-methylbutyl acetate	pears
2-phenyl ethanol	roses

Esters Experiments

Lab Report – Chemistry 9

        Student name: _____

        Experiment # _____

Name of Experiment: _____

List all apparatus used in experiment:

An ester is a product formed when an acid reacts with an alcohol. Do the following experiments in a test tube and note next to each what you think it smells like.

1. Put 10 drops butyric acid, 10 drops ethanol, and 3 drops of sulfuric acid in a test tube. Heat gently over a Bunsen burner and note smell. Let the oily product settle to the surface. With your medicine dropper, collect a few drops of the floating oily product and place a drop of the liquid here.

    Smell? ➢ ◯

2. Put 10 drops of acetic acid, 10 drops of ethanol, and 3 drops of sulfuric acid in a test tube. Heat gently over a Bunsen burner and note smell. With your medicine dropper, place a drop of the liquid here.

    Smell? ➢ ◯

3. Put 10 drops acetic acid, 10 drops amyl alcohol, and 3 drops of sulfuric acid in a test tube. Heat gently over a Bunsen burner and note smell. With your medicine dropper, place a drop of the liquid here.

Smell? ➤ ◯

4. Put 10 drops acetic acid, 10 drops octyl alcohol, and 3 drops of sulfuric acid in a test tube. Heat gently over a Bunsen burner and note smell. With your medicine dropper, place a drop of the liquid here.

Smell? ➤ ◯

What conclusions can you make?

☐ Teacher's approval

Proteins

The proteins are a huge family that make up about half the human body's dry weight. They are found everywhere in all living organisms. They can function as a building material in teeth and bones and muscles, and they can serve as enzymes, hormones and neurotransmitters. Their functions are the most diverse of any family. The word *protein* comes from the Greek *proteios*, or "of first rank."

Only plants can fashion simple proteins out of the mineral-bearing earth. They combine nitrates from the soil or air, water, carbon dioxide and light. Animals and humans are dependent upon ingested plant protein for forming their own protein.

When burned, protein gives off an acrid stench, and it does not burn easily. It will usually dissolve in water, forming a cloudy solution or colloid. When we digest protein, it is reduced to simpler substances out of which we then build the tissues for our bodies. In digestion the liver collects all the unused protein and forms non-toxic urea which is eliminated through the kidneys and the skin.

Proteins consist of macromolecules called *polypeptides*, made from monomers called *amino acids*. Most proteins also include traces of other organic molecules or metal ions, which give them their characteristic biological functions.

Enzymes

A very important function that proteins can serve is as catalysts. (A catalyst is a chemical that promotes but is not changed by a chemical reaction.) Enzymes are chemicals that act as organic catalysts. They speed up reactions inside an organism. The molecule which an enzyme catalyzes is called a substrate. Enzymes can only act on the substrate for which they were designed. If the substrate molecule's shape matches the enzyme's active site, it undergoes the reaction specified. This is called the lock-and-key theory of enzyme action.

Enzymes can either break up or put together substrates. And they can enhance the rate of a reaction to over half a million molecules per second. Because of the lock-and-key theory, enzymes must retain their shape to keep their function. If the temperature is too high, an enzyme will change its shape, becoming almost like a random mass of coils in a process called denaturation, and thus losing its function. Some dangerous poisons work by deactivating enzymes by changing their shapes.

Protein Experiment

Lab Report – Chemistry 9

       Student name: _____

       Experiment # _____

Name of Experiment: _____

List all apparatus used in experiment:

Materials: 3 test tubes; beakers, 3 types of proteins (yogurt, egg white and sunflower seed); cupric sulfate ($CuSO_4$) and Fehling solution, Bunsen burner

Procedure: In separate test tubes mix 1 part each protein and 2 parts sodium hydroxide with Fehling solution. Gently heat each solution.

Observations:

The base will make the protein soluble; the Fehling solution will indicate colors.

    The egg white will turn dark blue.

    The yogurt will turn blue violet.

    The sunflower seed will turn true blue.

                               ☐ Teacher's approval

Fats, Oils and Waxes

A fat is solid at room temperature, while an oil is a liquid under the same conditions. Oils and fats are not soluble in water. They will not mix with it even if stirred vigorously. They hold themselves separate and cluster into droplets. Like alcohol, oil is very flammable, but it burns slowly and steadily with a soft yellow flame. Ancient people used oil lamps as their primary source of light. The sun's warmth, stored in the oil, serves us as a food source, helps loosen tired tight muscles during massage, and, in the case of Eskimos and others who live in a cold climate, it provides lasting energy for heavy physical work and helps keep our bodies warm.

Oils and fats are produced when the chemistry of the plant weaves together dense esters. All of these substances are referred to scientifically as *lipids*, the Greek word for *fat*.

When lipids are removed from the plant, the chemist can break them down with caustic lye—splitting the lipid into fatty acid and oily glycerol. This process is the way in which earlier generations produced soap. This process is called *saponification*.

Fats and oils function to store energy. Animals convert excess sugars (beyond their glycogen storage capacities) into fats. Most plants store excess sugars as starch, although some seeds and fruits have energy stored as oils (e.g., corn oil, peanut oil, palm oil, canola oil and sunflower oil). Fats store six times as much energy as glycogen. Another use of fats is as insulators and cushions. The human body naturally accumulates some fats in the "posterior" area.

To my knowledge, there is no satisfactory definition of the word *wax* in chemical terms. It is derived from the Anglo-Saxon word *weax* for beeswax, so a practical definition of a wax is "a substance similar in composition and physical properties to beeswax."

Plant leaf surfaces are coated with a thin layer of waxy material that serves many functions. This layer is microcrystalline in structure and forms the "skin" of the membrane; it is the interface between the plant and the atmosphere. The wax limits the diffusion of water and solutes while permitting a controlled release of gases. It provides protection from disease and insects and helps the plants resist drought. As plants cover much of the earth's surface, it seems likely that plant waxes are the most abundant of all natural lipids.

Saponification
Soap Making

Lab Report – Chemistry 9

    Student name: _____

    Experiment # _____

Name of Experiment: _____

List all apparatus used in experiment:

Materials: magarine, sodium alkali, table salt

Procedure:

1. In a water bath boil 10 cm of magarine with 30 cm of sodium alkali. Stir constantly and a scum will rise to the surface and then disappear.

2. Allow the solution to cool. The fat from the margarine will merge with the alkali and form one substance.

3. Add a little of the table salt to the substance. Flakes of a semi-solid consistency will emerge and float to the top.

4. Carefully collect this substance. This is soap. Place a bit between your moistened thumb and forefinger and rub. Describe the feeling.

            ☐ Teacher's approval

Fatty Acid Experiment

Lab Report – Chemistry 9

        Student name: _____

        Experiment # _____

Name of Experiment: _____

List all apparatus used in experiment:

1. Place 0.5 g of lard in one test tube and 0.5 g of safflower oil (or olive oil or corn oil) in a second test tube. Mark each with a grease pencil so that you will remember the contents. To each test tube add 4 cm of perchloroethylene (dry cleaning solvent). Swirl the test tubes so that the fats are dissolved in the solvent. (Use care not to spill the solvent.)

2. To each test tube, add one drop of 0.05% iodine solution. Stir the contents thoroughly. If the pale violet color of the iodine disappears, add one more drop and stir again. Continue adding and counting drops of iodine until the color no longer disappears. Tally and record the number of drops used for each.

Which of the two fats used the most iodine drops and has, therefore, the highest concentration of fatty acids?

☐   Teacher's approval

Textiles

Since the remote periods of prehistoric times, human beings have clothed themselves, for both warmth and protection and also for personal adornment. We have come a long way from wearing skins, grasses, leaves and fur.

Today, the modern textile industry, which produces various fibers which, in turn, can be woven into cloth, is based on exact science. Natural fabrics come from plant and animal sources while synthetic fabrics have been created in the laboratory from chemicals.

Natural Textiles

Name	Chemical type	Uses	Problems
Cotton	polysaccharide (cellulose)	soft, cool	wrinkles
Wool	polypeptide (protein)	warm, insulating	shrinks in hot water
Silk	protein	strong, warm	expensive
Linen	flax fibers	cool, crisp	expensive

Synthetic Textiles

Name	Chemical type	Uses	Problems
Rayon	regenerated cellulose	absorbent, strong	does not breathe
Triacetate	treated cellulose	silky	flammable
Acrylic	poly acrilonitrile	soft, lightweight	does not breathe
Dacron	polyester	wrinkle-free wash & wear	does not breathe

Mineral Fibers

Name	Chemical type	Uses	Problems
Asbestos	asbestos	flame retardant	carcinogenic

Textiles Experiment

Lab Report – Chemistry 9

    Student name: _____

    Experiment # _____

Name of Experiment: _____

List all apparatus used in experiment:

Microscopic examination (Please draw each fiber as accurately as you can.)

   ◯   ◯   ◯   ◯   ◯   ◯

  Burlap Silk Polyester Cotton Acetate Plastic

Underneath each drawing above, attach with transparent tape one thread, approximately one-half inch in length, and then describe each fiber's qualities in a few words below.

Describe each fiber as it burns:

Burlap:

Silk:

Polyester:

Cotton:

Acetate:

Plastic:

NOTE: This experiment is available from Waldorf Publications as Science Kit #14.

Burning Test on Textiles

Cotton	burns easily yellow flame light, feathery ash	direct dye soluble
Wool	burns slowly flame flickers and sputters; strong protein odor	easily dyed with acid dyes
Silk	burns slowly slight odor	dyes easily with acid dye
Rayon	burns easily white ash woody smell	dyes like cotton
Nylon	melts first then burns black beads form pungent odor	acid dyes work
Polyester	melts away from flame black, hard beads form sweet, waxy odor	difficult to dye
Triacetate	bursts into flame drips flames vinegar-like fumes	insoluble disperses dyes

Dyes and Stains

Coloring has been applied to textiles for thousands of years. Originally all dyes came from pigmented soil, flowers, leaves, roots and animal sources. In 1856 aniline dye was produced from coal tar. Today most all dyes are made in the laboratory. The common dyes are acid dyes made from potassium and ammonium salts and basic dyes which are unaffected by washing but fade in sunlight.

We all eventually have to deal with stains in our clothes. In general we try to remove the stain by a mechanical method (hand or machine scrubbing), by chemical process (soaps and solvents), or by a combination of both. We can use bleach to take color out of a fabric or we can spread out our sheets early in the morning when the dew is still on the grass and the sun is rising to get a natural bleaching.

Each type of stain and material requires a different process. First, we must know our fabric and what caused the stain. A fresh stain is easier to remove than one which has been allowed to "set."

Dry cleaning is a process in which dirt is removed through the use of organic solvents rather than soap and water. This process is used when we do not wish a fabric to shrink. The solvents used originally were naptha and benzine, but they were found to be carcinogenic. Today perchloroethylene is used. It can be reclaimed and used repeatedly.

Below is a table showing the treatments for some stains.

STAIN	TREATMENT
Blood	Rub with cold water and then with water and a few drops of ammonium hydroxide.
Chewing gum	Rub with an ice cube; then work the gum off the fabric with a dull knife; then apply cleaning fluid.
Chocolate and cocoa	Rub with cool water and soap; then sponge with warm soap suds. If it still is not removed, use a few drops of cleaning fluid.
Coffee and tea	Stretch material and pour hot water through it. If necessary, use a solution of sodium hypochlorite (Javelle water) to bleach the stain.
Fruit	Apply boiling water. If this is not effective, sponge with Javelle water. Do not use soap—it will set the stain.
Grass	Soak in alcohol; then wash with warm soap suds.
Grease and oil	Sponge with carbon tetrachloride.
Ink and/or iron	Soak in oxalic acid, then apply Javelle water.
Iodine	Rub with alcohol.
Lipstick	Apply synthetic detergent soap directly and then rub and rinse thoroughly.
Mildew	Soak in oxalic acid; then wash with soap and water.
Nail polish	Sponge with amyl acetate (banana oil) or with acetone.
Paint	Apply turpentine to soften the paint; then sponge with benzine.
Rust	Moisten with oxalic acid; then apply ammonium hydroxide.
Tar	Work the tar off the fabric with a dull knife; then apply turpentine.

Synthetics

The pulp of wood is mainly cellulose which is a natural polymer. When chemists treat this pulp with different chemicals and solvents, it can be made flexible and when formed into sheets it makes cellophane.

The production of nylon in the 1930s was followed by the chemical synthesis of many other non-cellulose fibers. Some of the major contributions to the world of textiles include the acrylics, oleins, polyesters and spandex. Fibers in these various classes go by a variety of trade names. Acrilan is an acrylic. Some other generic names of synthetic fibers are:

acetate olefin
acrylic orlon
aramid rayon
glass rubber
metallic saran
modacrylic dacron
novoloid triacetate
nylon vinyon

There were further explorations to imitate nature and use her techniques to make new products.

Demonstration: Making Nylon 610

1. In a 100 ml beaker pour solution of sebacyl chloride.

2. Very carefully pour on top of this solution, a solution made by dissolving 2 g of 1.6 hexanediamine and 4 g of sodium carbonate in 50 ml of water.

3. It will slowly form two distinct layers with a milky layer in between.

4. With a pair of tweezers, loosen this film at the sides of the beaker and carefully lift it out of the beaker and wrap the string around a glass stirring rod. Wash the string in acetone and allow it to dry. This string is nylon. It can be melted and stretched into a long fiber by touching it with a glass stirring rod and pulling it out.

CAUTION! Ventilate well.

Plastics

Plastic is a material which is capable of being molded and shaped. It is produced from organic compounds. Some common plastics are described below.

- Celluloid was first made in 1868 by an American printer by the name of Hyatt. The first "plastic" ever made, it is made by dissolving nitrocellulose (cotton) in camphor and alcohol. It was primarily used to make motion picture film but has been replaced because it is highly flammable.

- Bakelite was invented in 1909 by an American chemist named Baekeland. It was the first synthetic plastic for commercial purpose. It is made by heating together phenol and formaldehyde under great pressure in the presence of a catalyst. One of its chief uses is for electrical boxes and for electrical insulation.

- Vinyl plastics are made by the polymerization of such compounds as vinyl chloride and vinyl acetate. One such compound is placed between two sheets of glass in automobile windshields so that they are shatterproof. Vinyl plastics are also used for lining tin cans and for coating cloth.

- Acrylic plastics are such plastics as lucite and plexiglass which are flexible, shatterproof, transparent sheets that can be made into windows, nose-cones of aircraft and lighting fixtures.

- Nitrogenous plastics are derived from animal protein to make plastic buttons and buckles. Plastics have been made from casein, the cheese solid in milk; albumin, the nitrogenous solid in egg-white; and urea, a product in urine which when mixed with formaldehyde makes a brightly colored plastic called "beetleware."

NOTE: Plastics can and should be recycled. Pick up a copy of your local guidelines and share the information with your class.

Making Bakelite Plastic

Some teachers feel better doing this experiment as a demonstration.

Lab Report – Chemistry 9
        Student name: _____
        Experiment # _____

Name of Experiment: _____

List all apparatus used in experiment:

1. In a fume hood, take 25 g formalin, 20 g phenol, and 55 ml glacial acetic acid [**DANGER!**] in a beaker and wrap it in a wet towel.

2. Set up a gas generator with concentrated HCl (hydrochloric acid) with concentrated H_2SO_4 dripping in to create bubbles and HCl gas [**CORROSIVE!**].

3. Wait one minute until the mixture in the beaker froths up forming a pink phenol-formaldehyde called Bakelite.

Drawing of setup:

Observations:

What conclusions can you make?

☐ Teacher's approval

Rubber

Rubber is a natural plastic which is derived from the sap or latex of specific rubber trees found in the Dutch East Indies. A slit is slashed into the bark of the tree with a machete. From the slit oozes a white latex which is collected in buckets. This latex is then treated with acetic acid which suspends tiny particles of rubber in the liquid. This rubber is coagulated and a soft, jelly-like mass is removed. This substance is then vulcanized by heating it and adding sulfur. The resulting rubber is then made black through the addition of lampblack.

During World War II, when rubber was in great demand but the rubber trees were not accessible, chemists created synthetic rubber. Some synthetic rubbers are described below.

- Neoprene was produced in 1931 and was the first successful rubber substitute. It is made from two simple raw materials: acetylene and hydrochloric acid. It is very resistant to decay by oils, sunshine and air and is a good insulator. I made a neoprene wetsuit when I was a scuba diver hunting lobsters off the Massachusetts coast during my teenage years.
- Buna S is made by polymerizing butadiene with sodium. It was first made in Germany and today makes up about 87% of all synthetic rubber. It is used to make automobile tires.
- Thiokol is a condensation product of etylene dichloride with sodium polysulfide. This rubber is very resistant to chemicals and is used in seals and sealants and to coat metal storage tanks.
- Koroseal is a rubbery material made by polymerizing vinyl chloride. It takes on colors easily and is used to make shower curtains, raincoats, umbrellas, belts and suspenders.

Demonstration:

1. Take a rubber balloon and partially inflate it. Allow it to sit overnight. The next morning it should be soft.
2. Take a long, sharp-pointed steel needle and carefully push and twist at the top of the balloon until the needle penetrates without bursting the balloon.
3. Push the needle and carefully spin it at the opposite inside wall until it comes out the other side. The soft rubber compresses against the needle and forms a seal around the hole as the needle goes through the rubber.

Making a Synthetic Rubber Ball

Lab Report – Chemistry 9

        Student name: _____

        Experiment # _____

Name of Experiment: _____

List all apparatus used in experiment:

1. Put approximately 100 ml of 1M NaOH (sodium hydroxide) into a 250 ml beaker. **CAUTION!** THIS SOLUTION CAN CAUSE SKIN BURNS!

2. Add 6 grams powdered sulfur and several drops of liquid detergent. Stir.

Observations:

3. Heat your solution carefully to boiling. BE CAREFUL NOT TO BOIL OVER! Boil for about one minute.

Observations:

4. When your beaker cools enough to handle, take it to the teacher. He will adjust the temperature to 85° C and add 20 ml of 1,2 dichlorethane solvent.

Observations:

5. Set your beaker in the hood for at least 20 minutes. Then discard the liquid carefully into the hazardous waste container. Look for a plug of solid material at the bottom of the beaker. Rinse it completely in clean water several times and squeeze all the water out.

Observations:

What conclusions can you make?

                                                      ☐ Teacher's approval

Making Synthetic Rubber
Alternative Method

Lab Report – Chemistry 9
        Student name: _____
        Experiment # _____

Name of Experiment: _____

List all apparatus used in experiment:

1. Dissolve 5 g of sodium sulfide and about 2.1 g of sodium hydroxide (25 pellets) in 50 ml of water in a 250 ml beaker. Heat to boiling and add 7 g of flower of sulfur with constant stirring. Allow the solution to boil for five minutes, then cool and filter through a coarse paper towel into another 250 ml beaker. Dilute this solution to about 200 ml with water.

2. Working in a hood with the exhaust fan on, warm this solution to about 75°C and add 10 ml of hot 5% soap solution to act as an emulsifier. Slowly add 10 ml of ethylene dichloride with vigorous stirring, keeping the reaction below 72°C by immersing the beaker in a 400 ml beaker containing cold water. Continue to stir until the color changes from a red to a light yellow. Add 5 ml of concentrated ammonia-water solution to stabilize the emulsion and allow to stand overnight.

3. Pour off the upper layer and resuspend the latex by adding 200 ml of water which contains 5 ml of concentrated ammonia-water. While stirring, add 40 ml of acetic acid to coagulate the latex. A rubber ball will form in the bottom of the beaker. Wash well in clear water before handling.

CAUTION! Be careful when squeezing the ball that the liquid does not squirt in your eye.

☐ Teacher's approval

Hydrocarbons

The element carbon is the basis for organic chemistry. Carbon gives form to a substance. It has the ability to combine itself with other elements strongly. There are more compounds containing carbon then any other element. Soot, charcoal, graphite and diamond are all different constructions of carbon.

Every living thing is made up of carbon, oxygen, nitrogen and hydrogen. When living things decompose, carbon dioxide is formed, the nitrogen forms proteins, and the carbon and hydrogen are left to combine to become what we call *natural gas*.

The Process of Refining Crude Oil

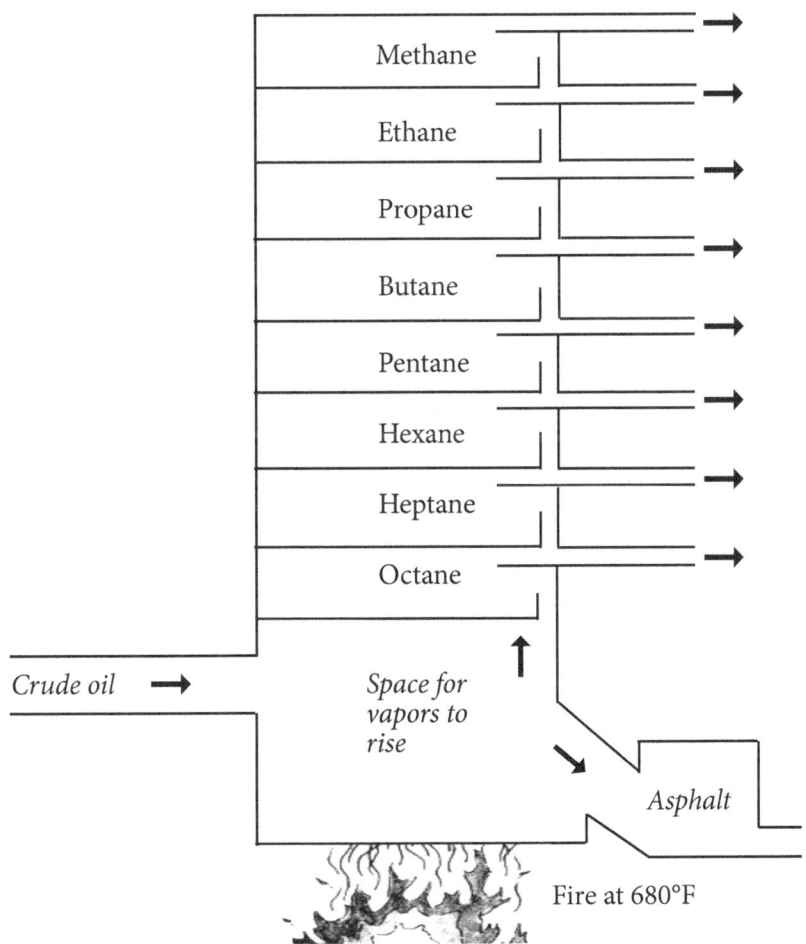

Each alkane has a different boiling point. Crude oil is pumped into the bottom and heated to 345.7°C (680°F). The lighter gases rise up and settle at different layers in the tank where they are drawn off in pipes. The heavy, gooey substance which settles to the bottom is asphalt.

Only 25% of the crude oil becomes suitable for gasoline.

Everything is then refined a second time in a cracking tower at 384.7°C (7500 F).

Additives are combined with gasoline to protect engines. For a long time lead was added to slow down the burning process. It was expelled into the air as a pollutant. When people became aware of how poisonous lead was, the refineries stopped using it.

Making Aspirin

Lab Report – Chemistry 9

    Student name: _____

    Experiment # _____

List all apparatus used in experiment:

1. Place 2 g of salicylic acid in a 25 ml Erlenmeyer flask.

2. Pour 5 ml of acetic anhydride down the walls of the flask in such a way as to wash any crystals of the acid down to the bottom.

3. Add 5 drops of concentrated (85%) phosphoric acid to the flask to serve as a catalyst.

4. Clamp the flask in place in a beaker of water supported on a ring stand over a Bunsen burner. Heat the water to 70° to 85°C and maintain this temperature for 10 minutes by which time the reaction should be complete.

5. Cautiously add 2 ml of water to the flask to decompose any excess acetic anhydride. Hot vapors of acetic acid will be emitted as the decomposition proceeds.

6. When the liquid has stopped giving off vapors, remove the flask from the water bath and add 20 ml of water. Let the flask cool to room temperature. As the solution cools, crystals of aspirin should appear. If crystallization does not occur spontaneously, scratch the inside of the flask with a glass stirring rod and cool the liquid further by placing it in an ice bath.

7. Collect the product by filtering the cold liquid on a Buchner funnel using suction. Wash the crystals with 5 ml of ice-cold water and draw air through the funnel to dry the ice crystals as much as possible. Transfer the crystals to a piece of dry filter paper and let them dry in air for at least 5 minutes. If time permits measure the melting point of your crystals. Now, turn the sample in to your teacher.

Observed MP of aspirin   _____
Correction   +_____
MP of aspirin   _____

    ☐ Teacher's approval

Drugs

While teaching chemistry the teacher may receive inquiries about drugs. The following is a brief overview of some of the more available street drugs.

Hallucinogens control the mind and affect the nervous system. They are found naturally in various cactus plants and wild mushrooms, and when ingested they cause illusions and fantasies. They can also be synthesized in the laboratory using chemicals. Frequently these chemicals are placed on a piece of blotting paper which is subsequently cut up and sold as acid "tabs."

The most common synthetic hallucinogen is **LSD** (lysergic acid diethylamide) which is made from the Morning Glory flower and a fungus called Ergot. While is has been claimed that LSD is not physically addictive, it is mentally addictive. It is frequently used as a prescription drug for the treatment of criminals suffering from sexual disorders, schizophrenic children, psychotics and alcoholics. LSD has also been used to alleviate pain in terminally-ill cancer patients. The normal dosage of LSD to produce any type of effect is 0.028 mg (one millionth of an ounce!) The purity and strength of LSD has raised questions about whether or not it causes cellular or chromosomal damage. Current evidence shows that small doses do not cause fetal damage or birth defects. It has not yet been proved to cause cancer or detectable genetic damage. However, impure LSD can cause these effects and increase the rates of occurrence.

Marijuana, on the other hand, has an active ingredient (tetrahydrocannabinol or THC) which can be addictive when used in large doses for sustained periods of time. "Pot" is taken from the female hemp plant and is sometimes used to make hashish. The hemp plant is also a source for rope which is used for tying things up! Marijuana has the same quality of tying up the psyches of users. The main chemical constituents of marijuana are stored in the fat cells of human beings and are now understood to paralyze short term memory and cause long-lasting effects upon the central nervous system. It is often used medically to help cancer patients overcome the severe nausea caused by chemotherapy.

Analgesics is a large group of drugs that covers everything from Ben-Gay and aspirin to novocaine and cocaine. While Ben-Gay is a topical ointment used to numb localized areas of skin, novocaine is used as an analgesic in minor operations and dental surgery. Mild analgesics, the most common of which is aspirin, are used to treat headaches. They have many side effects such as drowsiness and stomach discomfort. (Aspirin can eat a hole into the stomach lining and cause an ulcer.) Overdose can be a common problem. Allergic reactions and a thinning of the blood are other common side effects.

Cocaine can be called the drug of the 90s. It can cause a rush in circulation strong enough to cause heart failure, such as in the case of first-time user basketball star Len Bias who died after one dose. It can be inhaled through the nose (destroying the cilia,) injected directly into the vein (mainlining), or swallowed. A reduced form of cocaine called "crack" can be smoked. It has been found to arouse severe anti-social tendencies and violence. It is strongly addictive. Addiction means to "surrender oneself to something habitually or compulsively."

The strong analgesics are called **narcotics**. They are used medically to relieve intense pain. Usually they are illegal in their purest form and must be broken down into compounds that are legally usable. Examples of these narcotics in their purest forms are opium, morphine, codeine and heroin. The three latter mentioned are extracted from the first. When broken down, they are used in cough syrup, pain killers and tranquilizers. As drugs they are strongly addictive and personality-altering.

Tranquilizers and **sedatives** are used to calm and relax. Other uses are to tame anxiety and psychotic problems. They are addictive physically and psychologically, and users build up a tolerance over time. They are proven useless when used for long periods of time. The withdrawal symptoms are extreme, even fatal.

Ecstasy (methylenedioxymethamphetamine or MDMA) is a popular party drug which increases the flow of seratonin in the brain. This lowers inhibitions and provides a short-term sense of comfort, well-being and social inclusiveness. These are states of being that every adolescent longs for! Pills sold as ecstasy might contain other addictive, psychoactive substances—most commonly methamphetamine ("speed") which artificially stimulates certain areas of the brain, causing the sensation of a "rush." LSD has been found on occasion in ecstacy pills. 2-CB has appeared in ecstasy but is more often sold under its own name. Ephedrine and ketamine (a central nervous system depressant and hallucinogenic, respectively) are often added ingredients. Caffeine is frequently found in fake ecstasy. In January 2001 a sixteen-year old girl in Boulder, CO, went into a coma and later died as a result of ingesting one tab of ecstasy and subsequently gorging herself with water because of the dehydration that the ecstacy caused.

Drug use and drug addiction in our society are very scary ordeals when enough true facts are placed before you. Drugs tend to speed up life experiences artificially and, in the long term, leave individuals dried up in both body and spirit.

What Is Essential Is Invisible to the Eye

"All men have the stars," he answered. "But they are not the same things for different people. For some, who are travelers, the stars are guides. For others they are no more than little lights in the sky. For others, who are scholars, they are problems. For my businessman they were wealth. You—you alone—have the stars as no one else has them. …

"I wonder whether the stars are set alight in heaven so that one day each one of us may find his own again. …

"The stars, the desert—what gives them their beauty is something that is invisible!

"And now here is my secret, a very simple secret: It is only with the heart that one can see rightly; what is essential is invisible to the eye."

– Antoine de Saint Exupéry
from *The Little Prince*

Biographies of Selected Scientists

Imagination should give wings to our thoughts, but we always need decisive experimental proof, and when the moment comes to draw conclusions and to interpret the gathered observations, imagination must be checked and documented by the factual results of the experiment.

– Louis Pasteur

Instructions for Your Scientific Biography Paper

1. Read the summary of your scientist and study the photo that I gave you.

2. Go to the library and research the following questions:

   - Where did he/she live?
   - What was his/her upbringing like?
   - Describe what he/she looked like (physical appearance from photo you have studied).
   - Describe his/her family life.
   - Give a humorous anecdote about something that happened in his/her life.
   - How did he/she become interested in science?
   - What significant discoveries did he/she make?
   - Explain what those discoveries have meant to modern science.
   - What difficulties did he/she encounter in life and how did he/she overcome them?

From the above research, write a three page (minimum) essay and make a drawing of your scientist.

This essay is due on: _____

From your essay take index cards and prepare a short oral report to be given to the class. Concentrate your report on the questions above. You can use your note cards to refer to, but do not read them. Remember an oral report is different than a written one. Be sure you practice it out loud. (In front of a mirror or a friend can also be a help!)

Most importantly, be sure you feel very comfortable with your **introduction** and your **conclusion**—the rest will flow.

Please be prepared to give your oral report on: _____

Note Taking

The students should be asked to take notes from each oral presentation. They are not allowed to stop the presenter with questions; however at the conclusion they may ask that pertinent points be elaborated. The following is an example of guidelines that the students can use to focus their notes:

Scientific Biography Notes

Name of scientist:

Student giving report:

Dates of scientist's life:

Country of birth:

Country where work was accomplished:

Notable life experience:

Notable scientific achievements:

What obstacle did the scientist have to overcome in life?

Additional notes of interest:

Robert Boyle

Boyle was born on January 25, 1627, in Lismore, Ireland. He studied at Eton College from 1635 to 1639 and read Galileo's works while on a five-year European tour, with a private tutor, begun in 1639 when he was twelve years old. After the tour, he returned to Dorset in England where he began his experimental scientific work and wrote moral essays. He was an early proponent of the scientific method and a founder of modern chemistry. He strongly believed in "the necessity of objective observation and verifiable laboratory experiments" in science, which is why he is known as a founder of the modern scientific method.

Boyle was also the first chemist to isolate and collect a gas. Through his studies, he formulated a law of physics which states that if temperature is held constant, the pressure of a gas is inversely proportional to its volume (Boyle's Law).

In the field of chemistry, Boyle observed that air is absorbed in the process of combustion and that metals gain weight when they oxidize. He also recognized the difference between a compound and a mixture and formulated his atomic theory of matter on the basis of his laboratory experiments. Boyle was also the first to note the distinctions between acids, bases and salts.

He died on December 30, 1691, in London, England.

Isaac Newton

Destined to be the chief figure of the scientific revolution of the 17th century, Newton was born on December 25, 1642, in Woolsthorpe, England. Isaac was so frail at birth that he was not expected to live. His father had died before Isaac was born and left the family destitute. His mother soon remarried and had three new children.

Newton was a strange boy who was interested in constructing original mechanical devices. He was rather slow in school, and his major accomplishment was beating up the school bully.

He went to Cambridge University and graduated without particular distinction. Then the Plague hit London, and Newton went to the family farm for safety. It was here, in the solitude of the countryside, that he was able to listen to his own thoughts. He was 23 years old. (Einstein developed the formula $E=MC^2$ also at the age of 23.) Ideas exploded within him. He worked out the binomial theorem during this period and laid the foundations for calculus. He began his studies on the laws of gravity. Later in life he built the first reflecting telescope and worked on the laws of optics and the mechanics of planetary motion.

He had a nervous breakdown in 1692, spent years exploring mysticism, and died in London on March 20, 1727.

Henry Cavendish

Born of English parents in Nice, France, on October 10, 1731, Cavendish spent the rest of his life in England. His mother died when he was two years old. He came from a wealthy family, so he never suffered from economic hardship. At the age of forty he inherited a fortune of well over one million English pounds; however, he had not much use for his wealth because he was a recluse.

He attended Cambridge University but left after four years without taking his exams, partly because he was too shy to meet his professors face to face. He had great difficulty being with people, preferring instead the solemn isolated space of his laboratory. He especially had a psychotic fear of women. He was so eccentric that he had a second staircase built onto his house so that he would not have to meet the servants when he came and went.

His true love was scientific research, and he spent sixty years satisfying his own curiosity. He was the first to study the nature of the gas hydrogen. He demonstrated that water formed after hydrogen burned. He discovered the gas argon. He was the first person to calculate the mass of the earth.

He died on February 24, 1810.

Joseph Priestley

Priestley was born in Fieldhead, England, on March 13, 1733. He was raised by a pious and strict aunt—his mother had died when he was seven years old. His health was fragile, and his aunt would not allow him to go to school so he retreated to the attic where he taught himself French, Latin, algebra and geometry.

He attended the university and became a preacher. He was fond of dressing in fancy clothes and had delicate, almost feminine, features.

While attending a lecture by Benjamin Franklin on electricity, he was encouraged by Franklin to write. His writing led to his own experiments, and he discovered that carbon was a conductor of electricity.

Living next door to the Jakes & Nell alehouse, he observed the constant smell of beer fermenting. Experimenting with it, he found that the fermenting grain produced a gas which turned out to be carbon dioxide. He injected this gas into sweetened water and created the first soda pop.

His greatest discovery occurred in 1774 while he was experimenting with gases; he heated mercuric oxide and discovered a gas which was later to be named "oxygen." He noted that this gas encouraged materials to burn much more intensely.

Politically, he was sympathetic with the American Colonies and the French people's struggles against their monarchy. This led a mob with opposite views to burn down his house in 1791, and he had to flee to America. He spent his last decade teaching chemistry in the United States where he died on February 6, 1804.

Antoine Lavoisier

Lavoisier was born in Paris, France, on August 26, 1743, and is one of the best-known French scientists. His theories of combustion, his development of a new system of chemical nomenclature, along with his writing of the first modern chemistry textbook earned him the title "the father of modern chemistry."

He was loved and pampered as a youth by his mother and then after her early death by his aunt. He received an excellent education and was looked upon as a brilliant student by his professors.

Lavoisier recognized the importance of accurate measurement, and by practising this skill he proved that mass does not change during chemical reactions. With this information he postulated the law of conservation of mass. He demonstrated that both rusting and combustion have a common link—an active gas which he called "oxygen" supports both.

His investments of money into a private tax-collecting firm earned him the wrath of the common Frenchman. He was guillotined in Paris on May 8, 1794, during the French Revolution.

John Dalton

Born to Quaker parents around September 6, 1766, Dalton left school at the age of eleven and became a teacher at a Quaker school where he fell in love with meteorology. He was to keep detailed records of the weather for forty-six years. His meteorological observations initiated a study about the composition of air. He wondered if the air at the top of mountains was of different composition than at sea level. This led him to study the properties of gases; since the composition is essentially the same throughout the lower atmosphere, he wondered if the gases were made up of tiny particles which were mixed randomly.

He theorized that not only gases but all matter was made up of tiny particles. He took the Greek word "atom" as a name for these minute particles. Thinking further, he said what made the particles different was their individual weight. In 1803 he presented to the world his "atomic theory." He was the first to prepare a table of what we now call "atomic weights."

He was a rather clumsy experimenter and a poor public speaker. Colorblind himself, he was the first to describe color-blindness in a publication in 1794. In 1832, when he was introduced to King William IV, he shocked everyone because he mistakenly wore his red academic robe; he thought it was gray.

As a practicing Quaker he was opposed to receiving awards or honors. He passed away on July 27, 1844.

Amadeo Avogadro

Avogadro was born on June 9, 1776, in Turin, Italy. His academic life led him to receive a doctorate in law. He began his professional life as a lawyer; however, he was so interested in his private study of mathematics and physics that science became his career.

He was very interested in a discovery made by Gay-Lussac which showed that all gases expand to the same extent with a rise in temperature. This led Avogadro to make his famous statement in 1811—now called Avogadro's hypothesis—"Equal volumes of all gases under the same conditions of temperature contain the same number of molecules." The word "molecule" was used for the first time in this statement. He calculated the number of atoms or molecules present in an amount of a substance that has a mass of its atomic (or molecular) weight in grams. This number is 602,252,000,000,000,000,000,000 (6.023×10^{23}) and is called Avogadro's Number.

Avogadro's statement was more or less ignored for several decades. It was not until countryman Stanislao Cannizzaro resurrected his thoughts in 1861 at the Karlsruhre Congress that Avogadro was taken seriously. This was four years after his death on July 9, 1856.

Humphrey Davy

Davy was born on December 17, 1778, in Penzance on the Cornish Coast of England. The eldest of five children, his father died when he was sixteen years old, leaving the family in debt. Davy hated school even though he was very interested in reading.

He became employed as an apprentice for a surgeon/apothecary and began a program of self-education. He was an excellent fisherman and even wrote a book on the subject. However, chemistry was his first love.

He discovered nitrous oxide (laughing gas) in 1800 and experienced the light-headed giddy feeling it brought on. He also devised a method for passing electricity through molten compounds and isolated, for the first time, a whole series of metals such as potassium, barium, sodium, calcium, strontium and magnesium. He also invented the miner's safety lamp which saved a great many lives in the mines. He hired Michael Faraday, and gave him a start in his career in science.

He died on May 29, 1829, in Geneva, Switzerland.

Jöns Jakob Berzelius

Berzelius was born in Väversunda, Sweden, on August 20, 1779. Both his parents died while he was young, and he was brought up by his stepfather who helped him to attend medical school. He was a poor student in medicine, but he excelled in physics.

He studied and analyzed various inorganic compounds to determine the exact ratio of the weight of the different elements in their composition. Patiently, over ten years, he ran two thousand analyses and backed up Dalton's atomic theories.

He went on to discover new elements cerium, selenium, silicon and thorium. He published a textbook in 1803 and was proclaimed one of the greatest chemical authorities in the world.

At the age of 56 he married a young woman of 24. He became very conservative and dismissed younger chemists' work as insignificant compared to his own. He died in Stockholm on August 7, 1848.

Michael Faraday

The son of a blacksmith with ten children, Michael Faraday was born on September 22, 1791, in Newington, England. The family had no money for education, but at the age of fourteen Faraday apprenticed himself to a bookbinder and began his self-education by reading every book in the shop.

His employer allowed him to attend lectures by Sir Humphrey Davy, and he made beautiful, illustrated main lesson books after each of them. He accumulated 386 pages of notes, bound them in leather and sent them to Davy, who, impressed with the boy's zeal, hired him as a lab assistant. The boy then proceeded to outshine the jealous master.

He liquefied gas by compression, discovered the hydrocarbon benzene, the laws of electrolysis, and his greatest discovery—electromagnetic induction. In 1831 he found that when he moved a magnet through a coil of wire, a current was produced. From this discovery the electric generator, the heart of all modern power plants, was developed.

His employer, Davy, fumed with bitter envy at Faraday's every accomplishment and attempted to turn people against him. To his credit, Faraday never allowed himself to become angry. He died near London on August 25, 1867, regarded as one of the finest scientists ever.

Charles Darwin

Darwin was born in Shrewsbury, England, on February 12, 1809; on this same day Abraham Lincoln was born in America.

Darwin's family was wealthy. His father was a physician whose ambition was to have his son follow in his footsteps. Charles, however, showed no particular academic promise in his youth, and he was repulsed by medicine. His father admonished him by saying, "You care for nothing other than shooting, rat-catching and your dogs. You will be a disgrace to yourself and to your family."

His mother died when he was eight years old, and he was raised by his three older sisters who constantly found fault with him. Charles' passion was collecting shells, bird's eggs and coins. He also loves to observe wild and domesticated animals.

In 1831 he signed on to be a ship's naturalist on board Her Majesty's Ship *Beagle* which was off on a voyage to the Galapagos Islands off the coast of South America in the Pacific Ocean. While on the trip Darwin noticed many things with amazing powers of observation. In particular he noticed that there were fourteen species of finches in a relatively small area of islands. This led him to think about isolation and natural selection. He wrote a book entitled *The Origin of Species* which, although controversial, became a pillar in modern biology. He died in Down, Kent, on April 19, 1882.

Maria Mitchell

In 1818 Maria Mitchell was born on the island of Nantucket off the south coast of Massachusetts' Cape Cod. She was one of ten children. Her father, William, an officer at the local bank, taught astronomy and celestial navigation to all his children. Her mother, Lydia, urged her to "study, gain an occupation and independence." When she was twelve years old, she assisted her father in recording the time of an eclipse, and at the age of seventeen she created her own school for girls, training them in mathematics and the sciences.

Nantucket was a whaling town, and for most of the year the men were out to sea. Maria took the job of librarian at the Nantucket Atheneum. Here she gained exposure to great literary and scientific personalities. She continued her study of astronomy and was a keen observer of the night sky with a telescope in an observatory her father had built on the roof of the bank where he worked.

On October 1, 1847, she became the first person in America to sight and record a comet. For this the King of Denmark awarded her a gold medal. She became the first woman elected to fellowship in the American Academy of Arts and Sciences. She was also the first woman to become a Professor of Astronomy. Throughout her life she championed woman's rights and education. She died in 1889.

Louis Pasteur

Born in France on December 27, 1822, Pasteur was not a remarkably good student in his youth. He chief interest was painting. In chemistry, where he was to make major achievements later in life, his teachers thought him merely "mediocre."

As a professor of fine arts, he attended a lecture by the French chemist Jean Dumas, after which his life was redirected onto a path of chemical research. He discovered that fermentation, the process used to make beer and wine, is carried out by tiny animals. Pasteur called these microorganisms "germs" and learned that they are responsible for spreading contagious diseases. He thus solved the mystery behind rabies and created vaccines for this and other deadly illnesses, saving many lives.

He was approached with a contamination problem in alcoholic fermentation, which was thought to be an entirely chemical process at the time. After careful examination, he found that the fermenting solution contained optically active compounds and concluded that fermentation was a biological process carried out by microorganisms. This hypothesis, called the germ theory, was followed by many elegant experiments that showed unequivocally the existence of microorganisms and their effect on fermentation.

Pasteur's work served as the springboard for branches of science and medicine such as stereochemistry, microbiology, bacteriology, virology, immunology and molecular biology. Moreover, his work has protected millions of people from disease through vaccination and pasteurization. He died near Paris on September 28, 1895.

Dmitri Mendeleev

Born in Tobolsk, Siberia, on February 7, 1834, Mendeleev came from a large family of seventeen children of which he was the youngest. He received his first lessons in science from political prisoners who had been exiled to Siberia by the Russian government.

Just as he was finishing high school, his father died. His mother took him to the university in St. Petersburg and then she died. He finished college at the top of his class and then travelled to Europe for graduate studies.

In 1869 he devised and published the periodic table of the elements after recognizing that the properties of chemical elements recur in regular patterns when the elements are arranged according to their atomic weights. His table had blank places for unknown elements which were discovered later. He also discovered the phenomenon of critical temperature, the temperature at which a gas or vapor may be liquefied by pressure.

He died in St. Petersburg on February 2, 1907.

William Ramsay

Sir William Ramsay was born in Glascow, Scotland, on October 2, 1852. He was to be a renaissance man—accomplished in many areas. He was adept at music, languages, mathematics and science. He was a top-notch glass blower, and he made most of his own laboratory equipment.

He studied chemistry in the German language at the University of Tübingen where he became intrigued with the gas nitrogen. He found that the atomic weight of nitrogen from the air was different from the weight of nitrogen obtained from chemicals.

He copied Cavendish's experiment to liberate hydrogen and found a bubble of a different unknown gas which he named "argon." He then went on to discover the five noble gases—helium, neon, argon, krypton and xenon. His explanation of the nature of these elements led to important ideas about atomic structure. He was awarded the Nobel Prize in 1904.

He died on July 23, 1916.

Svante August Arrhenius

Born in Wijk, Sweden, on February 19, 1859, Arrhenius was a child prodigy. He taught himself to read at the age of three and graduated from high school as the youngest and brightest of his class.

While attending the University of Uppsala he experimented with how electricity passes through different solutions. From this he conceived the word "ions" for electrically charged particles. His ionic theory was developed for a doctoral dissertation, but he was too advanced for his professors who did not have the insight to see what he was doing. He barely passed.

He sought out and worked with friends who were interested in his theories. He evolved another theory of "energy of activation," which was essential to the theory of chemical reactions. In 1903 he received the Nobel Prize for his ground-breaking work.

He suggested the existence of a "greenhouse effect" in which small changes in the concentration of carbon dioxide in the atmosphere could considerably change the temperature of the planet. He also speculated that all life was blown to earth from spores from other life-bearing worlds.

He died in Stockholm on October 2, 1927.

George Washington Carver

Carver was born a slave in 1860 on German immigrant Moses Carver's thirty-two acre plantation near Diamond Grove, Missouri. As an infant, he and his mother were kidnapped by Confederate raiders. Later he was found in Arkansas and returned to the Carvers; his mother was never seen again. The Carvers raised him as their own son. As a boy, he wandered in the fields and woods day after day collecting flowers and caring for them in a secret garden.

He had a strong desire to obtain an education. Finally, at the age of thirty he was accepted at Simpson College in Iowa. He supported himself by ironing clothes for his fellow students. He studied botany and agriculture until he received a Master's degree.

He accepted a teaching job at Tuskegee Institute in Alabama where he also did research. His scientific discoveries include more than three hundred products derived from the peanut, one hundred from the sweet potato, seventy-five from the pecan and many more from Georgia clay. He developed processes for manufacturing paper, ink, shaving cream, linoleum, synthetic rubber, plastics, bleach and metal polish. He became an authority on plant diseases throughout the world.

Throughout his life he remained a simple and religious man. He never married, and money meant little to him. He died on January 5, 1943, and left his entire savings for the advancement of science.

Marie Curie

Marie Sklodowska was born in Warsaw, Poland, in 1867. Her father was a professor of physics and mathematics; as a young girl she lost her mother to tuberculosis. In 1895 she married Pierre Curie, a famous scientist. Along with her husband, she spent her entire life working in France and helped usher in the nuclear age by discovering the radioactive element radium. She was awarded two Nobel Prizes—one for physics and one for chemistry. She is the only scientist to have won two Nobel Prizes.

She faced profound difficulties as a woman scientist in turn-of-the-century France, and she also has personal tragedies—the untimely death in 1906 of her husband in Paris after his skull was crushed by the wheel of a heavily loaded horse-drawn wagon.

Marie worked in difficult conditions. She spent most of her money to buy laboratory equipment. She lived in poor quarters and used an old shed as her laboratory. It kept out neither wind or rain. She studied x-rays, radiation and the mysterious pitchblende, a highly radioactive rock in which uranium is found. Curie and other scientists handled the uranium with their bare hands, having no fear of the substances that were burning the tips of their fingers. Her cavalier attitudes fit into the craze over radiation that was gripping the world at the time.

Marie Curie founded the Radium Institute in Paris. She died in 1934, poisoned by the very radiation she labored to understand, from leukemia, which is caused by long exposure to radium. She is remembered today for discovering radium and polonium, two elements highly useful in the treatment of cancer.

Ernest Rutherford

The son of a farmer, Rutherford, was born in Nelson, New Zealand, on August 30, 1871, the second of twelve children. He placed second in a competition for a scholarship to Cambridge University in England. Because the first place winner decided to get married and stay in New Zealand, Rutherford was able to go. He received the news while he was digging potatoes.

At Cambridge he began to work in the exciting new field of radioactivity. He distinguished three different types of radiation, which he named "alpha," "beta," and "gamma." He also studied the rate at which radioactive atoms break down and coined the term "half-life." Rutherford was awarded the 1908 Nobel Prize for chemistry for his work in radioactivity.

Rutherford made his greatest discovery in 1909. Shortly after his move to Manchester, he found that a few "alpha" particles, when bombarding thin metal foils, were deflected from their incident beam through more than ninety degrees. "It was almost as incredible," Rutherford later responded in a now-classic statement, "as if you fired a fifteen-inch shell at a piece of tissue paper and it came back and hit you." Early in 1911 he finally announced his version of the structure of the atom: a very small, tightly packed and charged nucleus sprinkled with opposite negative charges in the surrounding void. He also discovered artificial disintegration—the artificial splitting of the atom—a signal discovery that presaged his entry into the field of nuclear physics.

He died on October 19, 1937.

Albert Einstein

Einstein was born in Ulm, Germany, on March 14, 1879, and spent his youth in Munich, where his family owned a small shop that manufactured electric machinery. At first there was some thought that Einstein was retarded. He did not talk until the age of three, but even as a youth he showed a brilliant curiosity about nature and an ability to understand difficult mathematical concepts. Because of his predominant interest in mathematics, one of his teachers invited him to leave school, admonishing him that "he would never amount to anything."

He was barely admitted to a college in Switzerland where he cut lectures to read theoretical physics. Upon graduation the only job he could find was a minor position at the patent office in Berne. There, without a laboratory and with no academic guidance, in his early twenties, he revolutionized the world of science. He created the special theory of relativity and made a bold hypothesis concerning the particle nature of light.

Einstein's prime concern was to understand the nature of electromagnetic radiation. Very few of his contemporary physicists understood or were sympathetic to his ideas.

Einstein predicted the bending of starlight in the vicinity of a massive body such as the sun. The confirmation of this phenomenon during an eclipse of the sun in 1919 became a media event, and Einstein's fame spread worldwide. After 1919, Einstein became internationally renowned. He received a number of honors and awards, including the Nobel Prize in physics in 1921.

When Hitler came to power, Einstein left Germany for the United States. He became the most well-known scientist of the 20th century. He took a position at Princeton University in New Jersey, where died on April 18, 1955.

Niels Bohr

Born on October 7, 1885, Bohr was a Danish physicist and Nobel Prize winner who made basic contributions to nuclear physics and to the understanding of atomic structure.

Bohr's theory of atomic structure was his most famous achievement. His atomic model suggests that an atom emits electromagnetic radiation only when an electron in the atom jumps from one quantum level to another. This model contributed enormously to future developments of theoretical atomic physics. Bohr demonstrated that uranium-235 is the particular isotope of uranium that undergoes nuclear fission.

Bohr was forced to remain in Denmark after the German occupation of the country in 1940. Eventually, however, because he had Jewish roots, he had to escape by fishing boat to Sweden, under peril of his life and the lives of his family. From Sweden the Bohrs traveled to England and eventually to the United States, where Bohr joined in the effort to develop the first atomic bomb, working at Los Alamos, New Mexico, until the first bomb's detonation in 1945. He opposed complete secrecy of the project, however, and feared the consequences of this ominous new development. He desired international control.

In 1945 Bohr returned to the University of Copenhagen, where he immediately began working to develop peaceful uses for atomic energy. He organized the first Atoms for Peace Conference in Geneva, held in 1955, and two years later he received the first Atoms for Peace Award. Bohr died in Copenhagen on November 18, 1962.

Harold Urey

Urey was born on April 29, 1893, in Walkerton, Indiana. He attended Montana State University, majoring in zoology and then went to Denmark to assist Niels Bohr in his research on the theory of atomic structure.

During World War I he worked to develop heavy explosives and became dedicated to chemistry. After the war he focused his attention on hydrogen and in 1934 was awarded the Nobel Prize for his discovery of the heavy form of hydrogen known as deuterium.

During World War II he directed a research project at Columbia University that became a vital part of the Manhattan Project, which developed the atomic energy program in the United States.

After the war he studied the temperature of the ocean and developed a method for determining what the ocean's temperature was 180 million years ago. He theorized that the early atmosphere of the earth was like the present atmosphere on Jupiter, which is very rich in ammonia.

Urey died in California on January 5, 1981.

Barbara McClintock

McClintock was born in Brooklyn, New York, in 1902, just before Mendel's work on genetics was rediscovered. She studied as an undergraduate in the College of Agriculture at Cornell University. She launched her scientific career at Cornell in 1919 and, in the face of social adversity and tremendous intellectual challenges, established herself among the great geneticists of her century.

Her first major contribution was made as a graduate student. At the time McClintock started her career, scientists were just becoming aware of the connections between heredity and events they could actually observe in cells under the microscope. McClintock pioneered the field of cytogenetics in corn. She learned to identify each of the ten maize (corn) chromosomes.

McClintock rose to many challenges throughout her career—not only scientific but personal—from other scientists who felt intimidated and threatened by what one of her colleagues described as her "independence, originality and extraordinary accomplishment." In the most notable case, Lowell Randolph, her advisor and colleague, became extremely irritated with McClintock's success in solving a problem he had spent his entire life working on.

In 1944 she was elected to the National Academy of Sciences and in 1945 to the presidency of the Genetics Society of America. In 1983 she received the Nobel Prize for her discovery thirty-five years earlier of transposable genetic elements. She died in 1992.

Rachel Carson

Born on May 27, 1907, in the rural river town of Springdale, Pennsylvania, Rachel Carson longed, from an early age, to become a writer. She credits her mother as having bequeathed her a lifelong love of nature and the living world. She was, however, able to combine her two loves by writing both clearly and beautifully about scientific issues.

Her fascination with the sea began in 1929 when, as a graduate of the Pennsylvania College for Women, she traveled to work as an aquatic biologist for the federal government at the Marine Biological Laboratory in Woods Hole, Massachusetts, as a beginning investigator. Once there, she changed her field of study from that of the cranial nerves of reptiles to that of marine biology.

She was hired by the U.S. Bureau of Fisheries to write radio scripts during the Depression and supplemented her income by writing feature articles on natural history for the *Baltimore Sun*. She returned to Woods Hole in 1932 as a graduate student from Johns Hopkins, where she earned her master's degree in biology.

She published articles and books about life in and around the ocean. Her second book, The Sea Around Us, became a best seller. This wonderfully illustrated book looks at sea life. The work she is most remembered for, though, is *Silent Spring*, published in 1962. This controversial work, which examines in alarming detail the environmental damage caused by the widespread use of chemical pesticides, led to a greater public awareness of the need to preserve and maintain our fragile environment.

Carson's major legacy was forcing issues about environmental awareness into the nation's consciousness. She died of bone cancer on April 14, 1964, at the age of 56.

Helen Caldicott

Born in Melbourne, Australia in 1938, Helen was the eldest of three children. Her father was a factory manager and her mother an interior designer. They considered ideas, books and music very important. At school Helen found the work easy, but making friends was difficult. "I was a loner. ... I think being alone as a child made me very independent and that I could handle any situation that arose."

She was one of only a few women accepted into the Medical School at the University of Adelaide in 1956. After graduating, Helen married William Caldicott, a fellow doctor, and they had three children. In 1966 the family moved to the United States to work at the Harvard Medical Centre and treat children with cystic fibrosis, a life-threatening disease of the lungs and digestive system. It was during this time that Helen realized how precious and special life was. She became an empassioned advocate for nuclear disarmament and a true woman of peace who has been recognized in every corner of the globe. Her awards, acknowledgments and citations fill pages. She has written several books and developed dozens of video tapes and films, written scores of articles which have appeared in nearly every major newspaper and magazine, and spoken at major universities throughout the world.

She founded and headed Physicians for Social Responsibility and Women's Action for Nuclear Disarmament (WAND).

In association with physicians and scientists, Dr. Caldicott and her husband, Bill Caldicott, play a major role in educating the people of New Zealand and Australia about the vast dangers to health of nuclear production and development. She currently resides on Long Island, New York.

Chemicals
and
Supplies

Chemistry Supplies for Grades 7 & 8

QUANTITY	DESCRIPTION
1 pr	Asbestos (ceramic fiber) gloves
1	Balance, weighing – triple beam
2 doz	Beakers, Pyrex, assorted sizes: 50–4000 ml
9	Bottles, wide mouth, 16 oz
6	Bottles, narrow mouth, 16 oz
2	Brushes, beaker
2	Brushes, flask
2	Brushes, test tube
2	Burner, Bunsen (hand torch), propane
1	Burner lighter (flint and steel striker)
1	Burner, wing top
1	Chimney, glass
2	Clamps, test tube
4	Clamps, hosecock 1/2", screw type
1	Chart, Dangerous Materials (Flinn catalog)
2	Clay triangles
1 set	Corks, assorted rubber (solid, one-hole and-two hole)
2	Crucibles, porcelain, medium size, with covers
2	Cylinders, graduated, 100 ml glass
1	Cylinder, graduated, 1000 ml glass
6	Dishes, watch glass, 5" diam. Pyrex
6	Dishes, petri, 100 mm diameter Pyrex
2	Dishes, porcelain, 3" diameter
1	Dish, porcelain, 10" diamster
1	Eye washer apparatus—water
2	Flasks, boiling, 500 ml flat bottom, Pyrex
2	Flasks, boiling, 500 ml round bottom, Pyrex
1	Flask, boiling, 2000 ml round bottom, Pyrex
2	Flasks, Erlenmeyer 500 ml Pyrex
2	Flasks, 250 ml Pyrex
1	First aid kit
2 pr	Forceps (tongs)
2 pr	Forceps (tweezers), 5"
2	Funnels, analytical, 75 mm, glass
1	Funnels, analytical, polypropylene
1	Fire extinguisher, dry chemical charge
1	Fire extinguisher, CO_2 charge

6	Funnels, thistle
1	Funnel, 8" diam., polypropylene

Gas cylinders, lecture bottle size:

1	Ammonia
1	Chlorine
1	Carbon dioxide
1	Hydrogen
1	Helium
1	Nitrogen
1	Oxygen
1	Sulfur dioxide
2	Gauze, wire, 6" square, ceramic center
6	Glass plates, 4" square
5 lbs	Glass tubing and rod, assorted diam.
2	Glass cutters (for tubing)
2	Glass-cutting files, triangular, 6" long
1/4 lb	Glass wool
2 doz	Goggles, safety (one pair for each student)
1	Hot plate, electric
2	Hydrometer cylinders, 600 ml
1	Hydrometer cylinders, 100 ml
2	Meter sticks
1	Mortar with pestle (medium size)
2	Medicine droppers
2	Spatulas, stainless steel, 5" length
2	Spoons, deflagrating, brass, 1/2" diam.
1	Spoon, measuring, 1 teaspoon
1	Spoon, measuring, 1 tablespoon
3	Support stands (tripods)
3	Support rods
2	Support rings, 3" diam.
2	Support clamps, "V" type, large
6	Support clamps
2	Support tripods, 10" high, 3" diam. top
2	Test tube racks
2 doz	Test tubes (3/4" x 6")
2	Thermometers: -20° C to +110° C
1	Tongs, beaker
2	Trowels, stainless steel
2	Triangles, clay
1	Trough, pneumatic

Chemicals

All chemicals are shipped with safety paperwork which you will need to place in a three-ring binder and have available for reference. You should mark the date of arrival on each batch with a grease pencil. Acids are corrosive and need to be safely stored in a locked, vented, cabinet. Consult your local "Health and Safety Code" for specific instructions.

concentrated H_2SO_4	sulfuric acid, reagent grades
concentrated HNO_3	nitric acid
concentrated HCl	hydrochloric acid
$NaCl$	table salt, not iodized
NH_4Cl	ammonium chloride
Zn	zinc powder
S	sulfur
P	phosphorus, "white" or "yellow"
Fe	iron wool fine
$KMnO_4$	potassium permanganate
litmus	granules and paper
Cu	copper metal chunks
$Ca(OH)_2$	calcium hydroxide, roasted lime lumps
H_2O_2	hydrogen peroxide, household
Zn	zinc, mossy
MnO_2	manganese dioxide
Na_2SO_3	sodium sulfite
$CaCO$	calcium carbonate, same as marble chips
Al	aluminum ribbon
NH_4NO_3	ammonium nitrate
$(NH_4)Cr_2O_7$	ammonium dichromate
Mg	magnesium ribbon
CCl_4	carbon tetrachloride
CS_2	carbon disulfide
CH_3OH	methyl alcohol
KCl	potassium chloride
$SrCl_2$	strontium chloride
H_3BO_3	boric acid
$CaCl_2$	calcium chloride
$CaOCl_2$	calcium oxychloride
$LiCl$	lithium chloride
$CuCl_2$	cupric chloride
$Na_2S_2O_2 * 5H_2O$	sodium thiosulfate

Materials and Chemicals for Grade 9

(based on 30 students)

15 Lab Stations with:

30	safety glasses
15	test tube racks
15	Erlenmeyer flasks 250 ml
15	beakers 50 ml
15	beakers 100 ml
15	beakers 250 ml
15	stirring rods
15	flint strikers
75	Pyrex test tubes
15	test tube holders
15	funnels
15	spatulas
15	wire gauzes for Bunsen burners
15	Bunsen burners with gas outlets
10 ft	glass tubing
5	deflagrating spoons
10 ft	rubber tubing
15	pinch clamps
5	crucibles with covers
15	graduated cylinders
15	pairs of tongs
15	watch glasses
15	tripods
15	medicine droppers
5	thermometers

Chromatography biokit from Carolina Biological

Chemicals needed:

    For making synthetic rubber:
        acetic acid
        ammonia water
        ethylene dichloride
        flower of sulfur
        sodium hydroxide
        sodium sulfide

General needs:
- acetic acid
- acetic anhydride
- ammonia
- amyl alcohol
- Benedict's solution
- benzene
- bleach
- brewer's yeast
- bromine
- butyric acid
- camphor
- carbon disulfide
- cellulose
- confectioners' sugar
- corn starch
- cotton balls
- cyclohexane
- cyclohexene
- ethyl alcohol
- ethyl dichloride
- Fehling solutions A & B
- gelatin
- hydrochloric acid
- iodine crystals
- lime water
- margarine
- methyl alcohol
- nitric acid
- one box of wooden splints
- phosphoric acid
- potassium chlorate
- potassium permanganate
- salicylic acid
- salt-free crackers
- sodium alkali
- sodium hydroxide
- sodium sulfate
- sodium sulfide
- sodium thiosulfate
- sulfuric acid
- table salt
- table sugar
- tolulene

Bibliography

Faraday, Michael. *Faraday's Chemical History of a Candle*. Chicago: Chicago Review Press, 1988.

Julius, Frits. *Fundamentals for a Phenomenological Study of Chemistry*. Fair Oaks, CA: AWSNA Publications, 2000.

_____. *The World of Matter and the Education of Man*. Forest Row, UK: Steiner Schools Fellowship,1987.

Kolisko, Eugen. *Elementary Chemistry*. Bournemouth, UK: Kolisko Archives, 1978.

_____. *First Lessons in Chemistry*. Manuscript copy in possession of author.

Mitchell, David, ed. Waldorf High School Research Project, *Chemistry Colloquium*. Fair Oaks, CA: AWSNA Publications, 2000.

Oelhaf, R.C. *A Waldorf High School Chemistry Program*, downloadable PDF, Online Waldorf Library, www.waldorflibrary.org, Chatham, NY: Waldorf Publications at the Research Institute for Waldorf Education, 2014.

Ott, Gerhard. *Grundriss einer Chemie nach phänomenologischer Methode*. Basel: Zbinden verlag, 1960.

Rohde, Dirk, ed. *Chemistry Reader: An Orientation to Developing Chemistry Instruction in Waldorf Schools*, downloadable PDF, Online Waldorf Library, www.waldorflibrary.org, Chatham, NY: Waldorf Publications at the Research Institute for Waldorf Education, 2015.

Schad, Wolfgang, et al. *Goethean Science in the Waldorf Curriculum*. Forest Row, UK: Steiner Schools Fellowship, 1978.

Sonner, Robert H. *Chemistry for Waldorf Middle Schools, Grades Seven and Eight: A Compendium of Phenomenological Experiments*. Teacher's Reference Book, Chatham, NY: Waldorf Publications, 2013.

von Mackensen, Manfred. *Feuer, Kalk, Metalle und Stärke, Eiweisz, Fett; Zu den Chemieepochen der 7. und 8. Klasse, mit Vesuchsbeshreibungen*. Kassel, Germany, 1986.